One Day Longer

A MEMOIR

One Day Longer

A MEMOIR

Lynn Williams

ILR Press
an imprint of Cornell University Press

Ithaca, New York

First published in the United States 2011 by Cornell University Press

Printed in the United States of America

Library of Congress Cataloging-in-Publication Data

Williams, Lynn R.
One day longer : a memoir / Lynn Williams.
p. cm.
Includes index.
ISBN 978-0-8014-5067-9 (alk. paper)
1. Williams, Lynn R. 2. Labor unions – Canada – Officials and employees – Biography. 3. Labor unions – United States – Officials and employees – Biography. 4. United Steelworkers – Employees – Biography. I. Title.
HD6525.W55 2011   331.88′169142092 – dc23 [B]
2011019331

Cornell University Press strives to use environmentally responsible suppliers and materials to the fullest extent possible in the publishing of its books. Such materials include vegetable-based, low-VOC inks and acid-free papers that are recycled, totally chlorine-free, or partly composed of nonwood fibers. For further information, visit our website at www.cornellpress.cornell.edu.

Cloth printing   10 9 8 7 6 5 4 3 2 1

CONTENTS

Illustrations follow page 146

FOREWORD

I was a young union activist and smelter worker in 1977 when Lynn Williams, the new international secretary of the Steelworkers, offered me a full-time job. If I accepted, my wife and I would have to leave our hometown of Sudbury and relocate to Toronto. What's more, I had just unsuccessfully managed a campaign for a candidate who almost won a union election to represent workers in Ontario. But it was a candidate whom Lynn did not support. Unsure whether he valued my organizing skills or if he intended to fire me at the first chance, I was faced with a life-changing decision. As the son of a union activist growing up in a town where the union was part of the community fabric and the salvation of the working class, I could only dream of the opportunity to serve the membership of my union in a higher capacity. Fortunately, I made the right choice. With Lynn's guidance and advice, I took the job and eventually progressed to become the international president of the United Steelworkers, a union with 1.2 million active and retired members.

I offer this Foreword because I want readers to know what kind of man Lynn is. He is intelligent and wise, thoughtful and even-tempered, invariably willing to listen to all sides in a debate and never vengeful or mean-spirited. Lynn always wanted to make decisions that were best for the members and our union. People reading this book who know him are already aware of that. He put the interests of the membership first, making whatever personal sacrifice was required.

Union activists, especially young activists, will learn a lot about the history of the North American labour movement during the last half of the twentieth century from reading this book. Lynn played a major role in that history. Rank-and-file members who may take their union for granted will come to understand that what they have was not handed to them by generous and benevolent employers but fought for through decades of perseverance by the generation that came out of the Great Depression of the 1930s. Casual readers or those studying business or commerce may be surprised and enlightened by Lynn's account, which presents views and lessons that are in stark contrast to what is commonly taught.

The union 'boss' is really a 'servant' not a master of his or her membership. Labour unions are unlike most major corporations and institutions. They are in fact among the most democratic organizations in society. Their decisions are not autocratic or dictatorial but are made after serious consultation and deliberation with workplace union leaders and members. A union leader derives his or her power from the membership, whether it be fifty people in a shop or more than a million workers across two countries. When a cause is just and the membership believes in it, the union leader is at the front line of the crusade, with passion and resolve. There is no time to rest. Workers are under attack and there are always challenges to be addressed. Communications and union education are therefore vital. Knowledge is power and an informed membership is a strong membership.

In the pages that follow, Lynn Williams tells his story. It is also the story of our union. It is the legacy that was handed to us and it is up to us to safeguard and continue to promote the ideals set forth here. I am eternally grateful to Lynn for helping me achieve the job of my dreams. But I am thankful for so much more than that – he served to nurture me, providing advice, counsel, and guidance. More than a mentor and friend, he treated me like a good father treats a favourite nephew.

On behalf of millions of workers and their families – thank you, Lynn Williams.

Leo W. Gerard
USW International President

PREFACE

Invariably, it is the lessons gleaned from our parents and the life experiences of our youth that shape our convictions and determine the paths we choose to follow. Reflections on those early road maps of life are usually most vivid in our moments of greatest triumph or deepest sorrow.

So it is not surprising that on the night of 29 March 1984, when the voting trend had clearly established that I was about to become the first Canadian president of the one-million-member United Steelworkers of America (USWA, now USW), my thoughts went back to my roots in Ontario. It was in the border city of Sarnia, across the St Clair River from Port Huron, Michigan, that the need to help people who were enduring unspeakable poverty and hopelessness was etched indelibly on my psyche. I was seven years old when our family moved there in 1931, and my father, a Protestant minister, would take over the pulpit of a church whose congregation was composed primarily of working-class people.

I was impressed by my father's selfless commitment to his congregation in its time of need. His ministry was much more than what he delivered from the pulpit on Sunday. He was truly living the creed of Christianity in the full sense and scope of its meaning.

After briefly thinking of following my father into the clergy, I found a new pathway to helping others – the union movement. My first real baptism by fire was as a foot soldier in the 1947–51 battle to certify the department store workers of the T. Eaton Company in Toronto. Further organizing efforts followed, leading to my becoming a staff representative of the Steelworkers in 1956. In this capacity, and later as an area supervisor, I assisted in various organizational efforts across the country. Appointed in 1965 to the District 6 office, which was then responsible for the sprawling region stretching from Ontario in the east to British Columbia in the west, plus the Yukon and Northwest Territories, I was elected the district's director, by a referendum vote of the membership, in 1973. Four years later, I became the USW's international secretary; in 1983 the USW's International Executive Board chose me to act as the union's temporary acting president; and in 1984, by a special membership referendum, I was elected to the presidency, holding the post until 1994. By then, thanks to the lessons I had absorbed in my youth and in my earlier work in the union movement, I had learned that helping better our members' lives and working conditions was not about vindictiveness and score settling; instead, it was about finding a balance between pushing hard for your workers and knowing when to make compromises that would protect their jobs in the long term. It was this ability to adapt – pragmatism if you like – that would set me apart from my rival in the election for the USW presidency. In the years that would follow, with Big Steel beset by strong competition from offshore producers, I believe it served our members well.

I have led a privileged life in the labour movement. Apart from my involvement with the Steelworkers, I was the first person to sit on the Executive Council of both the Canadian Labour Congress (CLC) and the American Federation of Labor-Congress of Industrial Organizations (AFL-CIO). I also was an internal auditor for the International Confederation of Free Trade Unions (ICFTU), a position to which I was elected by the various world congresses of the ICFTU, after being nominated and recommended by the AFL-CIO. That experience provided interesting insights on a remarkable range of work, such as supporting fledgling unions and encouraging economic development.

I sometimes think back on my life and marvel at how blessed I have been to have seen and experienced so much, both inside and outside the labour movement, 'on the ground' as well as in positions of union leadership. This book is my attempt to tell that story, and of the people who made it possible.

A few words about the book's title. In the North American labour movement, workers on strike frequently use the slogan 'One Day Longer' to emphasize their determination to hold out as long as it takes in order to have their demands met, as well as their conviction that change is indeed possible. The spirit underlying that slogan, with its combination of commitment and optimism, is also at the heart of this book. My entire career in the trade-union movement was based on the belief that, in the face of serious obstacles, workers, whether on strike or not, needed to remain united and committed over the long haul. If they did, they would be in a strong position both to achieve their collective-bargaining goals and to realize the broader objective of creating a more just and democratic society. I hold the same conviction today. And so 'One Day Longer,' encapsulating as it does the philosophy running through my entire life and career, a philosophy consisting of equal parts of determination and hope, is an apt title for the memoir that follows.

Having no expectation of ever writing another book, I wish to thank as many people as possible now, particularly since significant parts of the story that follows are as much theirs as mine.

I dedicate the book, above all, to my family, without whose support I could not have followed such a demanding career. I acknowledge in particular my debt to my late wife, Audrey, who was a devoted helpmate and spouse for nearly fifty-four years, and our four children and their families: our daughter Judy Hocking and her children, Sarah and Michael; our son David, his wife, Sharon, and their children, Rebecca, Jeremy, Evan, and Christopher; our daughter Barbara Williams, her husband, Christopher Dossett, and their children, Amanda, Kimberly, and Gregory; and our son Brian Williams, his wife, Julie Bélanger, and their children, Gabriel and Soline. I dedicate the book, too, to my parents, Waldemar Williams and Emma Fisher, and my sister, Carol Head, and her husband, Douglas.

I also wish to thank the members, staff, and leaders of the United Steelworkers, who, whenever circumstances required them to do so, faced unimaginably difficult and devastating crises with incredible courage, fortitude, imagination, and solidarity. To my late friend and colleague Chris Trower, without whose persuasive prodding this book would never have seen the light of day, I owe a particular debt of gratitude. Deserving of my heartfelt thanks as well are my principal mentors in the ways and principles of the democratic labour movement – Larry Sefton, Eileen Tallman Sufrin, and Howard Conquergood – and the enormous number of inspiring colleagues, teachers, advisers, and friends I have been privileged to be associated with inside and outside the labour movement, inside and outside North America, from whom I have learned so much and whose friendship and collegial association has been such a significant source of growth, learning, inspiration – indeed the substance of life itself.

In the area of the labour movement and collective bargaining, this list would also include a number of people from the 'other side' from whom I learned a great deal; in fact, failing to learn from them was, in some circumstances, at one's peril. I cannot begin to name all of these people. They know who they are. Many appear in the book, but many others do not, for the inclusion of someone in my story is largely a function of the incidents that I have chosen to describe. I hope that all those who are not named will be forgiving. I know inevitably that a large number of people who should be included have not been.

I have, therefore, chosen a handful of special people to represent themselves and to be stand-ins for all the rest. They are: Bernie Kleiman, I.W. ('Abe') Abel, Lloyd McBride, George Becker, Leo Gerard, and Jean Gérin-Lajoie. Bernie was our general counsel for a generation, but in ways much more than that term represents. He was a model of strength, character, and talent who demanded the best from all of us. He became my best friend and closest colleague in the darkest of times, and, by his very presence, he strengthened our resolve to persevere. Abe set a standard of strength and integrity that shone from his determined stance and his strong face, etched with the lines of struggle and experience. Lloyd's straightforward candour and honesty were legendary. 'Telling it like it is' wasn't just a saying with him, it was a way of life. George brought a shop-floor sense of fairness and outrage at injustice to every issue and an irresistible focus of energy, intelligence, and compassion to its resolution. Leo is a big man in body, head, and heart, all of it committed every moment of every day to building a better union, a better movement, and a better world. Jean was thinking out of the box long before the phrase was invented. The union owes more to his creativity than can be imagined. The temptation to go on in this vein is hard to resist, but resist I must.

There is one other person I wish to thank: my special friend Carmel St Amour, who has brought so much joy and happiness into my life in these recent years.

ABBREVIATIONS

AFL	American Federation of Labor
AFSCME	American Federation of State, County and Municipal Employees
AIW	Allied Industrial Workers
AWA	Aluminum Workers of America
BSIC	Basic Steel Industry Conference
CAW	Canadian Auto Workers
CCAA	Companies' Creditors Arrangement Act
CCAC	Campaign Conduct Administrative Committee
CCF	Co-operative Commonwealth Federation
CCL	Canadian Congress of Labour
CCYM	Co-operative Commonwealth Youth Movement
CIO	Congress of Industrial Organizations
CLC	Canadian Labour Congress
COLA	Cost-of-living Allowance
COTC	Canadian Officers Training Corps
CUPE	Canadian Union of Public Employees
CWA	Communications Workers of America
DNC	Democratic National Committee
EEC	European Economic Community
ENA	Experimental Negotiating Agreement
ERISA	Employment Retirement Income Security Act
ESOP	Employee Stock Ownership Plans
EU	European Union
EV	Extended Vacation
FTA	Free Trade Agreement
GE	General Electric
GSP	General System of Preferences

HERE	Hotel and Restaurant Employees
HMO	Health Management Organization
IAM	International Association of Machinists
ICD	Institute for Career Development
ICFTU	International Confederation of Free Trade Unions
IEB	International Executive Board
ILGWU	International Ladies' Garment Workers' Union
ILO	International Labour Organization
IRRA	Industrial Relations Research Association
IUD	Industrial Union Department
LERA	Labor and Employment Research Association
LMPT	Labor Management Participation Team
NAFTA	North American Free Trade Agreement
NDP	New Democratic Party
OCAW	Oil, Chemical and Atomic Workers
OPIC	Overseas Protection Insurance Corporation
OPSEU	Ontario Public Service Employees Union
PATCO	Professional Air Traffic Controllers Organization
RWDSU	Retail, Wholesale and Department Store Union
SEIU	Service Employees International Union
SOAR	Steelworkers Organization of Active Retirees
SUB	Supplementary Unemployment Benefit
SWOC	Steel Workers Organizing Committee
TAA	Trade Adjustment Assistance
TLC	Trades and Labour Congress
UAW	United Auto Workers
UE	United Electrical, Radio and Machine Workers of America
UFCW	United Food and Commercial Workers
USW	United Steel Workers of America
WTO	World Trade Organization

One Day Longer

A MEMOIR

1

IN THE BEGINNING

The driving force, the creative energy in my family, goes back to my father's mother, Eva Sherk. A devoutly religious person, she had been raised a Mennonite but left that denomination when she married my grandfather, Daniel Wilhelm (later Williams), at about the age of eighteen. She was very committed to education. Her fondest wish had been to pass her entrance to high school, but she was unable to accomplish that because, as the oldest child, she was required to work on the farm. Spring was planting season and fall was harvest time, so she was never able to have a full year at school.

All the same, she read voraciously and by the time I knew her she was an educated person. She read her Bible a great deal, but she read far beyond that, such as religious magazines that were around the house. I do not know if the family subscribed to a newspaper. They lived in New Hamburg in southern Ontario, which I imagine had only a weekly paper. She loved poetry – Bliss Carman is a name that comes to mind – and could recite many poems from memory. She took great pleasure from it and spoke to the grandchildren constantly about the importance of poetry and reading, of expanding one's knowledge and vocabulary, and, of course, about the importance of pursuing an education.

She was determined that her family members achieve the education she longed for and that they succeed beyond the confines of rural Ontario. My grandfather began married life as a farmer, but it was a time when there were not enough farms to go around, so many young farmers moved to the towns and cities. Religion was one mechanism through which to gain an education and open up more opportunities. It is something of a sociological description of upward mobility to observe that a common route for farm family members was a combination of religion and education, and that was true of my father's family. My father, Waldemar, was the oldest and he became a minister in the family's Evangelical Church, a branch of German Methodism. The second-oldest son, Wellington, died in a flu epidemic; the third-oldest, Morgan, also became an Evangelical minister; and the next-to-last boy, Russell, became a high school teacher and died in the First World War. A daughter who followed, Eva, became a nurse. The final baby, a boy named Harvey, resisted all his mother's pressure to follow the model of his older brothers and pursue either a religious education or education itself.

My father left school after completing his high school entrance and went to work in the general store in New Hamburg. Then he moved to Toronto and worked for some years as a salesman in a men's furnishing store on King Street. He was active in the church and became a lay preacher. He found an opportunity to return to school by combining it with missionary work in western Canada, while living with a Sherk uncle in Summerland, British Columbia. There, he began his high school studies in the church school at age twenty-two in 1907.

After completing two years of high school in Summerland, he moved to Alberta, where he worked in the mission field and finished high school. It was in Medicine Hat that he met my mother, Emma, whose own father was active in the church. She was considerably younger than my father but graduated from high school a year after he did. Accompanied by my mother, Dad moved on to the Evangelical Church college, North Central, in Naperville, Illinois, outside Chicago. His brother Morgan and his wife, Maude, were also there about the same time, both of them one a year ahead; however, my uncle went on to Divinity School at Northwestern University, in Evanston, another Chicago suburb. Dad completed his bachelor's degree at North Central and then proceeded to a master's degree in theology at the University of Chicago, wrapping up his formal education when he was thirty-one. He served as a pastor throughout his university education, which enabled him to graduate without any debt.

An interesting side note for me is that my dad's full pastorate, after my mother and he were married in 1917 and during his studies at the University of Chicago, was in Hammond, Indiana, one of the communities right in the heart of the steel complex in the northwestern part of the state. I've spent a good deal of my steel-related life in and around Hammond, dealing with matters of considerable importance to the citizens of that fine Indiana town.

My uncle Morgan's story, like my father's, is one of work and education somewhat interspersed. In the period between high school and attending Northwestern University, he apprenticed with a tailor in Seaforth, Ontario. He and his wife would raise four daughters and he maintained his tailoring skills by making their winter coats, and often jackets and suits as well. After college, my father and uncle pursued somewhat different directions. Although both were educated in the Evangelical Church, they both joined the Methodists after graduation. Both continued in the ministry, too, but my uncle remained in the United States. As have so many immigrants, he viewed it as the land of opportunity. My father was much more the Canadian and returned north of the border. However, they remained close throughout their lives, often sharing summer vacations and many ideas regarding sermons, church activities, and the direction of religious life.

Their careers were also quite different in other ways. My uncle remained around the Chicago area. His first church was in Chicago, and then he served for many years in Kankakee, Illinois, a few miles to the south. Later, he acted as a retired minister at the Chicago Temple, which is a Methodist church on the top of a skyscraper in the city's downtown. My father served in a succession of locations in Ontario, progressing from small rural communities to a larger rural town and only then to cities. The Methodist practice was that a minister should remain in a community only three or four years, a practice my father viewed as quite wrong in that it prevented ministers from becoming as integrated in the community as they should. In 1925 the United Church of Canada came into being, representing an amalgam of the Methodist Church, the Congregationalist Church, half of the Presbyterian Church, and ultimately a number of other denominations, including the Evangelical Church. This new body moved away from the three- and four-year tour, a change surely encouraged by many ministers who shared my father's opinion in that regard.

My father's first congregation in Ontario in the Methodist Church was in Tilbury, his next in Springfield, then, in succession, Aylmer, Sarnia, and Hamilton. He remained a little longer in each place: three years in Tilbury, four years in Springfield, six in Aylmer, seven in Sarnia, and seventeen in Hamilton. Then, as a retired pastor, he moved to Brantford and served as an assistant at Zion United Church there for some years.

I was the middle child. I had an older brother, Ross, who was born in 1919 when my dad was serving in Tilbury. I was born in 1924 in

Springfield, but the family moved almost immediately to Aylmer, a much larger town about ten kilometres down the road. My sister, Carol, the youngest in the family, was born in Aylmer just before Christmas, 1930, and we moved to Sarnia in July 1931, just in time for the Great Depression.

Sarnia was an industrial town, its economy built around the railway, the prospect of becoming an important border crossing, and the Imperial Oil refinery. It sits near the base of Lake Huron on the St Clair River, a geographically valuable location. There was, of course, also a variety of smaller industrial enterprises servicing the major ones and others related to some particular community need. At the time, there was no apparent sign of the massive chemical sector that would emerge in Sarnia in succeeding decades. My father's church was in the south end, near the railroad yards and shops and the Imperial Oil refinery, in the heart of the working-class area of town. His was almost entirely a working-class congregation, with two or three business people and executives mixed in.

My mother was an introverted person. She was an excellent pianist who enjoyed being home with her music and her books. Being a minister's wife was, at the best of times, a duty that she undertook because she felt it was required, not because she took much pleasure in it. When she attended a women's church meeting and made a speech, or a presentation of some kind, she did so to make a real contribution. It was not easily done.

My older brother was in many ways quite like my mother. He was musical and played the piano well. He was active and played on the football team in high school, but he enjoyed being home. He did his studying and, like Mother, enjoyed reading. We all read, but in truth they were both more committed readers than I. My character was more extroverted, and in this I resembled my father.

A major crisis in our family life occurred in Sarnia in 1935, when, at Christmas time, Ross, then sixteen, went to the hospital for a routine appendix operation and died unexpectedly. Although I don't believe a doctor ever said it, my father always believed that Ross was allergic to the anesthetic and had a terrible reaction that almost immediately caused his lungs to fill with blood. It was as traumatic a day in the life of the family as one could imagine. He went to the hospital at noon. I was home from school for lunch, as we were in those days. I remember Ross volunteering to drive the car when they went to the hospital because my father was too nervous. By the time I arrived home from school a little after 4 p.m., my mother and father were at the hospital and my grandmother, who was staying with us, was crying. They worked on my brother for hours, but they were not able to bring him back.

I was devastated, of course. He was a big brother who did all the things he was supposed to do. I remember one day when he was practising football in the field behind the school across from our house. As we often did, I and a few friends hid close by and listened in. He was then in the middle of high school and I was five years younger and in grade school. I heard him swearing vigorously in the scrum and he noticed that I had heard him. So he came over to the sidelines and threatened me every which way, up and down and sideways. He said if I told Mom and Dad that I heard him doing this I'd be in great trouble with him. I don't recall any desire to tell them what he was doing, but he certainly was protecting against that possibility.

My mother desperately missed her firstborn. His loss was a terrible blow and I think it shook her religious faith to some extent. It certainly tested it. How could this have happened?

I remember a song that was around in those years: 'My Bonny lies over the ocean, my Bonny lies over the Sea, my Bonny lies over the ocean, Oh bring back my Bonny to me!' I imagine it was a wartime song, but Mother just couldn't bear hearing anybody playing or singing it. Why? Ross had often played that very song on the piano.

In many ways, my mother never recovered from Ross's death and she was sick off and on for years. She had experienced no mental trouble before, at least not any that I was aware of, but she became a paranoid schizophrenic, a circumstance that dominated the life of the family as long as she lived. My father was a saint about it all. He looked after her during most of those years at home, usually without help while carrying a major workload himself. She was in hospital on a number of occasions during periods of extreme illness. My dad had a wonderful cousin, Hilda Weil, who came and cooked and looked after us when things became too difficult. But, mostly, my father soldiered along and looked after my mother until he died at nearly age ninety in 1974. She lived for ten more years in nursing homes close to wherever my sister happened to be living, dying at the age of ninety-one.

Every experience in life is a learning experience. My mother's illness certainly proved to be that for me. It aroused deep sympathies and profound curiosities in me, and provided, along with a multitude of memories and impressions, a significant measure of understanding that has remained with me throughout my life. As the years went on,

I read a great deal of psychological material, particularly Freud. There was a time I thought I would be interested in becoming a psychologist or a psychiatrist, but the cost of going to medical school followed by professional training in psychiatry made it all a fantasy. Nonetheless, I pushed, prodded, and explored to find out all I could about what kind of treatments were being developed for schizophrenia. I developed a basic sympathy – I think my whole family did – for people suffering from mental illness. And I came to acquire some new insights into human nature, ones that would be useful in my later career in the labour movement. My home experience in these early years awakened me to the importance of patience, understanding, and sympathy in dealing with people who are experiencing pressure and stress beyond the ordinary, from whatever sources, and what may be required to manage or overcome it.

The other important and formative experience in Sarnia was, of course, the Great Depression. When we moved there in 1931, I was seven years old and we left in 1938, when I was fourteen. The Depression was a transforming experience for everybody. The difference between the Depression in an industrial town such as Sarnia and subsequent situations of economic difficulty there and elsewhere was that, in Sarnia in the 1930s, virtually everybody was affected. All the workers were suffering periods of layoff, reduced hours, and reduced wages. All the businesses were short of customers. The entire town was reeling from the loss of jobs, of income, and of purchasing power. Business people, big and small, workers of all kinds, teachers, professionals, my father, everybody either took reductions in pay, lost benefits, or lost jobs altogether. Nothing like it has been seen since, which is not to minimize the suffering caused by subsequent recessions. Not only were the numbers of unemployed much greater than those in more recent economic downturns, but even those who were employed had virtually no protection against wage cuts, shorter hours, and the like. It was truly an awful time for workers, one without parallel in our history.

Because the effects of the Depression were so pervasive, there was a sense of solidarity in Sarnia in those days, with everyone realizing that they had to work together to tackle the problems they were confronting. And Sarnia was not unique. Canadians everywhere were witnessing the evolution of the political spectrum, from right to left, immediately before their eyes. The Co-operative Commonwealth Federation (CCF) delivered the Regina Manifesto in 1933 and Social Credit emerged in Alberta about the same time, under the leadership of William Aberhart, an evangelical preacher who became the premier of the province. Our house was a focal point for all of these swirling ideas and pressures of the 1930s. First of all, my father's was a working-class church, so there was a great deal of concern all the time about keeping the church afloat, and my father and the family afloat as well. But there was a much deeper and more emotional concern about those in the congregation who were having the most difficult time. My father helped these people look for work, even part-time work, or found some chores for them around somebody's house – anything to provide a little income. Finally, most heart-rending of all, he visited and tried to help the most seriously affected families.

I didn't see a great deal of that personally, except at Christmas when I would accompany my father on his rounds distributing Christmas baskets. The homes where these were to go were determined by need, and when one visited them, that need was abundantly clear. Another memory that sticks in my mind is weddings. People couldn't afford weddings – the contrast between weddings of that day and those of the present is dramatic. Many weddings were conducted at our house. We had a nice house. It was built just before we arrived, a final extravagance of the 1920s. There was a living room and a dining room, a kitchen, and a study on the main floor, all quite generously proportioned. For many couples in that era, my father's study served as the chapel for their weddings. Frequently, the couple would arrive alone, without guests or friends to witness for them, in which case my father would enlist me for service, even if it meant bringing me in from a pick-up football game. I do not recall many wedding pictures being taken, certainly not of the football-playing witness, no matter how much he had been scrubbed up.

A member of our family who was seriously affected by the Depression was my father's younger brother, Harvey. From the perspective of a young person at least, he was the most exciting member of the Williams clan, providing some counterpoint to the somewhat sombre atmosphere of the family's life. Unfortunately, Harvey became involved in a family disaster during the Depression. My grandfather had had to retire; he had been a furniture salesman for one of the furniture houses in Kitchener, with a regular route around southern Ontario that he covered by train. There was no pension or retirement benefit, except for maybe a watch. When you were finished, you were finished and presumably had enough savings to live on, which Harvey didn't. They still lived in New Hamburg, and Harvey was finding work where he could at the time, helping on relatives' farms and such, whatever it took to make a little money.

My father and his other brother, the two ministers, set up their younger brother and my grandfather in a little gasoline station. It was at the edge of New Hamburg, on the highway to Stratford. The Nith River ran behind their house, and a little way along it was crossed by the highway that then climbed up the hill on the other side of the valley. The gasoline station was at the top of the hill. My uncle, the American and the more entrepreneurial of the two ministers, and my father bought this station for my grandfather and Harvey to run to provide some income for themselves. Both Ross and I worked there quite a bit one summer, the summer before my brother died.

It didn't last long. Harvey was running the station and this didn't work out. He lost the business and left a considerable debt. My mother was aghast at this because my dad and his brother had to bail everybody out. From then on, my grandfather and grandmother lived with Morgan's family and ours, moving back and forth. Harvey left for the woods in British Columbia, where he became a logger. He was a man's man who could do anything; he was strong and well coordinated. He played a mean game of pool and knew all about the world with which his brothers were totally unfamiliar. My grandfather died shortly after all of this happened, but eventually Harvey came back east and more than made amends for the earlier difficulties. He paid back the money. My father and his brother set him up in a house in Hamilton and my grandmother lived with him for the rest of her life, with occasional visits to the other families.

Morgan's family and ours had never settled down entirely with my grandmother. It wasn't that they didn't care, but my mother wasn't in good health, to put it mildly, after my brother died. And the two women's relationship just didn't work very well in our house. My grandmother, a strong and independent person, simply couldn't help but take charge of various chores, just wanting to help out, I'm sure, but sometimes annoying the daughters-in-law in the process. To make matters worse, Grandmother was sometimes disapproving of the way they did things. Harvey's home in Hamilton was a solution for all concerned.

That said, my family and extended family were all people who were deeply affected by the plight of others, and so in the Depression years in Sarnia those in need would come to us. There were a lot of homeless people – they would have been called tramps then – who would stop by. People claimed that caring folks such as my family had houses marked, and the poor certainly stopped at ours regularly. They were always fed and made comfortable and given something if there was something to be given, from clothes to whatever they needed. While we were all growing up and when Grandma was there, she always told us that if we didn't finish off our plates we should think about all those starving people in India. To her, nothing was more important than going to terrible places in the world and introducing the pagans there to Christianity.

As for Mother, she was not, despite her illness, a weak character. On the contrary, in terms of the principles and ideas for which she stood, she was a tougher, somewhat more rigid, person than my father. I do not mean to suggest that my father was not consistent about his principles, but my mother simply was stricter. If someone had done something that was wrong, then there were consequences that should follow, unquestionably. My father was much more the conciliator, willing to give the person another chance. Mother was kind of a Robin Hood socialist in terms of her attitude regarding the obligation of the wealthy to share their riches with the poor. She held such ideas very specifically. There were in our family, as in many families, variations in the wealth – or lack of it – among the relatives. There were a couple of rich uncles and, during the Depression years, she would frequently proclaim quite vigorously that it was their duty to do more to help the less fortunate. These ideas were not intended for her own benefit particularly, nor for our family, since we were somewhere in the middle of the social structure. Rather, she was thinking of those in the family who were having a tough time in the Depression and she felt that they should have been helped much more by the richer relatives.

In these days, I didn't know much about the labour movement. I expect I knew the name of John L. Lewis, president of the United Mine Workers of America from 1920 to 1960 and one the most influential labour leaders in the first half of the twentieth century. Lewis was famous, and, living in Sarnia, we were close to the action in Detroit. I probably did not know who Philip Murray of the Steelworkers and CIO was, nor could I have named unions or other labour organizations, except possibly recognizing the initials CIO as meaning something important about labour.

I was, however, increasingly aware of the shortcomings of the capitalist system and the pressing need for greater social and economic justice. I was firmly committed to the cause of building a better world, to put it somewhat grandiosely, or to put it more specifically, to help create a new society built on the principles of social and economic justice. The capitalist society as we knew it was cruel, heartless, and destructive, and resulted in enormous hardship and suffering. We had to do better. This conviction was a good deal of my father's motivation in ministering to working-class congregations. In my own case, I was too young to know what contribution I could make, but the ideal of social change beckoned all the same.

I remember particularly one winter in which the Bible class theme for the young men's Sunday afternoon session was Christianity and communism, examining the values claimed by each, their similarities, and their differences. There would be material around the house relating to this program and I became interested in reading much of it, because it seemed so connected to all that was going on around us. Adding to this interest was my maternal grandfather, whom I had rarely seen and had no sense of as a person. He lived in Medicine Hat, Alberta, and his only trip east in my time had been when I was very young. I never saw him again. Not too much later, he entered a second marriage and my mother wasn't in any way close to her stepmother. Medicine Hat was a long way away and in the Depression you couldn't afford to go across the river to Port Huron, Michigan, much less travel across Canada. But, though far away, Grandfather was a presence in our home. An enthusiastic Social Credit supporter, he bombarded us with Social Credit literature, principally newspaper articles. Bundles of newspapers would arrive, all marked, circled, underlined and with arrows. I used to read them because I was interested, because they came from another part of the country, but mainly because they were so well marked. One could understand what grandfather was getting at quite easily.

Needless to say, we had many discussions in the family, especially as long as my brother was alive and was contributing his views as well. After Ross's death and the onset of my mother's illness, things were very different. The house now became a very quiet, terribly sad place to be a good deal of the time.

The atmosphere of the home encouraged my outgoing instincts, because it was more fun to attend the Boy Scouts and to play with friends on the street in our self-styled, self-organized Sarnia Sports Club. We played semi-organized games with other gangs around town and pushed our parents to allow as much time as possible for this activity. The result of all this was that, in our last two or three years in Sarnia, I led an active organizational life, increasingly in the Scouts and in the church. A couple of people were early mentors. One was Bob

Gates, a contemporary of my brother and his best friend. Bob went on to become a United Church minister. Another was Jack Kerns, who was at the beginning of a career with Imperial Oil that led to quite a senior position with the company at the head office in Toronto. They were both active and excellent Scout leaders, interesting, imaginative, energetic people with a commitment to the young people in their charge and to the highest quality of organizational life that could be achieved. I owe them a great deal for providing me outstanding examples of the best qualities of leadership. On a scale of one to ten, they were very near the top.

My first two years of high school were in Sarnia. I wanted to play football but was not sure I could make the team. In any case, because of my brother's death right after the football season, my parents would not hear of it: my playing the same sport, and on the same team, as Ross was too painful a prospect to bear. So I played in the school band. It was in Sarnia, too, that I saw my first sit-down strike, at Holmes Foundry in the north end of the city. This occurred towards the end of our years there. One day our group of friends heard that there was some excitement at the foundry, so we grabbed our bikes and headed for the north end of town. In time, my father learned what we were doing. Quite concerned, he drove up in the car to drag us all home.

For many years, I assumed that it was a United Auto Workers (UAW) sit-down, because Holmes Foundry was owned by Ford and made parts for the Ford Motor Company. However, I recently learned that it was really a Steelworker strike. Monty Montgomery, the first Steelworkers staff representative on the payroll in Canada, was the individual involved. Monty was the father of Don, who was our area supervisor in Toronto for many years and then was elected secretary-treasurer of the Canadian Labour Congress. It was later, in the interests of maintaining appropriate jurisdictional lines, that Philip Murray, who was president of the Congress of Industrial Organizations as well as the Steelworkers, persuaded the unions in some cases to exchange local unions back and forth. Obviously, a case was made that Holmes Foundry's natural interests lay with the auto industry. And that's where it is and has been for a long time.

There were always churches eager for my father's services during these years, and in 1938 he enthusiastically accepted a call to Hamilton. From his perspective, I'm sure, the move would remove my mother from all the painful memories of my brother and his tragic death. In fact, however, Mother's illness was at its worst during the early years in Hamilton.

Generally speaking, ministers in the United Church in those years were all moved at the same time, at the beginning of July. The church to which my father moved suited him perfectly. It was in a new suburb called Westdale, on the western edge of the city beside McMaster University. It was a small church that had been established only a few years before. It was certainly in one of the fastest growing, if not the fastest growing, suburb in Hamilton, and it prospered mightily. My father was well accepted by the congregation, and he enjoyed reaching out to new people as the suburb grew. His remaining the pastor there for seventeen years was quite against the traditions of the church until that time.

I was then beginning my third year of high school, and so much was going on that the next several years seemed to fly by. I graduated from Westdale Secondary School (at that time high school was still five years) and followed up with a three-year general bachelor of arts degree at McMaster. During these years my sister was also growing up. My father sent her to the University of Toronto so she might have an opportunity to live on her own away from the difficult atmosphere at home.

My mother spent her time mostly sitting in the kitchen, often crying, feeling terribly persecuted, with a great deal of anger directed at my father, who was, in her mind, responsible for all of her difficulties. I persuaded Father to find a psychiatrist in New York City who did some practising in Buffalo, so we could take Mother to see him. We did this a few times without success, but with new insight into how intractable the illness was. I was involved when sometimes we had to take her to the Buffalo hospital, despite her fears and protests. On a number of occasions she would receive electric-shock treatments and each time they were temporary miracles. She would be herself for a few weeks, and then the fears and the voices and the sense of persecution would return. She was terrified of the treatments. It was like dragging someone off to the electric chair to have her take them. What it must have been like to be so terrified I cannot imagine, but we concluded we had to do whatever we could to calm those fears, and we did.

During this time, most people had a decidedly negative view of mental hospitals, a view that eventually would lead to the campaign for de-institutionalization (which essentially came to mean turning patients onto the streets). But my perspective was different. I remember the hospital doctors and staff we encountered as being sensitive, caring, and concerned. It may be that my mother received better treatment than some would, as the wife of a person of some consequence in the city, but I am inclined to think not. When my mother was in hospital we spent as much time with her as possible and in those circumstances you come to know an institution, or at least develop some feel for the atmosphere. You also hear the views of the person whom you are visiting. I am not suggesting that my mother liked being there, far from it, but her resentment was directed at the idea of being in the hospital at all, not at the caregivers. I think that, the electric-shock treatments aside, she was often quite comfortable to be there because, from her perspective, the pressures of daily responsibilities were gone and Father was not in her face every day.

My mother was an intelligent, thoughtful person. Despite the illness and its complications, she read a good deal. She began with *Time* magazine every week and she read it from cover to cover. She read a great many other things too. She didn't do much else. My dad prepared many meals, though, in fairness, my mother did a good deal of the meal preparation as well. My dad did all the laundry and most of the cleaning. Of course, my mom also had time to read because she was not engaged in any activities involving other people.

In those years, a minister's wife in a Protestant church, certainly in the United Church, was in some ways almost an assistant minister. In a sense, the local church hired them both. The expectation was that the minister's wife would participate in the life of the congregation by leading organizations, teaching Sunday school, and accepting similar responsibilities. My mother did some of that in her best years, but never enthusiastically. It was not that she could not carry out such duties. When she accepted them, she performed well, with everything thought through and carefully planned. More careful, I must say, than the family extroverts were on some occasions. Essentially, however, even in the good years, she avoided these activities and when she was sick she rejected them entirely. They simply were not her cup of tea. As I've said, she was essentially an introverted, shy person. Fortunately, my father's congregations, both in Hamilton and in his earlier postings, afforded him, my sister, and me a great deal of sympathy, understanding, and support.

This whole experience left me with enormous concerns about the waste of life that my mother's illness represented, given her intelligence when her mental circumstances enabled her to exploit it. It contributed to my resolve to be active and attack life positively. It may be just that I'm a much more extroverted person, but I decided to act in order not to risk wasting my life as she had.

A postscript. In 1953, fifteen years after we had moved to Hamilton, my sister announced her intention to marry. Mother was still quite ill at the time, but, on hearing the news, she snapped back to normality overnight. It was an absolutely incredible transformation. For six months, she carried on as my father wished she would have carried on all the time, managing all her obligations, driven, it seemed, by her total determination that my sister's wedding should be just as it ought to be. She did all the things you would expect a mother to do, arranging events, planning every detail of the wedding, and acting as a charming and accomplished hostess. In a way, it almost made her whole circumstance the more tragic, underlining as it did what might have been. Yet, at the same time, it was a magic moment to be enjoyed to the full. There were no doctors involved and no consultations. It simply happened. My father felt that, having done it once, Mother could do it again, and simply decide to be herself. It was not to be. A few months later, the illness returned.

As she became older, the illness gradually eased to some degree. She became less paranoid, didn't hear voices as clearly, and was more amenable to going out a bit. But she was never the same woman as she was at the time of my sister's wedding, let alone the one of my childhood, before Ross's death.

2

WAR AND PEACE

On enrolling at McMaster in September 1941, I had intended to enter the ministry so I started out in a four-year honours program in English and philosophy, thinking it was a good introduction for the later study of theology. My plan to become a theological student had one enormous recreational advantage: it meant I could play on the theology football team in the intramural sports program. Had I been required to try out for the freshmen team, it would have been impossible for me to make the squad because it had a full complement of former high school stars who had not made the varsity team but still outdid me in talent and experience. In contrast, the theology team was always short of players and recruited whomever it could claim to be a theological student. Even with my limited experience, I was a sixty-minute man on the team, playing both ways, and really enjoyed it. We didn't have a spectacular record, but we had a good time.

McMaster had been created as a Baptist college. It always had a number of graduate students studying theology and several undergraduates headed in that direction as well. The university encouraged and, in a sense, watched over these students, arranging events for them and assignments with church congregations in the field. That was how it came about that I did some preaching a little before, during, and after my summer vacation in 1942. There were two churches near the YMCA camp on Lake Erie where I was then working. I was expected to preach every Sunday, at one of them during the spring, summer, and fall, the other only during July and August. One was a country church that functioned, one way or another, year-round in a place called Walsh, near the town of Simcoe. The other was at a summer resort community on Lake Erie called Normandale, where the church was open only in the summer months for the convenience of the cottagers. I was paid $7 for the morning service on Sunday and was given the collection at the evening service. I forget the precise sums of money, but I did very well with the evening congregation. I think there was a little bit of curiosity about this boy preacher.

That summer – I turned eighteen in July – was definitive in finishing any ideas about a career as a minister, mostly because I quickly came to realize that I was not grounded firmly enough in any religious beliefs to spend my life as an advocate for them. But there was more to it than that. I have always been very persuaded as to the wisdom of Christianity, as presented in the injunctions of Christ and his disciples to love thy neighbour, do unto others as you would have them do unto you, be thy brother's keeper, and so on. Yet I was deeply concerned about the failure of our society to carry out these beliefs and the considerable hypocrisy on the part of many who presented themselves as true believers. I didn't reject religion entirely, but I became very suspicious of it, although that word may be a little too strong. To live the Christian ideal was difficult for anybody, but I felt that many churchgoers did not even try. Certainly, I did not feel this way about my parents, whom I believed to be very consistent and strong in their convictions. With regard to the larger picture, however, I thought that the church and many of its members did not practise what they preached when it came to the pressing social questions of the day.

Partly because of my changing career ambitions, and partly because I was feeling conscience-stricken that so many of my friends were enlisting in the military while I was living the life of a student, I switched in my second year to a three-year general arts program. The university in those days was tiny, having moved over to Hamilton to establish itself in a more independent mode than was possible by continuing to be one of the many colleges at the University of Toronto. My recollection is that the entire student body, graduate and theological students included, was less than 1,000. One came to know almost everyone on campus. I enjoyed my time at McMaster immensely and learned a great deal. I also found that the opportunities for involvement in other activities were considerable. Despite the fact that I worked for twenty and more hours a week as an organizer at the YMCA, I was active in the Board of Publications, the International Relations Club, the University Air Training Corps (which was compulsory), and a variety of other campus organizations.

As I look back on my McMaster days now, I am struck by the quality

of the faculty. Given the size of the school, we had relatively small classes, conducted by very qualified professors, who in these circumstances
were able to know about and be interested in the growth and development of individual students. One of them, Professor William Waters of
the Psychology Department, who lived to be more than 100 years old,
wrote me a letter every two or three years during his retirement, giving
me words of encouragement and constructive criticism about what I
was doing or what the labour movement was doing generally.

My involvement with the YMCA in these years had a crucial impact
on the rest of my life. Before entering McMaster, I had continued my
activity in Scouts and Cubs at the church in Hamilton and had decided
to volunteer at the summer-camp program. I have no idea now how the
original contact was made, but in 1940 we took our group to the Hamilton Y camp on Lake Erie, known as Erie Heights, for the last two weeks
of summer, when the camp had room for us. It turned out that the Y's
Howard Conquergood was the camp's director in the summer. Conquergood and I worked together extremely well from the beginning.
He suggested that the next summer we simply integrate our group
into the regular camp and invited me to come back to camp as a counsellor. He also offered me work through the winter via a fellowship
while I was at university. The fellowship involved at least twenty hours
of work a week organizing boys clubs and ultimately some teenage
groups and parent-support groups out of the Dale Community Centre in the mountain section of Hamilton. In working with youngsters,
we were following the newest idea in YMCA programming, something
called N-Y clubs.

The theory of the N-Y clubs was that children naturally develop
neighbourhood groups of peers, and that the younger the children the
more such groups come together on the basis of their immediate neighbourhood. Expert opinion was that, while the neighbourhood groups
were often very good and essential, as my old Sarnia Sports Club was
for me, they often also had the potential to be the seedbed for problems. By organizing them a little and providing some adult leadership,
it was thought, they could be encouraged to pursue positive programs
to maximize child development.

Eventually we had a number of successful clubs and parent groups
and had established a Y Men's Club that later became the core of a full-
fledged YMCA on the mountain. Unfortunately, the Erie Heights camp
has not survived, but it did some useful work along the way in what
has become a large Y community in Hamilton. Erie Heights is gone too,

but camping is not – there is now a Hamilton Y camp in a much better location in Haliburton County. At the camp, I worked my way through the various leadership positions, starting as counsellor and then moving on to section director and program director.

Howard was a dedicated CCFer and a strong supporter of unions, and, of course, the Steelworkers were already an important organization in the life of the city. He had hired Eamon Park, another member of the key Co-operative Commonwealth Youth Movement (CCYM) group in Toronto, to be his secretary. Eamon had been out of work, as were virtually all of the CCYM group at that time, a number of whom became organizers for the Steelworkers. Eamon was much more open in his discussions about the CCF in those days than was Howard, who was somewhat restrained by his position with the Y.

In the summer of 1940, Eamon and I, both of us inclined to be pacifists, were involved in frequent discussions with the camp leadership group concerning war and peace and pacifism. The discussions were during the latter part of the evenings after the campers had gone to bed. Word of this quickly found its way back to the board of directors in Hamilton and, understandably, caused Howard a great deal of difficulty. He was required to appear before the board and was interrogated by the RCMP, but he managed to explain events adequately and prevent any adverse repercussions.

It was through Eamon that I joined the CCF that same year, at the tender age of sixteen, in time to work in a by-election in Hamilton West in which David Lewis – a future leader of the CCF's successor, the New Democratic Party (NDP) – was the candidate.[1] We campaigned with a five-point program, two of which I remember. One was to establish a national health-care program and the other to legislate a national labour code, as had been done in the United States. My punch line, when telling this story later, was that I was delighted that we succeeded in accomplishing the one and forgot about the other. By 1946, I was quite knowledgeable about the party and was taking my father to CCF

---

1 Over the years, I was privileged to work closely with the Lewis family. David Lewis, as recounted in chapter 3, was the union lawyer in our drive to organize Eaton employees just after the war. His son Stephen, as leader of the Ontario NDP, played a key role in efforts to rid the party of its 'Waffle' wing, as related in chapter 8. And Stephen's brother Michael also merits mention. Like Stephen, he has worn a variety of hats in his distinguished career, contributing in particular to the Women of Steel program and its work in building the leadership potential of women in the union. This program led to the emergence of Beverly Brown, Norma Berti, and Mary Spratt, among others, as leaders in the Steelworkers.

meetings whenever I could persuade him to attend. That was usually only when major speakers such as M.J. Coldwell, the CCF's leader, and David Lewis came to the city.

I learned a great deal at the Y about organizing, because I worked so much with Howard Conquergood, who was a master of how to organize people and was educated and skilled in the psychology of it. My political work with the CCF was also useful in this regard. At the same time, I was acquiring public-speaking skills. My short career as a preacher was a great help here, obviously, but valuable as well was my Y work, which required me to make presentations as a part of organizing clubs, building parent-support groups, reporting on activities, and matters of that kind. Also important in developing my ability to speak in public were the various university activities in which I was involved, such as the University Air Training Corps, in which, as a sergeant, I had to shout out orders, a kind of public speaking. In a variety of ways, leadership roles in these organizations required a fair amount of standing up and talking, if not a great deal of formal speechmaking.

For a time, I considered social work as a career after my interest in the church had declined. In the midst of my studies at McMaster, I applied to and was accepted at the Y College in Lynn, Massachusetts, which is an option that, in the end, I did not pursue. Over time, I came to appreciate that, for all its good works, the Y was a charitable institution, dependent for its success on the support of those in the community who had the financial resources to share with those who did not. That, at its heart, is a destructive, demeaning process, requiring recipients to ask for and live on whatever charity others are willing to provide. I couldn't imagine devoting my working life to such a system, as expressed in the annual United Way drive. It is not that such work is not worthwhile and indeed necessary – I have been an active supporter of the United Way throughout my life. It was only that I concluded it was not for me.

By now, I had learned a good deal about the labour movement, having read a considerable number of books on the subject. It was not nearly enough, but my early experiences with the Y and the CCF had greatly increased my knowledge and understanding. The result of all of this was that I was enthusiastically committed to the idea of the labour movement and to finding a way to become involved in it. I didn't want to help people through charity, as the Y did. Nor did I want any kind of research job, which would tie me to a desk preparing charts and compiling data. I wanted to be in the field, building and organizing.

Hamilton was then, as it still is today, a fairly segregated city. Production workers were mostly, or in large part, immigrants or members of immigrant families from various parts of Europe. Tradesmen were by and large hired from the British Isles. They were the people whom I came to know through my work with the YMCA in the mountain section of the city. In many instances, they were quite active trade unionists or had a pro-labour history from the old country. In my eyes, their example showed that the best way for people to improve their circumstances was to do it by their own actions, with their own organization, insisting on their right to a decent share of the economic pie, which they were helping to create. That struck me as a more honourable and more adult way of achieving a fairer distribution of wealth than either the Y model of charitable giving or academic study.

As the years in university moved along, I had begun to think more and more that work in the labour movement would provide an exciting, useful, and satisfying career. With graduation approaching, I asked our dean for his advice. I expected that he might be negative about the idea. Working for the labour movement did not fit into mainstream activity in our society any more significantly then than it does today, and probably less. However, he surprised me. He had some words of caution about labour unions being a different kind of institution than most. But he was positive about their value and told me that if I had a genuine interest I should pursue it. I have always appreciated his words, not that if he had spoken otherwise it necessarily would have changed my opinion. But it was encouraging to know he supported my objectives and was willing to help in any way he could.

In 1943 Howard Conquergood left the Y to become education director for the Steelworkers in Canada. The Steelworkers had organized two major war plants in Toronto, John Inglis and Research Enterprises. There were about 18,000 workers in each plant and the union wanted to do all it could to support this large number of members, many of whom had left home and familiar surroundings to support the war effort. One idea was to develop an extensive education and recreation program. I think Murray Cotterrill, another of the CCYM group and the union's public-relations director, was the champion of this idea and also the one who suggested that Howard was the best person to execute it. Howard was delighted with the challenge and the opportunity. He worked in the labour movement for the rest of his life, first for the Steelworkers, then as the director of education for the Canadian Congress of Labour, and finally as political education director for the Canadian Labour Congress.

Howard was one of the most important influences in my life. He opened my mind not only to a constructive approach to progressive politics but also to the philosophy of the progressive education movement. I can't think of anyone quite as imaginative as him, combined with a total commitment to the people and the cause and a *joie de vivre* that knew no bounds. He always kept track of me, as he did of a number of other people whose involvement in the labour movement he had encouraged. In his travels, he would stop by to see me, always with useful and imaginative recommendations and ideas about projects in which I was then involved. The last time I saw him was during the 1958 steel strike in Hamilton when, after visiting the picket lines and reviewing the recreation and support arrangements for the strikers, he dropped down to Welland, where I was living, for a visit. He had dinner and stayed overnight. Without either Howard or me saying anything about it, we knew we were saying goodbye. He died a few weeks later.

Through my last two years in university, I had intended to join the Air Force. As a member of the University Air Training Corps, the Air Force equivalent of the Canadian Officers Training Corps (COTC), I had been promoted to sergeant by the time of graduation in May 1944. However, my interest was in air crew and they were not recruiting air crew to any significant degree, not pilots at least, and the odd person who was recruited needed absolutely perfect eyesight. While mine was very good, it was not perfect. So I joined the Navy as a second choice, in the hope that if I was there for any length of time I might be able to find my way into the Fleet Air arm. I joined as a rating and was assigned to become a telegraphist.

My basic training was at HMCS *Montcalm*, a shore station in Quebec City beside the Plains of Abraham. My telegraph training took place in Saint-Hyacinth, Quebec. It was a six-month course and then I was shipped to Halifax for appointment to whatever my assignment was to be. Four of us met with the assignment officer at the same time. He had two positions at sea and two on shore. We all insisted we had joined the Navy to go to sea, so we drew lots for the positions. I drew one of the shore jobs, which turned out to be in Newfoundland, in a little fishing village called Harbour Grace, about one hundred kilometres from St John's.

My position there was to be one of the operators (S/O, meaning Special Operator, was our rank) of a small High Frequency Direction Finding station (HFDF). Our task was to monitor the airwaves to attempt to listen to German submarines as they reported to their central station, whose call letters were ADA, in Berlin. We were to take a bearing on them while they were reporting. It was a difficult assignment because they broadcast in very short time frames. The theory was that, with a number of stations like ours around the North Atlantic, if a number of us succeeded in taking a bearing, where the bearing lines came together there would be a sub. Then the Air Force would dispatch a flight immediately to the area in the hope of bombing the enemy vessel.

I wasn't too keen about the naval experience at the time, but it really was an important event in of my life. First of all, I learned a great deal about living in a barracks with many people and being exposed to a much wider variety of lifestyles than had been my experience until then. Secondly, the time in Quebec was most interesting, particularly during the six months of training in Saint-Hyacinth. I lived as one of a group of four, with two opposing double bunks and little space in between. One of the other three was a young Jewish man from an old Montreal family. He had many insights into what was happening even then, as the spirit of Quebec nationalism was beginning to stir.

One of the basic training experiences in Quebec City was to run around the Plains of Abraham in the early morning, frequently down Wolfe's Cove to the river and then back up the cove to see how many would drop off along the way. My time in Newfoundland was less demanding physically but equally educational, though in a different way. I had seen much poverty during my boyhood days in Sarnia, but it could not compare to what I witnessed in Harbour Grace. Half the main street had burned down. The Royal Canadian Air Force had provided some lumber from buildings they were dismantling, as a way of assisting the people in Harbour Grace to rebuild their main street. However, the government commission of the time, with Newfoundland still a direct colony of Britain, was attempting to sell this lumber to the residents, none of whom had the money to purchase it. The pile of lumber remained at the edge of town and half the main street remained in ruins.

The station was so small that we all lived in the homes of local citizens. As a result, we observed their economic struggles first hand every day. Our little group of naval personnel was one of the best things that had happened to the community economically in years. Those of us in the home where I stayed were fed from four basic meal plans, in rotation, three times a day. The meals were spam, potatoes, pork and beans, and dried cod. In each case that was the total menu.

I developed no admiration for the military mind or the naval sense of organization – it seemed enormously bureaucratic, slow, tradition-bound, and frustrating. I did, however, learn how it feels to be at the bottom of a bureaucratic organization in which one has no voice. Another thing I learned is what, I suspect, every worker discovers, namely, that there are bosses who are more concerned that you look busy than making sure you are doing something useful and productive. Saturday morning was clean-up time in our barracks. I quickly discovered that I could make a full morning project out of cleaning the same radiator but would be in immediate trouble if, having cleaned it in ten minutes or so, I was caught looking around for some other useful project but not appearing to be doing anything useful. I therefore concluded that the simplest way to stay out of trouble was to pick some narrow job and stay at it, if only I could stand the boredom of it all. It was an early lesson about the relationship between supervisors and workers, how non-productive it can be when supervisors pay little attention to what is really happening and ignore the opinions of those whom they are supervising.

I had been in Harbour Grace only a few months when VE day arrived, but I volunteered to continue in the Navy until Japan was defeated. As a result, I was shipped out of Harbour Grace two days after VE day and sent home to Hamilton on extended leave, since the Navy did not have facilities established for training in Japanese code. I did not have sufficient income to support myself during this extended period, so I found a job on the labour gang in the shipping department at Stelco. It was real work, shovelling slag in front of the furnaces, unloading raw materials such as manganese and brick, and generally doing whatever was required. It was my first exposure to the steel industry close up. It was work that was contracted out – we were really employed by an entity called the Hamilton Shipping Company. I worked there under the least articulate foreman one can imagine, with a group of long-time employees who impressed me enormously with their ability to handle big loads and heavy material. When I was wheeling manganese down a plank off a boxcar, if the wheelbarrow began to tip that was the end of it, but many of my fellow workers, some of whom were much older and much smaller than me, could handle these wheelbarrows with apparent ease and never did I see them dump a load.

Before my leave was over, Japan surrendered and honourable discharge became a possibility, if one had a job and if there was some particularly important family reason to be relieved of military service. I immediately went to the Y and secured a full-time job as a community organizer for the next year. I used my mother's illness as a reason, explaining that it would be helpful in my family if I were on the scene. Having met the conditions, I was discharged.

The end of the war brought momentous changes in my personal life. I had begun dating Audrey Hansuld in Grade 13 and the two of us continued going together when we both went on to McMaster. Graduating in the same year, 1944, we were married on 12 September 1946 when I was out of the Navy and had worked at the Y for a year. My goal of building a career in the labour movement was a novel idea for her, but, from the beginning, she was a loyal supporter and helper. At her parents' home, life was much more regular and moved at a much steadier and more predictable pace than what she would experience with me. She accepted all of that. Her father had been a management person in the meatpacking industry. In retirement, he began working as a salesman for a group of immigrants from Czechoslovakia, selling highly productive pasture seed around Ontario and Quebec. Eventually he became a partner in the company.

These were heady days for North American labour. In 1945 and 1946 CIO industrial unionism came of age in the United States and Canada. Emerging out of the Great Depression in 1935–6, the CIO, under the leadership of the legendary John L. Lewis, was committed to leaving behind the old model of craft unionism – in which workers were organized by craft – in favour of industrial unionism, whereby all workers in a given industry would be organized into a single union regardless of their specific occupation. Founded by eight international unions belonging to the American Federation of Labor, the CIO broke from the AFL in 1938 but years later, in 1955, the two bodies would come back together to form the AFL-CIO. In its early days, the CIO waged a number of high-profile battles, particularly in the automotive sector, and afterwards obtained unexpected leverage from the outbreak of the Second World War, as enormous increases in military production allowed unions to achieve economic gains for their members and improvements in recognition as well. However, with the end of the war, the major industrial corporations in both countries immediately went on the offensive to roll back recognition and economic gains, while the unions were similarly on the offensive to improve them. In 1945 the Rand formula came into effect, requiring all workers covered by a union contract to pay dues but not to join the union, thus avoiding compulsory unionism. That year and the following, there were major strikes in steel, auto, rubber, and many other industries in both countries. In one of those strikes, at Stelco's Hamilton operations, the company launched a particularly aggressive, even vicious, anti-union program – housing scabs inside the plant, wining and dining them and paying them twenty-four-hour wages for eight hours worked – without a care in the world that its actions were ripping the city in two, turning father against son, brother against brother, wife against husband. After a bitter struggle, the union emerged victorious, with its security intact and a wage increase in place.

These events began a period of significant progress for the labour movement. Organization grew in both countries, new sectors such as public employees joined the fold, and incomes and living standards improved. Certainly, for myself, the Stelco strike of 1946 was a critically important event in firming up my desire to be a front-line activist in the labour movement. I had decided by then that the labour movement was where I was heading, although I am sure I made a nuisance of myself by raising the subject constantly with Howard Conquergood and Larry Sefton, who was director of District 6, headquartered in Toronto, of the United Steelworkers of America. The problem was always that the union didn't hire college kids to be organizers. It was suggested that it would be easy for me to be a researcher or something like that. But I didn't want to sit behind a desk doing research. I wanted to be where the action was. The normal reply was that I would have to go to work in a plant and I said when that becomes appropriate that is what I'll do. But first I was going back to school.

In September 1946, after Audrey and I were married, I enrolled at the University of Toronto in a two-year master's program in industrial relations that had recently been established by the economics professor Vincent Bladen. In the summer break after the first year, I was hired at John Inglis, where the Steelworkers represented the workers. There, I volunteered for everything in the local union, including the first summer school the Canadian Congress of Labour had ever conducted. Not surprisingly, it was being conducted by my good friend Howard Conquergood. I offered to attend for two weeks at my own expense if the local union would designate me an official delegate. It was a deal they could not refuse.

At the end of the two weeks I discovered, unbeknownst to me, that Eileen Talman Sufrin had been attending, in part for a break but also to find someone to work with her on the Eaton's department store campaign. A former CCYM member who would go on to become one of the most celebrated organizers in Canadian union history, Eileen offered me a job on the Eaton campaign, which I accepted immediately. I went to work in the labour movement full time on the first working day in August 1947. Whether Howard and Larry Sefton had something to do with Eileen offering me a job, I have no idea. Neither she nor they ever mentioned it, but I also know that neither of them was shy about making recommendations.

I never did finish my degree at the university. I finished the course work after I started to work in the labour movement and had only a dissertation to do. The university agreed I could do it about the Eaton drive, but I never got around to it. A few years ago, the University of Toronto gave me an honorary doctorate. I thanked them for finally giving me a degree and apologized for my negligence.

These were exciting and hopeful times. By 1947, when I started on the Eaton drive, the war had been over for a couple of years, the United Nations had been established, and the labour movement had been through its crucial struggles in 1945 and 1946 in both the United States and Canada, with major struggles in the steel, auto, and electrical sectors in both countries. These were struggles about what the future was to hold. Were the unions to be beaten and battered by the employers and put in their place, if not destroyed? Or had they survived the fight and were on their way to achieving a better life for their members and a more secure position for themselves? Those of us in the union movement knew the answer. We were confident in 1947 that the future was ours.

My personal ambitions were focused on joining the labour movement, getting involved and being an activist, and seeing where it led. What I mean by that is that I simply wanted to be part of building. I had no fancy ambitions. I had come to know quite a bit about labour, but I don't think, in retrospect, that I had much political sense about it. I was not thinking of progressing to better jobs or any such thing. I was caught up in the idea of being part of the labour movement, of organizing people, of making a difference in working people's lives. That was what the labour movement was doing across the world in those years. Just the idea of being part of that was satisfying beyond belief or imagination.

3

THE EATON DRIVE

The Eaton campaign in the late 1940s had a critical impact on my involvement in the labour movement. Indeed, it is difficult for me to imagine any other way I could have learned as much as I did about the work of union organizing.

Those of us involved in the Eaton campaign saw it as the first step in organizing the department-store field in Canada. The decision to focus initially on Eaton's Toronto operations was essentially based on the large size of those operations relative to all others. There were five principal sites: three stores (the main store at Queen and Yonge, the Annex store at Albert and James, and the College St store at College and Yonge) plus the delivery and auto repair departments on Hayter St and the factory departments at James St and Trinity Square. The total workforce was 13,000, a number far greater than that of any other gathering of department-store employees anywhere else in the country. To approach department-store organizing by concentrating on some dramatically smaller operation somewhere else seemed an invitation to failure. Simpson's was a possibility. It was almost as prestigious as Eaton's though somewhat smaller, but there had quite recently – it was felt too recently – been a failed AFL campaign there.

The campaign was conducted in the name of the Retail, Wholesale and Department Store Union (RWDSU), and its organizing committee included the top leaders of the industrial union movement in Canada. Fred Dowling, Canadian director of the Packinghouse Workers, was the chairman; Charlie Millard, Canadian director of the Steelworkers, was the vice-chairman. The other members were: Norman Twist, Canadian director of the RWDSU; Pat Conroy, secretary treasurer of the Canadian Congress of Labour (CCL); George Burt, Canadian director of the United Auto Workers; and Eileen Tallman Sufrin, director of the campaign. All believed that, given the labour movement's accomplishments in the struggles of 1945 and 1946, the major battles were behind them and now it was a question of building and consolidating. So they were willing to tackle as traditionally difficult a target as Eaton's.

There were all the traditional difficulties presented by white-collar workers: their feeling that unions were for others, the 'workers,' not for people like them; their anxiety about losing their jobs; their concern that joining a union represented a loss of status and prestige, that unionization would subject them to rules and regulations which would take no account of their individual qualities and accomplishments; and their fear of the union itself as an unknown player in a work atmosphere that they viewed as congenial, sociable, and somewhat prestigious. In addition, there were some circumstances that were Eaton-specific. Pre-eminent among these were the emotional ties to Timothy Eaton's homeland of Northern Ireland, which meant that immigrants from there looking for a new life and new opportunities in Canada could count on Eaton's as a place to begin. Also, Eaton's policy of accepting returned goods with no questions asked was famous and popular and the employees to some extent lived in its reflected glory. Similarly, they lived to some degree in the reflected glory of the company's business success and its support of a variety of good works, not the least of which were the Eaton family's church activities and the company's sponsorship for many years of the annual Santa Claus parade. Many workers took much pride and satisfaction in this mix of business acumen and social role playing and overlooked the downside of low wages, lack of benefits, and limited future prospects.

None of this deterred Eileen Tallman Sufrin. One of the very best organizers in the early days of the Steelworkers, she had been a leader in the drive to organize Inglis, then a war plant with 18,000 people, half of whom were women. She and Bill Sefton, Larry Sefton's brother, had been the chief organizers in that campaign, and she had also been involved in a number of other organizing efforts, including an attempt to organize bank workers across Canada. She had developed and honed her skills in organizing out in the real world by doing it, successfully and otherwise. Over the course of her career, she would organize many thousands of women across Canada.

Eileen had been working on the Eaton drive for a few months before she hired me. She had devoted her time to learning the layout of the main store in downtown Toronto, at Yonge and Queen streets, and preparing some blueprints and pictures of the various floors and departments. In this way, along with reading every bit of available literature, she was able to know and understand the structure of the company. She also started the direct house-call part of the campaign, beginning with names that came out of the earlier Simpson's campaign but also involving people who were thought to have moved across the street to work at Eaton's, which at the time, in department store terms, was considered an institution in Canada.

We knew from the beginning that there was no way of conducting a campaign in a unit of this size without it becoming a public activity. There was a limit to how long we could only work from door to door. By the beginning of 1948, we felt we had done enough preparation and we launched Local 1000 with a meeting at the Wakanda Centre on Bloor Street. The place was chosen carefully in terms of location and size, readily reached by public transportation and not too big. We were granted an RWDSU charter for Local 1000 and that became the banner for our organizing efforts from then on.

All of our activity increased in intensity during that fall. The staff grew during those months to what became its basic size, with little change during the rest of the campaign. The person hired after me was Wally Ross, another protégé of Howard Conquergood. Wally was then working as an insurance agent but had been an active Steelworker during the war. Missing one eye, he had been unable to join the military and instead had gone to work at Research Enterprises, a major wartime plant in Leaside in the Toronto suburbs, where he had met Howard. Wally was an imaginative, energetic, adventuresome person who could not have been more suited for the work of the campaign. In later life he would go back to sales, this time in real estate. In terms of the Eaton campaign, the practical abilities of an insurance salesman were very valuable because in those days labour organizing was largely a door-to-door, person-to-person kind of business.

Wally not only brought many practical and thoughtful techniques to our work but was also a fascinating colleague. He had been in the mathematics and physics program at the University of Toronto, and though he did not graduate, his high intelligence was evident. He was a wonderful raconteur, knowledgeable about music, and a great reader. Eileen was also well read, particularly in political and economic matters, so that the quality of conversation in our group was high and often related in interesting ways to the work we were doing.

Another colleague, Ernie Arnold, who joined the drive in 1949, brought a practical, almost hard-headed realism to our work, while being as soft-hearted and caring a person as you could ever meet. He was the one among us who had the most experience as a union member. Wally's work at Research Enterprises had stopped at the end of the war. Eileen had never worked at the places she had organized and I had been a worker only briefly at John Inglis. In terms of how the labour movement operated, how people reacted, and why things were done in certain ways, Ernie brought a clear and useful understanding of what rank-and-file spirit was all about. He understood how people reacted to events, to each other, and to their employer. He was a model organizer in coming to know the people he was attempting to organize, and in his loyalty to them and identification with their concerns. His principal area of responsibility was the mail-order part of the business. I think that there were employees there with whom Ernie exchanged Christmas cards for the rest of his life.

Marjorie Gow joined us in the fall of 1948 to be our public-relations person. She had been a Steelworker employee/secretary and had excellent writing and general communication skills that she had developed and used, among other places, at the 1946 Stelco strike. There were also two secretaries in the original crew, one of whom was Olive Richardson (Chester). Olive was hired as office manager but demonstrated such outstanding interpersonal skills that by 1950 she was added to the organizing team. As she recalled in 2009, when she and I were the only surviving members of the core group of organizers:

> They thought I should go and organize 1,000 people on the main floor of Eaton's, so I did. I think it's a matter of being people oriented. God yes, I enjoyed it. You'd get up at six o'clock to be down at the factory or College Street for seven o'clock in the morning. Then we'd do the leaflet distribution and go down to the store. We never seemed to get into trouble for wandering around the store. I'd go all around the main floor and I'm sure I got known. I wouldn't spend a lot of time at the counter. What I would do is I'd go and meet somebody and then arrange a coffee time down in the Hub, which was a big restaurant in the basement (of the Eaton's store) at the time. And then we'd talk.

Olive, who is a 'people person' par excellence, never encountered difficulty in talking to employees during the organizing campaign. 'They may not have agreed with you or you might have had to explain to them why it was a good idea for them to join the union, but I don't remember ever running into any anti people. I don't remember any-body you couldn't talk to,' she said in 2009. 'People would say they're not interested, but you might still have a conversation with them. But there was a lot of acceptance. And the other thing that happened as we were giving out leaflets … they got wage increases. They got some benefits out of our organizing. They didn't really want to see us not keep organizing. They may not have been too keen about getting the union but they didn't want us not to be there. Us being there was very advantageous to them. They were getting a lot of benefits. A lot of things happened.' (Indeed, the pension plan put in place at Eaton's came towards the end of our organizing drive.) Before the campaign concluded, Olive emigrated to England where she worked for a time for Labour Party MPs in the House of Commons. She later returned to Canada and ultimately to an outstanding career in the conciliation department of the Ontario Ministry of Labour.

Our leader, Eileen, was an incredibly efficient worker. Her leader-ship style was not to expect anything of others that she didn't do in excess herself. She set an example for all of us. She also was disciplined. Following her cue, we took a break in the evening at 5 p.m. for a little while, and then worked the evenings again. We had staff parties regu-larly, in which she was an enthusiastic participant. But our real focus was on the campaign and its people, and the cause was not going to be lost by lack of effort on the part of the organizers.

Olive also has a clear and fond recollection of Eileen's leadership:

Eileen was a good boss. She knew the business and she taught us. We had weekly staff meetings where we had to write out what we had done all week. Then, we'd all read each other's report and we'd talk about it. These meetings were quite something. This is where all the ideas would come out. Whoever had been thinking of something while they were having a beer, you saved it and tried it out at the meeting to see if it would work. I can't imagine any other drive where the organizers had to write a report every week. It all made absolute sense because we all knew what each other was doing.

We all liked one another and we all assumed that everybody knew what they were doing. There wasn't any criticism about anybody. I don't remember anyone saying anything nasty about anybody. They were all very special people. We were all dedicated. We all cared a lot.

At the time, Eileen was the focus of a major article on the Eaton drive by the late June Callwood in *Maclean's* magazine, published on 1 October 1950. The lead paragraph got right to the point. 'Eileen Tallman is a five-foot-two blonde who works a 70-hour week organizing unions so that other people can have a 40-hour week.' It was a fitting description.

The house-call program was massive. Our employee list, which was the basis for the program, was compiled simply by talking to people and making note of the Eaton workers they knew. Later, we developed this list further through department and other meetings. Over the months and years – the Eaton campaign would last four years in all – we understandably became better organized and in the end developed an extremely accurate list of Eaton employees, all by word of mouth.

For about a year during our campaign, we had no automobile so we were doing our massive home-canvassing effort entirely by bus and streetcar. Any evening, Monday through Friday, when there was nothing else to do, it was expected that one would make house calls. Even then, Toronto was a big city, making it necessary to plan in order to use the time efficiently. To maximize the number of calls, we made visits as close to each other as possible, minimizing travel time. The assumption was that we would visit three prospective members in an evening. To accomplish that we would plan about ten calls, start early, and not bother people by calling too late.

Then I bought a car in 1948. It was the only car we had for some considerable time and we all used it. Eileen bought the next car, then Wally bought one, and we ultimately had enough cars to do the job without relying on the streetcars.

Phone calls were added to our program as we attempted to assess the situation as quickly as possible. This, too, was a major effort. We maintained index-card files on all the employees we had identified, with detailed information about our calls. We organized the filing system by department with four categories: very good, possible, unlikely, and opposed. Olive adds: 'The card information we gathered was important. We probably knew more about their workforce than they did.'

The systems we put in place brought in increasing amounts of information. We never made a house call without asking the person to list everybody they knew, along with addresses and phone numbers, and always with a program of follow-up and keeping in touch. Depending on the amount of information a person gave us and the quality of that information, we were able to test the effectiveness of our follow-up activity. It was considered a serious mistake, no matter how supportive a potential member of the union might appear, to fail to collect as much information as possible on every call.

By the end of the campaign, when we were examining bargaining units in the stores and other facilities, we indeed had more accurate information than the company at the Labour Board hearings, as Olive intimated earlier. This was an enormous tribute to the work that had been accomplished, and to Eileen's leadership and persistence in insisting and ensuring that it was done properly and carefully, with full accountability for timeliness and accuracy. As our lawyer, David Lewis, would later write in his memoirs:

> The people we had the pleasure of associating with in this case were incredibly hard working. Eileen Tallman, whom I knew as an active member of the CCF Youth, led them. Although there were others in the organizing group, we worked mainly with Lynn Williams, Wally Ross and Ernie Arnold, in addition to Tallman. They were undoubtedly one of the most competent teams of organizers, communicators, and planners one could wish to see. Nothing was overlooked, nothing was done sloppily; the information lawyers received was always reliable and logically organized. They deserved to win.[1]

To my surprise, my experiences in the YMCA were very relevant to organizing work. In fact, to some degree, the skills I picked up there were more easily applied in this campaign, in that we were doing something new in a different, largely white-collar setting. That in itself, of course, presented its own challenges, making traditional organizing inappropriate.

The techniques I refer to were such things as running social events to encourage participation, having competitions among teams and groups to sign cards, and using a large thermometer-style chart on our building to spur competition and publicize progress in various sections and departments. These were virtually exact duplicates of the fund-raising techniques used in social-agency campaigns, such as the ones I had experienced at the Y. The Y strategy of bringing groups of people together to solve problems and determine objectives was also directly applicable to a union organizing project. Certainly, in our circumstances we could not simply knock on doors and sign cards. It was necessary

---

1 David Lewis, *The Good Fight: Political Memoirs, 1909–1958* (Toronto: Macmillan of Canada 1981), 394.

to create an organization with leaders and commitment, with internal direction, organizational structure, and accountability. In this part of our work as well, all the skills and techniques of group work had a direct application.

Another point I would make is that, because of these unusual circumstances, nothing quite like this campaign had been attempted before, with such focus, discipline, and determination. There was a great deal of what is now called 'thinking outside of the box.' It was a most imaginative effort. We were, for example, conscious of the fact that we were dealing with white-collar workers. We had our critics within the labour movement at the time, and when we had difficulties these people would say that one of our problems was that we were not sensitive to white-collar workers' needs and points of view. My strongly held opinion is that these comments came from ignorance of the realities of the campaign.

Our leafleting of the stores was built around a publication we had created, called *Unionize*. At various stages we published as frequently as once a week. 'Through the pages of Unionize, the union keeps employees of Eaton's informed of alleged inequalities in pay, raises in various departments and airs charges of unfair treatment of employees and poor working conditions,' Callwood wrote in *Maclean's*. *Unionize* had original cartoons, mostly created in the beginning by George Luscombe, later of Workshop Theatre fame. When an issue came to our attention, Marjorie would write a story about it and George would do a cartoon. Much thought went into the make-up of *Unionize*, which, as early as 1948, was promoting the causes of women's rights and equal pay for equal work.

Given the length and complexity of the campaign, we developed a variety of techniques to keep interest up and attention focused. We had many stunts, such as handing out helium-filled balloons at Christmas with 'Join Local 1000' printed on them. The children took them with great enthusiasm, but they frequently slipped out of their hands, whereupon the balloons would rise to the ceiling. Then kids would cry, wanting their balloons back. Many managers spent a good part of the day scrambling up ladders to pull down helium-filled balloons. The greatest balloon show was on the first floor of the main store, a large, busy, customer-filled floor with a high ceiling.

Of course, our people enjoyed all this and the public received information that the news media of the day would not provide, so intimidated were they by the large advertising business of Eaton's. Over the four years of the campaign, being carried out every day in the heart of the city, the newspapers carried only two items of news – one on the day we applied for certification, the other on the day we lost the vote. Our stunts had many purposes, the principal ones being maintaining morale and informing the public. On another occasion we printed thousands of duplicates of Eaton's pay envelopes. We put two or three peanuts in each and printed a slogan on them: 'Why work for peanuts?' Everybody enjoyed that event. There were also dinners for Eaton's employees, dances, and fashion shows. The intention was to entertain the people being organized and get them interested in joining the union. Olive has a picture of two men at one of the dances covering their faces when a photographer appeared, so they couldn't be identified.

It was a time of enormous turnover at Eaton's. As I've said, the business was the first stop for many immigrants coming from the old country, particularly from Northern Ireland. The word was that, if you were from Northern Ireland and went to Eaton's looking for a job, you would be hired without difficulty. And, regardless of what Timothy Eaton's Northern Irish roots might have had to do with that hiring, it seemed there was always a job at Eaton's because it had so many people going out the door all the time. Yet, despite the high turnover, we encountered a large number of fence sitters among the workforce. A great many people, when we asked them to join the union, would say, 'Well, I would but I am not going to stay.' Some of the same people said that to us for four years, but a great many left, too, and neither group made our work any easier.

Then there were the people who told us they didn't want to join but would vote for us if given the opportunity. They simply were not telling the truth. It became standard for me to tell organizers that, usually when people say they do not wish to join the union but will vote for you, they don't have the courage to say they want nothing to do with you. They're trying to let you down easily. The reality of organizing campaigns is that the number of voters is always somewhat less than the number of cards you have signed up, rarely more.

When you're organizing in more traditional areas, such as the steel industry, everyone knows there's a good effective union and that it works. Some whom you approach may argue, but you need not scratch too deeply and they will admit, 'Sure it works and the people do very well, but I don't want to join.' However, when it came to organizing a huge department store like Eaton's for the first time, the situation was completely different. It was such a big, dominant company in Toronto and we had no comparable union organization to point to in Canada, as do the Steelworkers when they approach workers in an unorganized steel facility. In some ways, it was as if we had to reinvent the rules of organizing.

We were constantly being asked if we really understood department stores. Part of the Hudson's Bay store in Winnipeg was organized and so was Woodward's in Vancouver, but both were much smaller stores and a long way from Toronto. U.S. politician Tip O'Neill famously said, 'All politics is local,' and union organizing is no different. The people, as they must, make their own decisions in terms of their own needs. It was necessary for us to come to understand their situation as quickly as we could. There were a multitude of questions because, as far as our Eaton members were concerned, we were creating department store unionism from the ground up, starting with the very basics.

This is a helpful way to think about the organizer's task, however strong or weak the union may be. The organizer's job is to help the people create an instrument and learn how to use that instrument most effectively. In the Eaton campaign, we had many meetings with the members about how the union would work in their department. A great deal of creativity went into that. Of course, having them understand how the union would work for them was a principal means by which we won their interest and confidence.

Talent and thinking outside the box go together. Our group had talent in abundance, and the circumstances permitted ideas and imagination to enjoy free rein. These went far beyond what might have been likely in a traditional campaign. The fact that we were dealing with a department store, with large numbers of people coming to work at the same time, and on downtown sidewalks, created a place for visiting and something of a stage. To be sure, handing out leaflets was a challenge. To cover properly the number of entrances, we needed twenty-three people for every leaflet distribution, which in turn required the support of the broader labour movement and of other volunteers from all over town. For years, many people who said they worked on the Eaton campaign meant that they were volunteer leaflet distributors. We encouraged them to be proud of their contribution. It was a miserable job in the winter, often pleasurable in the good weather, and always interesting in terms of the chit-chat with the folks going to work. After the distributions, we would all have breakfast together, gatherings that were a kind of Toronto labour forum of the week.

Towards the end of the campaign, we were focusing on the undecided workers and the reasons for their indecision. We asked the members in merchandise display to make us a mugwump costume, a bird that sits with its mug on one side of the fence and its wump on the other. They did a beautiful job, constructing a mugwump big enough for a person to stand inside. Wally was usually the person who took on the mugwump role. Adding a special touch of his own – one of those rubber devices that makes a blabbing noise when blown through, acting as a sort of microphone – he would put this creation on and go to the gates blowing on his blabber and say, 'Why be a Mugwump with your mug on one side of the fence and your wump on the other'? It is time to make up your mind.' We thought that it helped. It certainly helped in providing some fun, too, an important part of any campaign – a lesson that stuck with me in later years. In a strike, if you can keep morale high and people have a good time, their solidarity and determination benefit enormously and boost the chances of success. The same is true in an organizing campaign. Indeed, keeping morale high is sometimes more easily accomplished in an organizing campaign because the pressures involved may not be as great as those in a strike.

We also did a couple of dumb things, though, of course, we did not realize until afterwards how dumb we had been. On one occasion during the campaign, the Eaton family went away for a summer vacation in Europe. While they were gone, their house in north Toronto, in Forest Hill Village, up the street from Timothy Eaton Church, was redecorated from top to bottom. It was a lovely home, in the white, flat-roofed, round-cornered, modern style with which architects and builders were experimenting at the time, and it remains today one of the outstanding examples of this style in Toronto. The security people who looked after it at night were mostly members of ours and one evening a couple of them who were close to us called the office to see if we were around. Of course, we were around every evening; we might be out knocking on doors but one of us would usually be tending the office as well. The guards asked us if we would like to come up and see this house and we leapt at the opportunity.

So as to be quiet and not too obvious, we waited until fairly late and went up and did the tour. None of us had seen a home like this in our lives. Among its features were thirteen bathrooms, a particularly elegant dining room with a vast etched-glass mirror on one wall, a built-in theatre complete with plush theatre seats and a projection booth, an elevator, and a turntable in the garage so you could drive a car in and turn it around and drive it out. I don't recall how many cars could fit in the garage, nor how the turntable worked. By our standards, the house simply had everything that could be imagined.

We, of course, were scandalized by all of this luxury and the inequality that it demonstrated and symbolized. Here are these people with all this wealth and living in all this luxury, in such contrast to the people working for them in their department store, mostly for miserable wages and often living in very modest circumstances. We prepared a leaflet emphasizing all these points, including a picture of the house. We thought it would be a real hit. Instead, it was anything but and we endured a storm of criticism, which went like this: 'We, the employees, the members of Local 1000, do not want the family to be attacked personally. That is not why we have joined the union. We have joined in order to win representation and improve our circumstances. Our purpose is not to attack the Eaton family.' Not all the employees felt this way, but it was very difficult for us with those who did. They tended to be impressed with the Eatons, loyal to them for a variety of reasons and often enjoying their association with the family's reputation for good works around the city. Our leaflet turned out to be absolutely the wrong thing to do. The mistake we made was that, in our certainty that the leaflet would be a hit, we had consulted only ourselves. We had not shown the leaflet to anyone before handing it out, so as to maximize its impact. In terms of impact, we succeeded, but not as we had intended.

It is so easy for a group of professionals, or a group of outsiders, or the people who are working full time on the campaign to wind themselves up about something that sounds terrific to them but just does not resonate with the group they are trying to persuade. Needless to say, we were more cautious during the rest of the Eaton campaign. Personally, I learned that lesson well and tried hard to apply it in every subsequent campaign in which I was involved.

Funding the Eaton drive was never easy, since the Retail, Wholesale and Department Store Union did not have the resources to sustain such a campaign over a long period of time. At one point, when the RWDSU was in some difficulty, the CIO offered the jurisdiction to the Amalgamated Clothing Workers. As a result, Amalgamated paid for us for a while, but they decided they were not interested in keeping the jurisdiction or in keeping us.

We had to raise our own money to some degree, and we did this by going around to local unions affiliated to the Canadian Congress of Labour and persuading them to donate money to the Eaton drive, preferably, as charitable institutions request today, on the basis of a monthly contribution rather than a single, one-time donation. It fell to me, in the way our work was divided up, to do most of the fundraising. Eileen looked after the key major local unions and everyone on the staff spoke to groups. The fundraising was intermittent rather than constant and was usually built around a major labour event, such as CCL conventions, at which we would contact local leaders and arrange visits to their locals. More frequently than was comfortable, we would run out of money and needed to seek support if the organizing campaign was to continue.

It frequently happened that a major donation from one union or another would set us up for a few months, but then we would face a crisis, and the fundraising would begin again in earnest. For me, fundraising was a wonderful way to meet many people in a variety of unions and learn a great deal on the ground floor about labour. I came to know well the more generous unions, and most particularly the Steelworkers (locals 1005 and 2251 were especially helpful to us), the UAW, and Textile and Rubber. I met local union activists across Canada and learned much about the labour movement, knowledge that would have taken a long time to accumulate in other circumstances. Exposure to other unions and their leaders gave me a frame of reference in which to compare union models, assess the value of various initiatives, and determine whether there were any useful ideas or activities being pursued in the wider labour movement that I could take back to our campaign.

This experience stood me in good stead in many ways. One recurrent issue in these sessions, for example, was that someone always wanted to run a boycott. We were forever explaining that, in trying to persuade employees to come into a union, a boycott wasn't helpful. The employees, with a little push from their managers, usually interpreted a boycott as a threat to their ability to earn a living from people not wanting to shop there. So we had to take a different approach, using the presence of shoppers as an opportunity to 'talk union' and persuade people to join.

The Eaton drive also gave me a chance to see one of Canada's best minds and best speakers at work, up close. One of our important decisions, and more contentious it seems in retrospect than it should have been, was who should be our lawyer, because it was anticipated by everybody involved that there would be a real struggle before the Labour

Relations Board. Whatever the issues might be, that would be a battle-
ground where the company would be most active and not spare anything in the use of its considerable resources. David Lewis had been
called to the bar many years before and by 1950 was a partner in a
new labour law firm in Toronto, along with Ted Jolliffe, who had been
leader of the CCF in Ontario, and John Osler. It was recognized as a
prestigious firm with partners of prominence and importance. However, Charles Dubbin, active in the Conservative Party, was then regarded
as probably the most effective and most expensive labour lawyer in
the city. And so we were faced with a dilemma. Should a campaign
of this consequence be put in the hands of the most experienced person available or in those of someone who was somewhat lacking in
experience but of unquestioned talent and obviously totally committed
to our cause? Dubbin could not have begun to match David Lewis's
commitment. The decision was made clearly in David's favour and he
performed magnificently.

Over the course of the campaign, Eaton's fought the union vigorously, but for the most part in its own underground way, not with open
hostility. It was known that the company did not like the union. Its
sentiments were given expression from time to time by a manager here
or an Eaton official there. Lady Eaton stopped one day when she was
going into the College Street store at the time the workers were arriving. She approached Ernie, who was handing out leaflets. Why was he
bothering to hand out leaflets in a place that did not need them? Why
he didn't go and organize a place that really needed a union? Ernie
replied that that was precisely why he was there.

That was about as overt as Eaton's became for most of the campaign
and there was no firing of people that could be challenged. Some of our
key people were let go over the years, and the company undoubtedly
was pleased to see them go, but there was always some reason that
made the discharge defensible on other grounds. We never really knew,
in such instances, the extent to which their activity in the union played
a role in the firing or if it did at all. The most common reason was theft.
There is a significant amount of petty theft in a department store, at
least there was in those days, and some wonderful people engaged in it.
There was a pervasive feeling that they were paid so poorly that any little thing they could pick up was only fair compensation for their inadequate pay. I am not suggesting that there was an enormous amount of
this going on, but it did happen.

In a store such as Eaton's, there was a hierarchy of departments in terms of earnings. The further up the hierarchy you were, the more likely you were to be on an Eaton's committee to raise money for the United Way or to be a representative of the company in some similar public capacity. It was the straight commission salesmen, rug salesmen particularly, who headed the hierarchy, followed by appliances, men's clothing and women's clothing, and so on, straight commission changing to salary plus commission along the way. The idea, of course, was to encourage sales by rewarding those who sold more with relatively higher earnings. As you moved down further, the wages became worse and worse and, of course, these were the jobs with the highest turnover, often filled by newcomers working there while they looked for better employment or by young people as entry jobs into the workforce.

Finally, towards the end of the campaign, the company did conduct a highly publicized campaign against the union. During the final six to eight weeks before the vote, it formed an organization called Loyal Eatonians, which began with a leaflet-distribution effort, gathering as many people as they could around the entrances on the days they distributed their material. One of their most famous leaflets carried the headline, 'Get Your Hands out of Our Pockets.' The story was about union dues and how we would be pursuing a compulsory check-off and that all employees would have to pay dues to an organization that they did not need anyway. They described us as representing third-party interference in their relations with the company.

This sudden switch to an attack mode should not have surprised us, but it did. We all learned from the experience, but we were not prepared for it. Our people were somewhat in a state of shock because Eaton's had not played it negatively until then. We disagreed among ourselves on how to respond. Therefore, we did not respond at all for a time, while we debated whether just to laugh it off or fight it vigorously. One concern was that attacking the company's claims too seriously might make them seem more legitimate than they were. We kept discussing what to do, changing direction often, but failed to establish a steady strategic approach with which everyone was satisfied. Over the years, I have learned from many campaigns that it is better to have a strategy and pursue it consistently, even if it isn't the best strategy, than to have none.

We continued hopping around and presenting, I am afraid, an image of considerable indecision, rather like neophyte political candidates when they are on the receiving end of some really brutal and disgraceful negative campaigning. They want so badly to believe that nobody would believe such outrageous charges. Should we simply ignore them, pretend that they were not there, and carry on with our campaign? That was a very inviting strategy because it did not demand anything new or different of the campaign, but it obviously was not remotely adequate – our activists and supporters needed much more. In retrospect, we probably had a little too much of that approach.

The other strategy under debate was to go right after the company and challenge its facts and assumptions, indeed its entire line of attack. This option was regarded fairly negatively by a lot of our people. I'm inclined to think, however, that the company's charges had a significant impact on the people in the middle whose votes were critical. They inclined many to be afraid of the union, afraid of what it might do and how things might change. The end of any campaign that involves change is nearly always the most difficult time as people hesitate to cross the line to something new.

My funniest anecdote about this issue involved an employee in one of the women's departments. She had been planning to vote for us and admitted she had not. When I asked why, she answered, 'You know, except for the wages and the working conditions, this isn't a bad place to work.' It was always good for a laugh when I told a union audience that story, but I repeatedly admonished them to think about what she was really saying. Her point was that she enjoyed the atmosphere of the work, though she did not like the poor wages and conditions, and she was concerned that the union would interfere with the parts of the job she enjoyed. So she was wary of change. I think that fear was the result of, or at least encouraged by, the company campaign in that it stirred up the fear of change among the workforce.

Despite the company's offensive, we remained supremely confident that, given the opportunity to vote, many who had not signed union cards would be certain to vote for the union. It was almost inconceivable to us that they would not do so because of all the things we knew about their circumstances, their wages, and their struggles. I remember making a house call on a fine person who was in one of the better departments. He had a relatively large family and when I went to visit him I was shocked that his living room had not one stick of furniture. It wasn't that they were waiting for new furniture to arrive. I think he just did not have enough money yet to furnish the room, but he and his wife needed the house for their kids. It was unthinkable to us that people such as him would not at least vote to have a union.

The final act began with our application for certification in October 1950. The delays in procedure held up the voting for more than a year, until December 1951. During that time, there were three major rounds of hearings, each of which lasted for two days. There was also a six-week investigation into the bargaining unit. The issues in the investigation were all created by the company, as it attempted to load the bargaining unit with supervisors, while we endeavoured to draw as rational a line as possible between the positions that were truly supervisory and those that were not. Looking back, we were far more confident of winning than obviously we should have been. Had we known better, we might have been tempted to try to shape the bargaining unit towards 'yes' voters. But we were sincerely trying to find the appropriate line. We were, after all, in essentially new territory in Canada. There were not many department stores organized and those that were had been so for a long time. We saw ourselves as pioneers, leading the way in making determinations about appropriate bargaining units and in many other ways. We envisaged the Eaton campaign, if it succeeded, as signalling the beginning of significant retail union organization in Canada.

Faced with a multitude of bargaining-unit issues, the Labour Relations Board asked its examiners, A.M. Brunskill and J.M. Flannery, to conduct an investigation into these matters. David, Eileen, and I represented the union. It was quite an experience to sit with David for six straight weeks, involved in the multitude of confrontations that were required. On the company side of the table sat Irving Webster Ford, head of its employee-relations operation, J.C. Adams, dean of the company's labour lawyers, and J.T. Weir, of the firm that served as general counsel for the company. From a personal perspective, there was enormous satisfaction in seeing the value of all the diligent work we had done in gathering and checking information. We had put great effort into canvassing, keeping records on index cards, and poring over lists of department employees. We had maintained such activity constantly throughout the campaign to ensure that we understood the unit, knew what was happening, knew how many people were there, where they were, and what they were doing. We had done our work so well that frequently our records about the unit were much more accurate than the company's.

I remember one day when Ford, unable to contain his annoyance and frustration, blurted out to Art Brunskill, registrar of the Department of Labour and in charge of the investigation: 'You might as well ask Williams, he seems to know the answers to all these questions.' Of course, the backhanded compliment was misplaced: it was not that I was so well informed, but that I happened to be custodian of information that all of us had put together. In any case, I took a great deal of satisfaction from Ford's comment, for all of us. The truth is that we never did see or find an official list of employees. The lists we had were all the result of painstakingly asking people, holding department meetings, making house calls, telephoning, and going over and over the lists to be sure that we were accurate and that we knew who was signed up and who was not, who did what, and on and on.

On the day of the vote, Eileen and I walked down from our office at Bay and Dundas streets to the main store. The route passed Toronto's only cocktail bar of that time, the Silver Rail at Yonge and Shuter, so we stopped in to have a drink. We were a little early. During the entire time we walked and stopped for the drink we talked only about what we were going to do next, after the victory. The thought that we could lose never entered our conversation and certainly, as far as I am concerned, never crossed my mind.

This was in December 1951. We had begun this journey in the summer of 1947. We had worked so hard and so long and had so many promises and so many people interested that, even though we knew our margin to be close in terms of having enough to apply for certification and successfully win the right to a vote, we were certain we would win. We believed that people who wouldn't sign a card but promised to vote for us would do as they promised, but they didn't. It was a terrible shock. I'll never forget it.

On voting day, the counting of the ballots took place in the 5th floor cafeteria, a large space where tables could easily be moved about to accommodate ballots and the government, company, and union representatives who would be counting them. There were ninety people counting ballots, thirty from the Department of Labour, thirty from the company, and thirty from the union. They counted in groups of three – there were twenty groups in all – and they piled ballots up in groups of fifty, either union or no union.

While the others were counting, David, Eileen, and I were involved in the adjudication of the extraordinarily large number of ballots the company vote counters were challenging. The company clearly was frightened to death that we were going to win. One of their tactics was to make it as difficult as possible for us by challenging every ballot they could, no matter how weak the argument or how clear the intention of the voter to vote for the union might be. They challenged on almost any pretense. For example, if an 'X' was not centred exactly in the box but a little off to the side, no matter how obvious which box the person was marking, the company would challenge.

The next part of the story Eileen and I always told differently, reversing our roles. As we grew increasingly impatient and curious about how the count was going, one of us took a walk around the counting tables and came back white as a sheet. Although there were many ballots to count, one could tell quite early the direction of the trend. In most elections, once a trend is clearly established, the end result in terms of winners and losers remains the same. In this instance, there could be no doubt. We were losing.

By then, we were winning the battle of challenged ballots in that many were counted that would not have been otherwise. However, once the counting formalities were concluded, our defeat signed and witnessed, it was time to leave. It was almost impossible to conceive of remaining longer that evening to deal with the challenged ballots and it didn't seem that important. In retrospect, had I thought about the situation more, I might have been inclined to propose that we lock it all up and complete the details the next day. Of course, I am not at all sure whether the government and/or the company would have gone along with such a proposal, certainly not without screaming their objections, because everybody was worn out with the tension and the struggles.

The company had ringed the cafeteria with bosses standing shoulder to shoulder, enclosing the area and forming a walkway to the elevators. The elevators were in the middle of the floor, and when we arrived at the main floor they had a similar group of bosses, shoulder to shoulder, lined up on opposite sides to mark a walkway to the exit. That was the longest walk of my life. I remember feeling that I wanted to kick the shins of every person in that line, on both sides, on the way out.

We had come so close. The official record shows that we lost by a few hundred out of a bargaining unit of about 10,000. I have always somewhat regretted that we did not conclude the exercise of dealing with the company's challenged ballots. I am confident that, had we pursued that procedure to the end, the official record would be considerably better, though it is unlikely the result would have been any different.

Most of us wanted to believe that we could pick ourselves up off the ground and shake off our defeat. We had done so well and built such a fine campaign that we believed we could try again. But it was clearly not to be. We tried everything we could think of, but we simply could not restart the engine. I think the explanation is that we had worked the ground too hard. Our people had worked with total commitment, persistence, and all-out effort, and with every strategy we could conceive of. And we failed. There was no energy left. We and our supporters were devastated. It took years and many new employees before an attempt to organize Eaton's could be mounted again.

4

JOINING THE STEELWORKERS

Following the Eaton defeat, Wally was the first person to go. Although Ernie had less seniority, Eileen felt that Wally, who was younger and had more education and more varied experience, could more easily find work either within or outside the labour movement. I took it upon myself to meet and talk with Charlie Millard about him and the Steelworkers took him on. So we were short Wally and, after a few months went by, Eileen decided to leave too.

Only Olive, Ernie, and I remained. Continuing to pursue the goal of department store organizing, we developed a two-prong strategy. The first was to pursue organizing in one of the best union towns we could think of in Ontario – best in the sense of the highest percentage of unionization, or, as we say today, the highest union density. The second prong, if we were successful with the first, was to attempt organizing in the province with the best possible labour laws, so we could avoid hindrances such as the long delay we had experienced at Eaton's. Windsor was the high-union-density city that we chose and Saskatchewan, with the Simpson-Sears mail-order house in Regina, was the target province. With funds raised from several Canadian Congress of Labour affiliates, we set to work.

Smith's was the name of the department store in downtown Windsor. There were a couple of hundred employees, and, with the beginnings of a list, we started house calling in 1953. The big UAW union gave us an office in its hall. It was such a good labour town that the local union newspaper was a weekly. It filled a whole back page with a member interview on a question of the week by standing on the street and asking everybody who came along. Nearly everybody questioned was a UAW member, and in short order the newspaper publishers had their interviews without having to budge from the main street.

This campaign was on and completed before the company ever found out. When the manager did, he was furious. He arranged to call all the workers in one at a time and had them sign resignations from the union. That was not yet illegal at this point in the evolution of labour law in Ontario. So the issue for us was what to do. We decided to find out who had the most influence with this largely female workforce, the boss or their union fathers or husbands and/or boyfriends.

It was a manageable list to work our way through. We went to the UAW in order to work through its lists and ours in order to make every family connection we could and through those connections complete the more difficult ones, involving changes to married names, girlfriend names, and other such complications. The purpose of all this was to put on a last-minute campaign, too late for the company to catch on before the hearing, to visit as many employees as we could, along with their families and friends, and have them sign a form stating that they had resigned from the union under pressure in the presence of a company manager. It further said that they had no intention of changing their minds and wished to be represented by the union in bargaining with the company.

At the hearing, we took the company completely by surprise, won hands down, and were certified without a vote. I believe we established some new labour law along the way. The next hurdle was collective bargaining. I had never been near a collective-bargaining table, though, of course, I knew what collective agreements were. I had heard people talk about them a lot and had spoken about their benefits when organizing. We looked at what other department store unions in the United States and the few that were in Canada had done. We prepared proposals and headed for the bargaining table. The mood of the company was even angrier by then and I was totally inexperienced, so we wandered along through bargaining and finally had to apply for conciliation[1] and hold a strike vote.

I was far from confident about the strike vote. I did not know that much about strikes and had not been through any, and our group seemed an unlikely one to head into a labour struggle. But my concerns

---

1 There are three basic forms of labour-dispute resolution: conciliation, mediation, and arbitration. Conciliation is the least formal and structured of the three and is led, as the word suggests, by a conciliator, who meets the parties separately and tries to resolve their differences. It differs from arbitration in that the process has no legal standing and the conciliator makes no award, and from mediation in that, unlike the latter process, the parties seldom meet each other face to face.

were entirely misplaced. These were good people, willing to do whatever was necessary. In any case, what we did was set down a strike deadline some weeks away so we would have some time to think about what to do.

These were the early days of television and only Detroit had stations, and just two or three at that. The technology was still all very new but it seemed that everybody had a set with its little miracle screen. It was a terrible nuisance when we were out canvassing. In fact, we had developed a whole set of techniques for moving the person we wished to talk to off by themselves in the kitchen, or out on the front porch, or by distracting them in some other way so that we could have a conversation. Of course, we also had to resist the temptation of becoming too interested in the little pictures ourselves.

On one of these stations, the UAW sponsored a popular newscaster named Guy Nunn. He was the anchor of a noon newscast, which had a big audience among workers. There are many viewers in a shift-worker town. There's the day shift at work, but everybody who could had access to television sets, and at noon the night shift is beginning to stir and the afternoon shift is up. So the noon broadcast was popular.

I went over to see Nunn. I told him about our department store campaign. I described what a miserable company this was and how badly it treated the employees, how richly these people deserved a union, and how obstinately the company was behaving. They hadn't made a decent counter-proposal. I also told him what reasonable people we were.

So Guy Nunn took up our cause. For three or four days running, he told the story or different aspects of it and, on his own initiative, made it into a serial. He said, for example, that viewers should tune in tomorrow and see the next rotten thing the company had done. He emptied the store for us. It was like a miracle. It was like having the most effective picket line in the world without bothering with a strike. Windsor was such a good union town that, when word was out that Smith was behaving this badly, it was all over. That won us our contract and a pretty good one, and it established us in the community. It also helped the company quickly understand that, in a union town, it makes a lot more sense to be sympathetic to unions than to fight them tooth and nail.

The store is now gone, but the local organized additional retail outlets and I think continues to exist. We called it Local 1003. One of the women involved, Doris St Pierre, became secretary of the Windsor

Labour Council and held that position for years. A number of the other people became activists too, building a fine local union and a great reputation in the labour movement. They were most appreciative of our organizing campaign. Among my prized memorabilia is a scroll they made, decorated like a charter and signed by every employee. The heading is: 'To Ernie and Lynn for their work as organizers.' All in all, it was a great experience. I find it interesting as well that the Smith campaign was an early demonstration of the power of television, in this case used to the advantage of working people and the labour movement.

We began to work on the second prong of our strategy even before we were altogether finished in Windsor. This was to take place in Regina, Saskatchewan. Though its labour movement was small, Saskatchewan, with a CCF government, had the best labour laws in the country. We calculated that this would make for a favourable atmosphere in which to campaign, and Simpsons-Sears, with a mail-order house staffed by a workforce of about 2,000, was a significant employer in Regina. Away we went.

Starting in March 1955, with the significant support of Walter Smishek of the RWDSU, we made a number of house calls to assess the situation and decided it was possible to organize and that we would begin a campaign when the good weather arrived the next year. We spent the winter finishing up in Windsor and began the campaign in Regina in the spring. We had a few contacts, one of whom turned out to be a company person, which was a great embarrassment later on. We did not know at the time he was a company informer, so we kept in touch with him, with the result that the company knew everything we had in mind.

The reaction of Simpson-Sears was the exact opposite of Eaton's. It fought us publicly and noisily from day one, even establishing an anti-union employee group. We believed what we learned from the grapevine, that the company had brought in anti-union consultants from Chicago. Certainly, in subsequent years I had more than enough experience with anti-union consultants and have no doubt this was what we were up against.

We discovered quickly that, although the work was confined to one building, there was a clear distinction between blue-collar workers and white-collar ones. Undoubtedly, in ordinary factory circumstances, there would have been two buildings, one the factory proper and the other the office. In the mail-order world we confronted, however, there was an assembly line on one floor gathering orders for mailing, and on the next floor above might be the auditing department. There was no simple way to look at the building and say, for example, the first three floors are office and the next three order assembly. We also quickly discovered there was a great difference between the white-collar workers and the blue-collar ones in their reception to the union message. We were having considerable success signing up the latter, very little with the former.

We decided that the best way to proceed was to propose to the Labour Relations Board that we be granted collective-bargaining rights for a blue-collar unit. This was clearly desired by the employees, as evidenced by their support for the union. We argued that the basic structure of collective-bargaining units across the country in all the provincial jurisdictions provided for the recognition of separate blue-collar and white-collar units, with blue-collar units normally the first to be established. We had an outstanding lawyer, George Taylor, from Saskatoon, later appointed to the bench, who prepared and presented our case magnificently. The Labour Relations Board agreed to a bargaining unit essentially as we had outlined it and ordered a vote.

It was a contentious campaign. We had a loudspeaker, permanently hooked onto my car, in order to run rallies at lunchtime and present union messages. The employee organization established by the company had a public-address system in the plant window, through which it shouted back. The atmosphere was raucous. There were not many people on the fence; they were on one side or the other. But we seemed to have the upper hand. At that time, Saskatchewan's very progressive labour laws allowed union representatives to join with the government and company representatives in posting the notices of the vote, so I had the pleasure of walking through the building and deciding with the others where the notices should go. As the walk proceeded, one could tell from the friendly interest of the workers in what we were doing that we were off to a great start.

At that point, however, the company appealed to the Supreme Court of Saskatchewan to have the Labour Relation Board's decision set aside. We came to court and had 'hearings' that I will never forget. Although the government was CCF, the court was composed entirely of old party politicians, mostly Liberals. The chief justice was William M. Martin. When George Taylor was presenting our case, Martin sat with his back to him, having turned around to put his feet up on the wall behind. Never before or since have I seen the chairperson of a public appeal committee, or a committee of any kind, behave so outrageously.

The company's case was presented by Murdo McPherson, who, in addition to his law practice, was president of the Conservative Party of Canada. The court was fully attentive. However, the chief justice, after about ten minutes, interrupted him and said words to this effect: 'Well, Mr. McPherson we know why you're here, what exactly is it you want?' McPherson told him what kind of an order he wanted and in a matter of a few minutes it was all locked up and done. That was the end of our vote.

I and the other officials had to take down all the notices of a vote. The only thing left to do was to appeal to the Supreme Court of Canada. As I recall, that would have cost $5,000. Though the demarcation between white collar and blue collar was dramatically clear and we therefore stood a good chance on appeal, Donald MacDonald, secretary-treasurer of the Canadian Congress of Labour, wouldn't hear of it. I was furious. I thought that, after all that had been invested and all the money we raised, it was ridiculous not to spend another $5,000. I could not be certain that we were going to win the vote, but I knew I had a real shot at it, well worth the $5,000.

I concluded from this experience that I had to seek another route to the labour movement so I phoned Larry Sefton. Over the years, the Steelworkers had offered me various jobs. Cleve Kidd, on the Steelworkers staff, invited me once to go into the research department. I thanked him but indicated that I wanted to be where the action was, not sitting at a desk in the national office or any other office for that matter. Through the grapevine I heard that Cleve had said, 'I think that kid wants to become president of the union.' I thought that was terribly unfair at the time, but I guess I had created some clearly unintended impression of that nature. Gower Markle had also proposed that I should be appointed to his job when he resigned as education director and went on to something else. My response was the same. Larry had not really offered me anything, but he was where the action was, he was the leader I most admired, and it was time to move.

One thing one can count on in the labour movement is that, if a little time goes by, things will begin to change one way or another. Not long after my talk with Larry, he came and met me in Regina. He offered me employment as a staff representative for the Steelworkers and I eagerly accepted. Of course, Audrey and I had to pack up and move back east, which took a little time. Then, instead of moving directly to the Niagara peninsula, as I had expected, it was decided to send me directly to a major organizing effort that the Steelworkers were then conducting on the west coast, in Kitimat, British Columbia, under the direction of my old friend and colleague from the days of the Eaton drive, Wally Ross. It was in effect a raid; our objective was to represent the workers at a large new aluminum smelter being built there by Alcan, dislodging the unions currently on the scene, a group of eight AFL craft unions and the Aluminum Workers, one of the AFL's industrial unions. From a Canadian perspective, we had never achieved the status in the aluminum industry that we had in the United States. Alcan workers in Canada, even with the big spin-off of their company from Alcoa, remained in an independent union. Our goal continued to be to bring everyone into the same house of labour, and so we had a great interest in Alcan's Kitimat project. The thought was that the Steelworkers could provide the workers with something they then lacked, a unified voice. Alcan seemed to have a parallel interest in keeping us out, for it proceeded to make a backdoor deal with the craft unions and the Aluminum Workers, which, as the drive progressed, it would use to deny us any access to company property, simply throwing any of our representatives out of the company-owned hotel, restaurants, and town. I was to work on the campaign until its conclusion, which was expected in a few months.

I had picked a propitious time to join the Steelworkers. In the early years of the union, the 1930s, there had been enormous challenges and intense battles, but far-reaching change had been accomplished incredibly quickly. The union grew from nothing in 1936 to 600,000 members in 1942, when the Steelworkers of Canada became part of the United Steelworkers of America. It was almost a revolutionary era, with workers on the move as they had rarely been before. The task facing leaders, beginning in the 1940s and continuing through the 1950s, was one of institution building, of bringing all of these members into a permanent, effective structure. The Steelworkers took pride in doing this work, in their eyes at least, better than anyone else. An expert on the steel industry, Jack Metzgar, whose father was a shop steward in the 1950s and 1960s, writes that steelworkers' wages in the United States increased by 100 per cent in the 1950s, a decade that culminated in a three-month U.S.-wide steel strike in 1959, when 500,000 steelworkers went on strike, shutting down more than 85 per cent of the nation's steel production. Given the dramatic wage increases of the time, one could argue that the 1950s were a watershed decade for steelworkers. Certainly, Metzgar has good reason to have positive memories of that decade. The Steelworker household in which he grew up did not own a home, car, refrigerator, or television at the beginning of the decade. It owned all four by the end.[2]

This was the context in which my career in the Steelworkers was launched, and Kitimat provided a useful setting in which to cut my teeth as an organizer. Kitimat was a company town. Alcan had recognized the construction unions during the building of this massive project, which involved erecting dams high in the mountains to bring water down to a power house in the mountain's base in Kemano, then sending the power over several kilometres to Kitimat. Whenever a Steelworker representative would appear, he would be prevented from staying in town, since everything there, including the hotel, was controlled by the company. Wally had offered to go underground, seek a job at Alcan, and become established as an employee. His offer was accepted by the union, his 'resignation' was announced, and he used his wartime experience as an instrument mechanic to apply for employment, in which he was successful. He became active in the union and was elected chairman of the joint bargaining committee of all the unions.

It was toward the conclusion of his first round of bargaining in this capacity that the company advised the government-appointed mediator that it had some very important information that would have a serious impact on the situation. It said there were some details to be finalized and asked for an adjournment for a few days so these outstanding matters could be cleared.

Three or four days later, the company called the parties together and announced that Wally Ross, who presented himself as the leader of the American Federation of Labor group, was in fact an underground agent for the Steelworkers. When Wally was asked if this were true, he answered promptly, clearly, and simply, 'Yes, of course that's true.' The negotiations were thrown into total confusion, which the company used to insist that an agreement be reached before any harm – whatever that might be – could be done.

However, one critical element had changed. In the interim, Wally had purchased a home from the company so he could not be thrown out of the community. That home became the union office, social gathering place, and schoolroom, whatever was required. By the time I was asked to go to Kitimat, Wally had been through one campaign, which had ended with the dismissal of the application for certification by the Labour Relations Board on technical grounds. He was now heading

---

2 *Striking Steel: Solidarity Remembered* (Philadelphia: Temple University Press 2000).

into a second campaign with excellent prospects. He had asked Larry for two additional people to come to help. I was one of them. The other was Terry Mancini, then a rank-and-file leader in Local 2251 at Algoma Steel in Sault Ste Marie.

The staff prior to our arrival in March 1956 consisted of Wally and Don Dunphy, one of our regular staff persons in British Columbia, who was an excellent leaflet writer and publicity person. Terry and I moved into the same house occupied by Wally and Don. It was where the action was and where we could be available all the time.

The ground was covered with many feet of snow. On the street you had to remember which particular hole in the snow bank was your driveway because you could not see your house. People living in these homes had to shovel snow off the roofs to relieve the weight, yet they had to throw the snow up because the snow banks beside many of the homes were taller than the buildings themselves. It was quite a sight. Then there was the country itself, the green, rich forest, mountains – everything on a gigantic scale. The town site had been cleared out of the rain forest. We were advised that it was unwise to wander into the rain forest without knowing what you were doing, or without having experienced people with you, because the forest was so dense that one could quickly become disoriented and lost. Going over a deadfall was very different from any woods I had ever walked in before. One climbed up one side of a trunk lying across the ground, walked across, and climbed down the other side. These were enormous trees. The main peak nearby was Mount Elizabeth. She disappeared often behind the clouds, snow, and rain, but when she did deign to appear she provided us with an ever-changing spectacle as different amounts of light at different times of day often transformed her appearance dramatically.

The company was functioning on what might be considered a grand scale as well, in that it had built this extravagantly expensive project. The smelting of aluminum requires enormous amounts of electricity. The most economical way to find electricity in such massive quantities is through hydroelectric power, which is why the aluminum industry the world over builds its smelters near hydroelectric sites. In one way of thinking, Alcan created Kitimat. It dammed lakes up in the high mountains and dug a tunnel through a mountain at Kemano, which was eighty kilometres up the inlet from Kitimat. Alcan built a powerhouse inside the mountain to generate energy from the water that flowed down giant penstocks through the mountain, then transmitted that energy across the mountains to Kitimat to power the smelter and its surrounding communities. We used to have data showing how much the power used in Kitimat would accomplish in serving the public and the comparisons were staggering. The smelter used up enough power day after day to look after a great many cities and villages in the area.

In terms of the workforce, I had never encountered before one with such a large proportion of immigrants. These men – Italians, Portuguese, and Germans were the largest groups but there were many other smaller ones too – came to Kitimat with virtually no direct understanding of the way things operate in North America, since nearly all of them arrived first in Vancouver and then were transported almost immediately to Kitimat. Terry and I used to think about what they must have felt about Canada when the first part of it they saw, apart from a fleeting glimpse of Vancouver, was all the snow and rain and the magnificent landscape of Kitimat. Though we put out leaflets in at least a half a dozen languages, we didn't begin to meet the linguistic needs of the smaller groups we were dealing with.

All things considered, this was very different from my previous experiences. On reflection now, I suppose it wasn't that dissimilar from what pulp and paper and lumber workers face in their work around the province of British Columbia. Nor was it different from major mining camps around Canada, which are often located in harsh climates, require the building of town sites for accommodation, and have a much younger workforce than is the general average. But for me it was all new. What a change from department stores!

Wally had the whole campaign in excellent shape by the time we arrived. Certainly, I think one could make a defensible argument that the additional staff probably added more confusion and unnecessary points of view to the mix, as compared to what would have happened had Wally and Don been simply left alone. Wally had clearly established himself as the trade-union leader in the community. I can imagine circumstances in which such a person would have been considered an outlaw for his secret activity in becoming a member of the opposing union. But Wally did all this with such charm that he intrigued the whole community. With his height – six feet plus – one eye, and big boots, he was hard to miss walking around town.

He made a point of having his jeep equipped for road service in terms of a cable jumper, chains, and shovels. If you're going to risk driving into the ditch or getting stuck in the snow, and we had vast numbers of such incidents, you might as well be prepared and Wally was. It's true there were only twenty kilometres of road from one end of Kitimat to the other, as well as a few neighbouring streets in the developing town site, so there weren't a lot of places to get in trouble. But there were enough. To get the angle right to cross the river on the bridge that had been built, one had to manoeuvre past awkward curves at each end of the bridge. One of the first things we had to find out Sunday mornings was how many people had run into the bridge on Saturday night. I frankly don't recall a weekend when somebody hadn't run into the bridge; we could always count on at least one driver hitting it.

Our schedule was hectic but we were able to fit in some recreation from time to time. We tenderfeet were being told constantly that we were privileged to be in the west anywhere, but particularly on the coast, in the rain forest and on a great salmon-fishing river. I was easily persuaded to buy a fishing rod and tackle and borrow some hip boots and to get out into the river and be a fisherman. While there are some pictures of me fishing that are quite good, they give the impression that I had some clue what I was doing. I didn't. Standing in the middle of the rapidly moving river in hip boots was an interesting experience, one that I never repeated in my subsequent union career.

But back to the work. Though Alcan had not been running the smelter particularly well, as far as we could tell, by the time our campaign was under way it appeared to have overcome the problems. Yet the company had been plagued for some time with what it called in French *defancé*. These were pots blowing up because of some malfunction in the way hydroelectric power was being fed into them. The explosions were quite dramatic, taking the roof right off the factory building and opening sections of it to the sky. I don't recall a *defancé* during the months I was there, nor do I remember hearing of anyone being seriously hurt in such incidents. But they had occurred and there is no doubt they were dangerous.

Too many accidents of this kind made safety one of our more prominent campaign themes. We aimed to provide felt hats for people who worked in the pot lines to prevent them from being burnt by flying sparks. These caps were in Steelworkers colours, orange and black. We had our committee men and shop stewards wear orange caps with a black peak, while regular members wore caps with a black crown and an orange peak. The idea was to have a distinction to make sure the stewards and activists were readily visible and could easily be found by a committee man on the job. Still, I can't imagine why we opted for felt rather than hard hats.

The campaign structure that Wally had put in place was divided into three areas. Wally's area was the town site because that's where all the veterans and old-timers were and he was a veteran and old-timer himself. In Kitimat, if you were there a few months you were there a long time. In general terms, Terry had the tradesmen and I had the operators and labourers. We functioned cooperatively and there was a good deal of overlap. Terry, of course, had practically a lifetime of such experience in a fine local union. And he was living proof that employers are wrong when they maintain that union workers cannot be loyal to both the employer and the union. When we would go for a walk down by the railway tracks, sometimes he would look at every rail and kick some of them and say that they were terrible and came from such and such a shop. Then he'd say, 'Look at this beautiful rail coming up. That's one of ours from Algoma.' He took enormous pride in the work of the plant and knew a great deal about it and was enormously loyal to Algoma in its role as a steel company in competition with other steel companies.

Another element of the organizing structure that was required by law in British Columbia was that the operation be run through a local union. We had officers and elections, committees, and regular meetings. Much of the normal campaign activities were structured around activities of the local union. This has many advantages in a campaign, including providing a sense of ownership to people. It's for their local union that they hope to win.

In circumstances such as those in Kitimat, where we were trying to persuade people that they should move from one union to another, the presence of a local made the transition much easier. The shift didn't seem quite as radical as going into a new union in some unknown country without knowing what kind of a local union you'll have. In Kitimat, the argument was that everybody would be in one local union run and directed and with all of its officers right in Kitimat. It was an attractive arrangement for workers, holding much more appeal than a group of local unions administered out of Vancouver, as was the case with the Alcan craft unions and Aluminum Workers. In retrospect, we were simply doing what we had done in the Eaton campaign, establishing that our ideas worked just as well in a blue-collar setting as in a white-collar one.

Ironically, the idea of leading an organizing campaign through a local union structure was rooted in the AFL tradition: the AFL's base was the craft union, which liked to use its local unions as its hiring halls and power base. However, this approach was foreign to the basic Steelworkers strategy, which held that workers were to join the parent union and all the details of establishing the local and electing officers were to be left until certification had been won. It was a strategy that dated back to the start of the CIO, when the union was swamped with certifications and didn't have the time to, or see any particular reason to, try to establish local unions during the organizing campaign. It was hard enough in some circumstances to keep up with the pace without adding that element.

Of course, organizing changed, more dramatically in the United States than in Canada, but in a negative direction in both countries. Early on, employers vigorously contested the right of workers to organize. In the United States, a whole industry of anti-labour consultants sprang up. They created techniques, methods, and ways and means of avoiding the law and pressuring people into being frightened of unions. So unions intent on successful organizing had to hone their skills to respond to every conceivable technique, strategy, and approach to increase their chances of success. That flexibility proved a great asset in Kitimat, for in Canada each province has its own labour laws and the laws in British Columbia required that only a local union could apply for certification. So it was through a local union on the ground in Kitimat that we proceeded.

Despite the fact that our campaign was moving so well, it was faced with the power of incumbency. For all of our noise and talk, issue raising, and the rest of it, the existing union representatives had the bargaining rights on the job. They were in a position to look after the problems and do something for the members in a way that we could not because we did not represent them.

My thought, which I kept mostly to myself, was that our rivals should have concentrated on their strength. They shouldn't have let themselves be dragged into arguments with us on other matters. Then they might have fared much better. They remained a threat potentially throughout the campaign, but it would have been much more serious had they adopted such an approach. Of course, such restraint isn't easy, because if a reasonably clever group without bargaining responsibility is simply attacking you, it can get away with saying many things without having to prove its words with deeds. Yet the advantage of incumbency in really being able to do something for people places a union in a much stronger position, in my judgment. Ultimately, workers want someone to represent them and solve their problems. If a union establishes a reputation for doing that, it's difficult for a raider to dislodge it – a principle that I would come to appreciate all the more in a later organizing effort in Sudbury, where the roles were reversed and I had to follow a defensive strategy.

The AFL-CIO merger in the United States had occurred, as noted earlier, in 1955, while the Canadian Congress of Labour and the Trades and Labour Congress merged in Canada in 1956 to become the CLC. These organizations tried to encourage people to do as we were doing in Kitimat, that is, work with affiliates rather than stay in central bodies which were bound to be significantly overstaffed. To promote this, they included a provision in the merger agreements in both countries that a person carried their seniority with them to the affiliate, their new union. As far as the Kitimat contest itself was concerned, the basic understanding in each of the mergers, the AFL-CIO and the CLC, was that a circle would be drawn around Kitimat until the vote was taken to determine which union would prevail, and the local would be recognized as belonging to whichever union won the vote.

Another important element in the Kitimat campaign was the teaching of English. This represented some unconventional thinking compared to most campaigns at that time. It was recognition of one of the critical needs in the community. The workers were recent immigrants in nearly all cases. Some had some knowledge of English but many had none. Obviously, nothing is as important when settling in a new land as learning the language. So it was critical for the union to provide that opportunity. Wally was sensitive to the importance of this early on and was fortunate to find an excellent teacher who gave English classes throughout the whole campaign and beyond.

The Steelworkers and its services were very visible. My recollection is that the other union had many more representatives in Kitimat than we did, certainly at times of peak activity, because each of its eight constituent unions had staff of its own. Each one also had a business agent in town from time to time, so the number of staff added up quickly. Our general view was they were often in each other's way, and having a bunch of staff from Vancouver talking in a bar didn't do much for an organizing campaign. In our case, however, we were always on the go, visiting the bunkhouses and organizing, keeping tabs on the situation and how many members we had.

We each had rented cars with a rack on top with the Steelworkers sign attached, so we had three cars charging up and down the twenty kilometres of road most of the day and half of the night. We might have had four cars, but Dunphy never let us put a sign on his. In the daytime, having these cars cruising around gave the impression of a very active organization and, of course, we lent the cars to whoever needed them.

Our house served full time as a social centre, rather like entertaining people in your own home in an informal way. It also served as the office, meeting hall, and storeroom. There was always a lot of chatter along the way and sharing and learning. Above all, it was a participatory campaign. Everybody was involved in everything. The staff was patient with people in terms of listening to their suggestions, brainstorming with them, and using their ideas.

Although the opposition unions were not slouches either, generally we did things first and they copied us, though that may not have been the case entirely. They adopted 'western'-style slogans, probably to send the message that they were the appropriate group for this place on the west coast, 800 kilometres north of Vancouver. They certainly were vigorous and matched us in terms of the quantity of leaflets, if not the quality. They ran an interesting campaign, one that was good enough that, had it pushed the incumbency angle a little more and not permitted us to engage them in many arguments along on the way, it might have done considerably better. They also seemed to lack our focus. We prepared for bargaining more than they did, even though they held representation rights and clearly, until someone proved otherwise, they had the right and the responsibility to lead.

We had one distinct advantage. Before Terry and I arrived, Wally had spent more than two years establishing himself, the Steelworkers, and its supporters as part of the community. Two of our supporters had been elected as members of the town council and they were active in that capacity. In the summer before our arrival, we had sponsored a town beauty contest, which was won by a member of a Steelworker family. In addition to English classes for Alcan's immigrant workers, we also helped them with their income-tax returns. This union had become an essential part of the community.

On the other side, the local representing the smelter workers was the only B.C. local of a union from Washington State. It had not settled an experienced staff man in Kitimat. Instead, by the time of the campaign, it followed the AFL practice and elected a local business agent. He was young but had no aluminum smelter experience. He had little if any experience as a business agent either and I doubt if he had that much talent. More senior people handled their campaign, but they were not settled in Kitimat. They would have had to devote a lot more thought and effort into servicing the Kitimat local than they did to have realized the benefits of incumbency. In the end, the vote, held in August 1956, was Steelworkers 1,700, incumbents 400. It was decisive.

Victory finally was ours. It was sweet indeed. So much had gone into the Kitimat struggle, from the early forays into the community, which resulted in people literally being escorted out of town, to Wally's dramatic success in establishing himself as an underground leader ('salting' is a word often used for that activity in the American labour movement), and then through two campaigns above ground, if you will, each one more interesting by the day and the second one more interesting than the first.

In the house where we lived and worked (and many visited) there was always music and fortunately the four of us had pretty similar musical tastes, or at least three of us did. There was a lot of jazz played and the record player we had purchased together – I think it cost about $200 – was a nice portable. We engaged in almost constant discussions about what were we going to do with the record player when we left, because it belonged to all four of us and we were going in four different directions after the campaign. So we decided we'd raffle it off; we would file secret estimates of how many votes we were going to get in the ultimate vote and whoever was closest would take the record player home.

I didn't tell the others, but my colleagues were all such enthusiastic talkers that they couldn't resist chattering about what they had guessed. My sense was that their guesses were all wildly optimistic. So I waited until I knew all three, then came in just under the lowest, which covered everything from just under the bottom all the way down. I won quite handily. Because they were all such optimists, I was reasonably convinced that there was no way the campaign would produce as many votes as they estimated. Still, we had very decent results.

A postscript. Pressures eventually pulled the Kitimat union apart and out of the Steelworkers. I believe we lost it just as we had won it. We won by paying a great deal of attention to the immigrant community and its needs. We were helping them, encouraging them, offering learning opportunities for them, providing leadership roles for them, and demonstrating by actions rather than words that we were a new and better kind of union. We were a union that would be involved in the needs of the members, whatever the difficulties might be, and indeed we wished to help them in achieving their goals. All of this was subsequently lost sight of, as the union came under the control of 'anglos.'

There was nothing underhanded about this process. One can almost imagine a scenario where an immigrant is nominated to be recording secretary, with an English-speaking person nominated as well. And the immigrant modestly says that he thinks the local union would be better served by a person more familiar with English and the customs of the country. He thereby withdraws from the race and hands it by acclamation to one of his friends, one who speaks English, one of the other candidates for the job. It's a difficult line to defeat or oppose. So it doesn't take long until the majority of the executive positions have been turned over to people of English-speaking background, whoever their predecessors may have been and whatever the general circumstances might be.

Natural or not, however, the changing complexion of the union ultimately undid what Wally and the rest of us had achieved. It was a shame.

On a personal note, a few years later, after I was long since settled in the United Steelworkers, Larry Sefton called me. He gave me the good news that I had just picked up pension service credits for time that included the Eaton drive. The result of this provision added almost ten years to my length of service for pension purposes, moving it from the spring of 1956 back to the summer of 1947. It was a most welcome addition, which paid off handsomely for me in retirement.

5

BACK EAST

Going to work for the Steelworkers was a very positive move for me in monetary terms, as my income effectively doubled. Not so pleasant, however, as we pursued our department-store strategy, were assignments away from home. My first taste of this was in Windsor. Then came Regina, but this time my family accompanied me. Olive and I had done the preliminary work for the Simpsons-Sears campaign in the summer of 1954, and the following spring Audrey and I and our two children moved to a rented house in Regina. We lived there until Christmas, which meant that, instead of suffering the pangs of separation from each other, we were able to share the new experience of living on the Canadian prairie with a field of golden wheat waving in the breeze at the end of our street. We also shared the joys of being attacked by huge, well-organized squadrons of mosquitoes, which buzzed our neighbouring park with the setting of the sun, requiring me to put two-year-old David on my shoulders, grab the hand of four-year-old Judy, and run for our lives to the shelter of our house half a block away.

Kitmat represented another period of separation from Audrey and the kids, following which we moved together again – this time back to Toronto. Home base was the first house Audrey and I had purchased, located in a new subdivision in the west end of Toronto. Our particular part of the subdivision was between Browns Line and Etobicoke Creek, the latter forming the western boundary of Toronto. Our community formed a new northern end to an older community called Alderwood, which was as progressively militant and humanely decent a neighborhood as existed anywhere in the city. It was in many ways an adjunct to Long Branch, which, along with New Toronto and Mimico, stretched along Lake Ontario between the Humber River and the Etobicoke

Creek. Good working-class territory, it was the home of many industrial plants. The largest was a Goodyear Rubber plant represented by
Local 232 of the Rubber Workers, while the Steelworkers represented
the workers at a number of other plants. In short, it was a relatively
high-wage, unionized community.

Politically, these were exciting times for those of us in the CCF. Supported by the Steelworkers, among many other unions, the CCF had
achieved considerable electoral success in Ontario in the 1940s. In 1943
we elected the largest delegation to the Legislative Assembly in Ontario
we ever achieved until the New Democratic Party formed the government in 1990. We suffered a setback in the next election, in 1945, but in
1948 we came back strongly, although not quite as strongly as in 1943.
A number of trade unionists were elected to the provincial legislature
over those years. They included Charlie Millard, the national director
of our union, who was probably the most famous of the group. He had
been the successful candidate in my riding, York West, in the 1943 and
1948 elections, his one defeat coming in 1945.

I had been active in York West from the time we moved there in 1950.
Bill Punnett, who became the Canadian director of the Rubber Workers,
and I were in some ways a team working in the riding: in one election
one of us would be the campaign manager and in the next election the
other would be. When I arrived home from the west in 1956, there was
a by-election to be held in York West and Charlie Millard wanted me
to be the candidate. Larry Sefton, however, as the Steelworkers director
with authority over me, had already decided that I was going to move
to the Niagara peninsula. This was a prospect that I relished, since it
was my opportunity to become involved in the full range of a staff person's job. I had been organizing for a long time and felt it was time, for
a period at least, to gain experience on the 'servicing' side of a union
official's work – the job of addressing workers' specific grievances, be
they wages, working conditions, and so on, outside the framework of
organizing, bargaining, and strike action.

Still, since the by-election was an intriguing option as well, I simply
went to Larry and said, 'You'll have to let me know your decision and
I'll get to it. Either the campaign or I'll get started on moving to the
peninsula.' Larry met with Charlie and advised me they had agreed
that I should run for the seat in York West and, since victory was unlikely, I would proceed to the peninsula afterwards.

Before all this played out, I had the opportunity to go to the peninsula for a couple of events. The principal one was a strike that had

been going on for about four months involving three plants, two in the peninsula and one in London, Ontario, all owned by the same company. We had separate contracts with them, United Steel in Welland, Standard Steel in Port Robinson, and London Steel in London. One of the objectives of the strike was to bring these contracts together. Obviously, the termination dates of the contracts were close enough that the workers were off the job at the same time, but it was proving to be a difficult strike. Larry had sent his brother, Bill, to pull it together the best he could and reach a settlement, which Bill succeeded in doing.

I went with him to a couple of the ratification meetings. These were stormy sessions and many members were upset the day they voted for the agreements, which were ratified. One member in Welland was so worked up that, when Bill and I were removing the material for the meeting from the trunk of his car, he drove his vehicle directly at us. Had we not moved quickly, we would have had our legs crushed.

Various experienced negotiators have said that often one cannot tell how effective a strike has been until negotiations for the next agreement begin. Only then does it become clear whether the company involved seeks further confrontation or whether it has become more reasonable and more problem-solving in its approach. In the case of the 1956 strike in the Niagara peninsula, the latter was true: many of the objectives we failed to accomplish in the strike settlement were achieved in the next round. The company continued to use the same firm of labour consultants, but with a different representative, and its dealings with the union, although not a textbook example of the best of industrial relations, were much better than they had been before and during the strike. In due course, we reached a settlement with which the members were very satisfied. This result put the relationships involved, between the union and the company, the local and the international, and among myself (as staff representative), the local union leaders, and the representatives of the company, on a much more positive footing. In other words, the 1956 strike had been successful.

Once back from the peninsula and immersed in the by-election contest, I found that campaigning was not that different from organizing generally, although I have always considered organizing unorganized workers to gain collective-bargaining rights, as compared with political organizing, the more difficult. In union organizing, one is always struggling with the demon of fear that is behind every conversation with the workers you are attempting to organize. Sometimes it is out front and centre, sometimes it is not, but it is the backdrop to everything you do.

In contrast, political organizing is hard work and certainly campaigning, and the strategies involved are demanding and challenging. But, in a political campaign, there is no element of fear and intimidation of one party by the other, at least in a democracy such as Canada. Essentially, political campaigning is a rational process in which people are asked to make up their minds. There are hidden arguments or motives and certainly circumstances that might prevent a person from doing what he or she otherwise might like to do, such as voting for an outsider party such as ours. But there is no one with the power and influence that a boss or employer has over employees. In that sense, political organizing is much easier and much more a matter of working and campaigning hard, keeping on message, having a reasonable strategy, and pursuing it consistently.

York West was a vast riding, and, as in all ridings in Toronto at that time, it was a long narrow rectangle stretching from Lake Ontario a considerable distance to the north. This configuration of constituencies had the effect of including in every riding, to some degree, a working-class south, a middle-class middle, and an upper-class upper, and it was mixed somewhat between middle and upper as you moved north. In York West, workers lived in the industrial suburbs along the western lakeshore. To the north, you first came to the Queensway, with basic housing developments, and then to the Kingsway, where much fancier housing was the norm. At the top end were rural suburbs interspersed with some estates and even horse farms, all of which have been overwhelmed with a variety of urban developments of various quality in recent years.

The long-standing tradition in the riding, where there were many community associations, was for these organizations to hold political all-candidates nights, to which the candidates were invited to present their case for election and debate each other. There were a number of these events in the by-election, but only the Liberal candidate, Arthur Nagels, and I attended. The Conservative candidate, Leslie Rowntree, never did show up. I'm not sure whether he accepted invitations or not. I assume not. In fact, I did not meet him until sometime after the campaign when he was appointed to the provincial cabinet and became the minister of labour. At that point, of course, many of us in the labour movement came to know him well.

Nagels and I slugged it out at meeting after meeting, and I am proud that on election day, 18 October 1956, I came in second, with 6,115 votes, and he came in third, with 4,461 votes. The frustrating element is that the Conservative, who never participated in a single debate, came in first, winning 11,089 votes. He had spent his time in the middle- and upper-class areas of the riding, attending coffee socials for the most part, and he beat us both. The reality of it is that people in those more prosperous areas voted in much greater numbers than did our supporters. There were more of us than there were of them, but it was much more difficult to persuade our people to vote – a fact of life that prevails in ridings across the province and country to this day.

Despite the result, the by-election was a great experience, with lots of practice at public speaking, and lots of door knocking, and it contributed to building the party base. In subsequent years, with the rearrangement of ridings in Ontario, the long narrow style was changed and more square ridings emerged. One result was that a much more reasonably proportioned riding, named Etobicoke-Lakeshore, was created out of the south end of the old York West, and for many years it was an NDP stronghold. Pat Lawlor was the first to win it for the NDP, in 1967, and Ruth Grier was the NDP member who held it most recently, from 1985 to 1995. If the new boundaries had existed in my time, I would have won as well.

With the by-election behind us, Audrey and I started focusing on the move to the Niagara peninsula. In fact, that move took us longer to complete than any of the many future moves would. Thinking that the kids should finish school before we relocated, we stayed put until the summer of 1957. By that time, we had examined the housing market in the peninsula thoroughly and had almost purchased a home on a couple of occasions. Initially, we house hunted in St Catharines and then in Fonthill, near Welland. In the end, we concluded that we should live in Welland, partly because Fonthill was known to be the home of company managers but more because Welland would be the focus of my work and also had better schools. I never regretted the decision. Welland was then, as it is today, essentially a working-class community, in a trade-union setting. It provided good wages and a good living standard, with decent facilities for growing children in terms of schools, libraries, and recreation. We could not have chosen a better place to live and enjoyed our nine years in the peninsula as much as our time anywhere. Audrey often used to say that it was perhaps the best experience of all.

By the summer, we had bought a house in the northwest corner of Welland. It was not completed by the time we sold the house in Toronto, so we rented a cottage at Long Beach on Lake Erie and lived there until September. Long Beach was in fine shape then, though it would not remain so for much longer. By the time we had moved back to Toronto in 1965, Long Beach would be terribly polluted, with horribly smelling algae piled up on the beach. There is no mystery regarding the causes of the deterioration. Lake Erie is the shallowest of all the lakes and in some places I found that one could almost walk across it, from Point Pelee to Sandusky, for example. The shallowness is a particular problem because there is so much industry on, or close to, the lake. When we lived in Long Beach, there was the steel industry in Buffalo and Cleveland at the eastern end, and the automobile industry at the western end, all producing at full capacity. On the Ontario side, there was no comparably sized industrial development, with the exception of a Stelco steel mill – then North America's newest, most modern facility – and some chemical plants. Nonetheless, to make a bad situation worse, agricultural fertilizer runoff from tobacco country and the other farming developments on the north shore of the lake contributed significantly to the pollution problem. Thankfully, in the last few decades, considerable progress has been achieved in cleaning up the Great Lakes, including Lake Erie.

As a Steelworker representative, my first objective was to assist in the effort to win certification at a new pipe mill that Page Hershey, through a separate company called Welland Tubes, was building as a joint venture with Stelco. That involved cracking the United Electrical, Radio and Machine Workers of America (UE) monopoly on the Page Hershey workforce. We hoped to acquire something of a base in the middle of the UE's territory and work towards the day when we might be able to take over everything. Secondly, as a much longer-term project, the plan was to conduct an organizing campaign at Atlas Steel, also in Welland. Atlas was one of a handful of major steel mills in both Canada and the United States that had not been organized in the early thrust of the CIO. Many of these mills remained a thorn in the side of the union and an obstacle to achieving full bargaining strength across the industry. Atlas was a specialty steel mill employing a couple of thousand workers 'represented' by a company union. That circumstance had resulted from an organizing failure during the first mass movement into the CIO. In most cases, such as Atlas, the companies were sensitive to what was going on and understood the appeal of the CIO. They generally attempted to blunt its appeal by providing benefits equal to those that the unions won and sometimes topping them up a little bit. This was true at Dofasco in Hamilton, Atlas in Welland, Weirton Steel in Weirton, West Virginia, Middletown Steel in Middletown, Ohio, Wisconsin Steel in Chicago, and a handful of others.

Union struggles among the Steelworkers, the UE, and the Mine Mill and Smelter Workers (commonly known as Mine Mill) and their allies were then at their peak. At the same time, the foundations of the Canadian and American labour movements were being built in both similar and quite different ways. In the beginning of all of this, in southern Ontario, the lay of the land was somewhat as follows. Windsor was the centre of the automobile industry and the UAW was predominant in southwestern Ontario; steel was the leader in industrial Hamilton; and the Niagara peninsula was, to a degree, UE territory. Because of allegations concerning Communist Party influence within the ranks of the UE leadership and that union's expulsion from the CCL – communist ties, real or imagined, could be fatal in the 1950s – there were a larger number of company unions in the peninsula than in the other parts of industrial Ontario. Independent unions was the term their leaders preferred, but they were mostly company-inspired, company-financed, and company-coddled organizations, although over time many became legitimate and joined the mainstream of the movement. Before and after I arrived in the peninsula, these 'independent' unions were the subject of constant competition among three of us: the UAW with its General Motors base in St Catharines, the UE with its base in Welland with Page Hershey and Union Carbide particularly, and ourselves. We were just starting to build a base of our own.

Life in the peninsula began at a hectic pace and never changed. In those days, we normally had three staff persons and three secretaries, working out of offices in St Catharines and Port Colborne. We rented vacant store space in Welland for meetings, but it didn't have any office equipment. In the beginning, I operated mostly out of the trunk of my car but also used both offices, whichever was more convenient for me. We set up a temporary organizing office in Welland but continued working towards setting up a real office there, and in some sense using that as a central office for the peninsula.

There were a few people, particularly one of my fellow staff representatives who had come from the UE, who thought that I should not live in Welland for fear of intimidation and worse. I was advised, if I insisted on living there, that I should be careful in the pubs and have an unlisted phone number. The staff member was Joe Bacon, an interesting and intelligent man who had been the president of the local union at English Electric in St Catharines. He had led the local out of the UE and into the Steelworkers and I don't think there is any question that he went through some rough experiences in the process.

I had no trouble in Welland. I did not have an unlisted phone. I have never believed in that. My position has always been that, if there is trouble some place, I want to hear about it as soon as possible. I never had any crank calls from the UE, although I had a few from some of our own members. But I was pleased to receive them because I knew something was amiss and I was usually able to address the concern quickly, if not immediately. There were some incidents that my wife sometimes imagined I put people up to, but I hadn't. Members would become involved in discussions in the pub in the evenings, sometimes a disagreement would develop, and it would occur to somebody, 'Well, why don't we call Lynn and see what he has to say about it?' Welland is not a large community and when such a call would arrive the simplest way to respond was to join in. I would become part of the discussion. It was often a worthwhile meeting.

The large pipe mill that Welland Tubes was building in Welland duplicated the large tube mill in Pittsburgh owned by National Steel Tube. I said to Larry that it would be helpful to me in the organizing effort if I could travel to Pittsburgh and visit that mill. This would give me an opportunity to see how it worked and how the workers viewed it in terms of the job and the skills required, the dangers involved, and other relevant information. Larry agreed and so I set off for my first exposure to Pittsburgh.

My initial view of the city was of its magnificent new airport terminal building, with pillars across the front and a beautiful fountain, quite a handsome terminal by the standards of that time. I would be around long enough to see the day when it was considered old, rundown, and disgraceful, to be replaced by a beautiful and functional new terminal. Back in 1957, however, the old terminal was quite impressive, particularly when compared to Malton airport in Toronto, where, in the original little terminal building, the food counter was located on one side of the main aisle, the ticket counter was on the other, and the aircraft, in turn, were parked immediately outside the front door.

Pittsburgh was an old industrial town and area. The mill I had come to see was in one of the suburbs, McKeesport, south of Pittsburgh down the Monongahela River. Typical of large steel mills all over North America, the mill occupied a section of an old plant. (In newer locations you have these nice new buildings and they're specific in purpose and modern in organization. But you can't tell how up-to-date the equipment in the steel mill is by looking at the outside of the building and I have seen many of these old buildings house quite modern equipment.) It was not a terribly complicated industrial operation. Giant presses compressed big sheets of steel first into a 'u' shape and then into an 'o,' and automatic welders brought it together to produce a tube.

Back in Welland, I immediately found myself in the midst of a bitter controversy about an increase in union dues. In September 1956 the Steelworkers had held its biannual convention in San Francisco. I did not attend the convention because I had just returned from Kitimat and was involved in the by-election. Since the convention was on the west coast and involved an expensive trip if a local was to send a delegate, and most of our locals on the peninsula at that time were quite small, the only persons who had attended from the Niagara area were the two staff representatives. Without advance notice, when the delegates arrived at the convention they were faced with a recommendation from the international union that the dues be increased from $3 to $5 monthly. Such an increase does not sound large today, but if one thinks of the wage and price levels at that time and the percentage increase that represented, 66.6 per cent, it was significant. The situation was aggravated by the feeling that a trick was being played on the locals and the membership, and that having the convention out west put it out of the reach of many union members, preventing their voices from being heard.

Though spread throughout both countries, the union's membership was much more concentrated in the east than in the west. Many concluded that the dues increase was all part of a deliberate design by the leadership of the union and that conclusion produced an enormous uproar. It was intensified on the peninsula, I think, by the fact that only the staff representatives had attended. There were no rank-and-file leaders there to hear the arguments that the union put forward for an increase, the justification for it, and the debate around it. The members simply received notices that the dues had gone up. Whether it was intended or not, the decision had every appearance of being contrived and appearance becomes reality in an issue of this kind. Another disturbing aspect of the affair – I remembered it years later when it became my turn to promote a dues increase – was that no persuasive rationale for the higher dues was presented to the members.

In my early days in Welland, I wanted to avoid becoming a fixture in either the St Catharines or Port Colborne office. I wanted to focus on getting to know the lay of the land around Welland, although the issue around the dues increase involved me with a number of the locals to a greater extent than I had intended, at least initially. Two of the most challenging cases were Local 1177, representing the workers at the iron plant in Port Colborne, Canadian Furnace, and Local 4923, representing the workers at a rope plant, Welland's first industrial enterprise, Plymouth Cordage. Each of these two locals had signed as the union party to the contracts with their respective employers, but, by union constitution, the union party to a collective agreement is supposed to be the United Steelworkers, that is, the international, not the local. When it came to issue of the dues increase, this arrangement by the signatory parties meant that the companies simply ignored dues-increase notifications from the international. The two local unions, for their part, certainly did not want to deliver such notices.

I got off to a roaring start with Local 1177. At the first meeting I attended I arrived a little late, sat at the back, and found myself listening to a vicious attack on the international union for all kinds of sins by a member named 'Pinker' Pine. I heard this out for a few minutes, then leapt to my feet and started screaming, 'Point of order!'

I had not met the president by then, a fine person named Bill Adams. He first asked me who I was. I told him. Bill, it turned out, attended conventions when he could and greatly admired the way Steelworkers President David J. McDonald conducted business. Bill had only a small local union, but he did his best to emulate McDonald and it made for interesting and effective meetings. He was clearly in charge and he brooked no nonsense and was quite entertaining. He was, therefore, quite intrigued with my outburst.

My point was that a local member had the right of free speech and nobody could take that away from him, but we all had an obligation to tell the truth. What Pine was saying included a number of claims that he and I both knew to be absolute falsehoods, and Bill and I could easily persuade anyone else in the room that such was the case. It was a useful intervention and I repeated it several more times.

Joe Bacon, who was the staff representative for each of these two locals, and I went to every meeting for some months, making the same case for the dues increase. Along the way, I reminded Bill of his admiration for David J. McDonald, and told him the president would not put up with the decision not to comply with the ruling of the convention. Bill replied that he would talk to the membership and the executive and he was as good as his word. The issue was quickly resolved.

Local 4923 was in the same circumstance as 1177 in that it had not accepted the dues increase, but it was a very different local union. It was larger, with about 300 members compared to 100 or so at Canadian Furnace. The membership was almost entirely Italian, not recent immigrants as in Kitimat but persons who had been in Welland for some time. As for the dues increase, we were working at the same process, attending every local meeting and urging the members to pass a motion requesting the company to check off the dues at the new level. They did not make any noise about it as did Local 1177, nor indulge in any wildly critical speeches about the international union. They simply smiled and quietly refused, and another month went by.

After a few months, I concluded that this could go on for a long time. Of course, the international union was concerned about having the dues in place. The district was requiring reports of how we were doing as it began to focus in on the places where nothing was happening. Our situation was a little bit of an embarrassment, since other locals around the peninsula were paying the increased dues. I finally suggested to Joe Bacon that I could not think of anything except to begin knocking on doors and visiting every member of the local union. Joe was a little taken aback, but when I asked him what alternatives we had, he offered none and agreed that we could go on for months in the same position.

So we picked up some check-off cards and started out. We quickly discovered that these people could not have welcomed us into their homes more warmly nor been more pleased to see us. They were, for the most part, vintners of some skill and experience and urged us to sample the fine results of their efforts. They were delighted to have us visit and, after a little conversation and an appreciation of their fine wine, were quite prepared to sign a check-off card.

We had a bit of an angle with the check-off cards in that we promised we would not use them until everybody had signed. In other words, we would not have the first people who signed paying $5 while others were still paying $3. But we were going to visit everyone and hoped they would sign, and when they had, then we would turn in the cards. It seemed to be taking something of a chance, but it was the only fair way to proceed. Everyone signed. All we could manage in an evening was three homes, after indulging in some wine at each of them. It was a little difficult to persuade our wives when we arrived home that we really had been out working. I was so pleased with the experience that, at the end, for the only time in all my years in the Steelworkers, I moved my membership from Local 2900 in Toronto to Local 4923 in Welland. For the rest of my time in the peninsula, that was where I paid my dues.

I have often talked about this experience and reflected upon how wonderful it would be if we came to know the membership of every local union as well as we knew this group. Just imagine if every local union had a staff representative who had been in every home, talked with each member individually, shared a drink with him or her, and shared the knowledge of when a union card was signed. The results were clear in Welland: Local 4923 became one of our most loyal and supportive unions. As well, from my own perspective, these home visits were a cultural experience in themselves. You often receive a very different perception of a person when you visit with him or her in their home. These were home-loving people. What appeared to be quite modest houses from the exterior were often quite impressive in the inside, obviously the recipients of a great deal of tasteful attention. The good news was that the members had these lovely homes. The bad news was they were destined years later, in 1969, to lose their jobs, early victims of the corporate search for lower wage areas.

When I arrived in the peninsula, there was a functioning area council, a grouping of Steelworker local unions. It met every month in a pub in Welland, whose owner, in appreciation of the business, donated a case of beer to the meeting. The principal agenda item, it seemed to me, was to give the staff reps a hard time. On many occasions, staff members displayed extraordinary patience in reacting as calmly as they did. The sessions had their good moments, but from my perspective they seemed destructive. It was essential that we change the style, have a different format and a different purpose. We accomplished that by emulating most of the other area councils in moving from a monthly meeting in the evening to a quarterly meeting on a weekend. We decided on daytime meetings with diverse educational, political, and other content. We also would invite a leading person from the peninsula, such as candidates for office, sitting members of Parliament, members of councils and school boards, or leading activists in social and other issues.

The idea of the area council in the Steelworkers, given the one-plant-one-local structure and the resulting proliferation of small locals, was to give voice to the larger issues facing the union with the united strength of all the locals. From that perspective, our area councils provided a mechanism for small local unions to make their voices heard collectively in ways that were not possible if they functioned separately. We worked that side of the street quite vigorously during my years in the peninsula. We did not overwhelm the other unions with our public relations, or anything like that, but we did begin to be heard.

The UAW, by way of contrast, had one large amalgamated local based in St Catharines around the General Motors plant. It had thousands of members, serviced by one staff person, one secretary, and many other full-time people – all holding jobs created by the local union. It had a high profile. For our part, the peninsula was a good example of the difficulties posed by a small local structure. Still, the area councils helped to offset our shortcomings. We had many fewer members than some, but our numbers were sufficient to make an impact.

Our group was greatly strengthened by the arrival of a veteran organizer from Sudbury, Jim Kidd, to replace Scotty Reid, who had been made an auditor at the international office. Jim was not very happy when he arrived. He had been one of the originals in the CIO's effort in Sudbury but had always been a Steelworker supporter and been the target of considerable hostility from the leadership of Mine Mill. Now, when things were stirring there and many were looking to the Steelworkers, Jim was upset that he had been transferred away, the feeling being that the need to focus on new issues was pre-eminent and that Jim's presence made that more difficult. The two of us had many conversations about this. I don't know that I ever persuaded him that the decision was correct, but I did persuade him that we had the need and the opportunity to make full use of his talents. He was a great pamphleteer and no organizing effort was too much trouble. We added a newsletter to the list of area council projects and Jim made a most valuable contribution to our work in the peninsula.

George Marshall and I were the organizers on the Welland Tubes campaign, with help from Local 1005 in Hamilton. We worked hard, house calling, leafleting, phoning, and meeting people face-to-face. Since the company was a new one and a joint venture with Stelco, where we represented the workers, we had a sound reason to be on the scene. However, the UE, whether by company connivance or by the right of their agreement, had full access to the plant and had an organizing committee transferred over from Page Hershey that worked inside. Although we had gained a foothold over the years, the UE was the largest union in Welland.

The major industrial complex was at the south end of the city where Page Hershey and Electrometals were the two big companies, operating side by side. Workers there belonged to the UE. This combination of community influence and cultural togetherness, access to the workers in the plant, and at least implicit support from the company gave the UE the edge. In the end I don't recall what the vote was but we lost decisively. However, from our point of view, it was no inconsiderable achievement to have signed enough cards to be on the ballot. Further, our efforts at Welland Tubes allowed us to establish a presence in the community, and, if my recollection is correct, this victory by the UE was its last in the Niagara peninsula.

Our defeat at Welland Tubes was a disappointment, but, given the odds and the activity against us, we felt we had done well to be on the ballot, to win a respectable level of support, and to let it be known that we were in town. When the vote was over, we began working on Atlas Steel. George was principally responsible for that effort and we began digging away at it. The company's strategy was to match the wages and benefits in Steelworker contracts, and often it even tried to put in a little extra something so it could say that its contracts were even better.

Our goal at Atlas was to find and develop enough support to build a major campaign. We managed to create sufficient interest that we were able, from time to time, to take some carloads of people over to see Stelco's Hamilton operations and visit with the workers there. They would visit the union hall and see what the set-up was like and they were usually reasonably impressed. On one occasion, when George and I were both involved and had each taken a carload over, we sorted out a question we had discussed many times and it provided some teasing material that I used in the days that followed.

I had always been interested in the fact that basic steelworkers went to work far ahead of the time their jobs began. So, if the shift began at 8 a.m., a great many of the workers were going in by 7 a.m., quite unlike any other plant I had encountered. Part of the explanation obviously relates to the huge territory covered by these big steel plants, which, from the air, seem to extend into the middle of Hamilton harbour. In addition, however, George always insisted that the early arrival was related to the tension of working in the plant and the need to prepare for the pressures and responsibilities of the day's work by having some coffee and being up to date on happenings in the department.

On the day in question, I inquired if we were going to see George's old job and he assured me we would. He really conducted these tours, having worked at Stelco a long time and knowing the plant well. He knew everybody and everybody knew him. So the excitement kept building between the two of us during this tour. I kept asking him if we were getting closer. Finally he said, 'It is the next building,' and we walked into a building that was a vast warehouse of a place with a five-stand mill in the centre of it. In those days, there was a worker's seat in front of a panel of gauges and buttons at each stand. George told me that, by the time he left Stelco, he had enough seniority that he was the first man. The person sitting in the first chair would be the one who took George's place. He noticed George, put down his *Globe and Mail* newspaper, and charged across the floor to say hello, quite some distance because we were not up to the mill yet. I could not resist needling George: 'I see now. I understand that the tension of this job is so great you somehow must read the *Globe and Mail* every day.'

However, George did persuade me that day that the tension involved in the job was real. It was not that you worked that steadily or that hard physically. It was that, when anything went wrong, you were expected to know immediately what the problem was, what to do about it, and then do it coolly, properly, and efficiently. Tons of valuable steel was at risk and preventing damage was entirely a function of how quickly one knew how to stop the mill, or change the steel, or whatever was required in any particular circumstance.

One of the distinctive differences about Welland is that it has a rather significant French-speaking section of town, including a French school and a French church. This is a result of workers migrating into Welland from Quebec during the Second World War, when there was a need for skilled people in Atlas Steel, particularly, and in the industrial area in the peninsula, generally. Because of this, we asked that Albert Desbiens, a Steelworkers employee, be sent down to work with us for awhile. Albert was an outstanding organizer and had done great work in the mines in northern Ontario.

It was the only campaign in which Albert had ever been involved where people were very polite and interested in talking with him, particularly in the French community. Everywhere he went, among French-speaking people or not, he attracted a following. He was an interesting person with a great sense of humour. People of whatever nationality or age group picked up a great deal of enthusiasm whenever they were involved with Albert in a campaign effort. From his perspective, though, he felt that the people in Atlas were just too nice. What he meant was that, in a successful campaign, feelings of enthusiasm are aroused in those supporting the drive and feelings of antagonism in those opposed. This helps you sense whether the campaign is really moving and likely to accomplish its goals. We received no such insight at the Atlas gates. Leaflet distributions were mostly to cars going in. The difference of the quality of the leaflet distribution in the morning at a plant can depend on whether you're handing leaflets into open car windows or through a crack in the window in the wintertime, or whether you are meeting people face to face. The latter circumstance is the most effective in any organizing campaign, but we didn't have much of that at Atlas Steel. All our hard work got us nowhere.

So we had suffered two defeats in quick succession, first at Welland Tubes and then at Atlas. But there was no time to dwell on any of this – there were too many organizing challenges needing our attention. In the years I was in the peninsula, there were a number of plants that the UAW, ourselves, and the UE were all interested in organizing. At one point, when the UAW and the Steelworkers were bumping into each other constantly, I approached Frank Fairchild, the UAW staff representative in the peninsula. He was a fine person, I had always felt, and we had cooperated well. I suggested to Frank that we look at these unorganized plants with a view to agreeing which ones each of our unions would pursue. I proposed that we each have a list and that we not involve our directors because the organizing would then become more complicated and political. Instead, we would just do it quietly between ourselves, and if our strategy succeeded in organizing more members, it would clearly be the right thing to do and everyone would be pleased. It would also be right in terms of the broader labour movement and would assure our directors that something worthwhile was happening in the peninsula. It was a win-win situation. After a couple of conversations, we agreed and the lists were appropriately agreed upon and exchanged.

One of the companies on our list was Columbus McKinnon Chain in St Catharines, where we had, at the time we were putting the lists together, just completed an organizing campaign and lost the vote by a few ballots. Labour Board rules prohibited further organizing activity in the same year by the union that had lost the vote. We kept tabs on the place and began to become more active as the year-end approached. Then we discovered that the UAW was working in the plant, too, in fact was a little bit ahead of us and had made an application. I was furious, and when I expressed my feelings to Fairchild, his reply was something along the lines of: 'Well, you just can't pass up a group of workers that want to be organized and want to be in your union.' I think it was an embarrassment to the UAW that we had managed our earlier application, even though the UAW had blanketed St Catharines with their amalgamated local union structure. That structure consisted of one local with a base at McKinnon's and then a number of satellite units, all of which contributed to providing full-time staff of significant size for the amalgamated local. The result was the UAW serviced a much larger membership in the peninsula than ours, with just one staff person and one secretary.

The events at Columbus McKinnon brought about the end of our arrangement with the UAW. It also marked the end of what until then had been a warm personal relationship between Frank Fairchild and me.

6

ORGANIZING

On moving to the Niagara peninsula in 1957, I hoped to learn more about the work of the union in the field in its various facets: collective bargaining, arbitrating, community organizing, and all the rest. In this, I succeeded. During my time in the area, from 1957 to 1965, I was involved in a number of organizing efforts and labour disputes, starting with Welland Tubes and Atlas and continuing through a succession of other cases which broadened my experience and deepened my knowledge. Along the way, I also pursued political causes and helped to found a university. These years were full, immensely rewarding ones.

The cornerstone local in the peninsula when I arrived was the English Electric local in St Catharines. English Electric at this point in its history was a wholly owned subsidiary of John Inglis. As a result, in 1957 we were involved in John Inglis company-wide bargaining, which was headed up by Don Montgomery, then the area supervisor in Toronto, later to be elected secretary treasurer of the Canadian Labour Congress.

The English Electric plant was a good plant, employing upwards of 1,000 workers in its good years, and a great British trade unionist named Art Riseley was president of our local there. Grievances were heard every Friday afternoon and, since there was a steady flow of them, I was usually there for the occasion. As the depression of 1957–8 became more serious, the electric business deteriorated badly and English Electric shut down. It was first announced as a temporary move, but by 1960 it had become permanent. We lost a number of small plants around the peninsula about that period. It was very upsetting.

It was these events that started me once more thinking seriously about workers' rights concerning the management of their plants. When I would have a drink with laid-off members, in order to understand their situation, share their misery, and hear about the difficult events they were experiencing, time and again they would tell stories about the dumb moves the company had made. These would range from inappropriate equipment that had been purchased to inadequate or incorrect ways it was used. I concluded, as I listened to all of this, that while all these opinions might not be right, they could not all be wrong either, and it was a shame that these people, with all their ideas about what should have been done, had lost their jobs. By and large, no one in management had paid any attention to their views or even listened to them. I began to feel strongly that there must be a better way. One issue that I became excited about was retraining programs. It seemed that there should be some retraining activity, particularly in the event of a major plant shutdown as had occurred at English Electric. We fired off a brief to Prime Minister John Diefenbaker asking for a meeting with him concerning plant shutdowns and retraining. To my amazement, he agreed to meet with us. We headed to Ottawa and appeared at the prime minister's office at the appointed time and, sure enough, they ushered us right in and there he was. He welcomed us warmly and delivered a summary of my brief that was much more eloquent and better than I could have done. I guess he was demonstrating his lawyer's mind. He had a great reputation as a lawyer. He knew that brief, had read and absorbed it, and he delivered a five- or ten-minute pitch about it that left me feeling his reputation as a lawyer was surely deserved.

Then he said, 'Mr. Williams, I understood all this, but we simply do not agree with it. This is socialism you are preaching in your brief and this government does not believe that is the solution to these difficulties.' What followed was a little lecture about the free-enterprise system, which his government believed would best provide answers to the problems we were experiencing. I responded mostly by addressing the retraining issue, making the point that we needed better labour-market studies to understand its dynamics more clearly. But I also noted that, even with that difficulty acknowledged, it was better that unemployed people have a learning opportunity than be expected to sit until something turned up.

I don't know if our little Ottawa invasion had anything to do with it, but some retraining programs were developed for the peninsula. A number of them involved welder training, which led to a good deal of criticism, based on the argument that automatic welding had arrived, eliminating the need for welding skills. In reality, when the recession of 1957–8 ended, there was a great boom at the General Motors plant in St Catharines. Despite the automatic welders, GM could not find enough welders, including all the people from our union and other unions. That was because the work was being managed through the labour councils, for those who had gone through the training programs. The result is that some welders who have retired during the last few years spent virtually their entire working lives at General Motors and made good money.

We had had a local for officeworkers at English Electric, too. It was a separate local and provided good support for general union purposes, but its own regular meeting attendance was almost non-existent. There usually were only three people, the president, the secretary-treasurer, and me. After a few months of this I spoke with Jim McAvoy, the president, who was a conscientious person, and said, 'Jim we must do better than this. There is no point in sitting around every month talking to each other and complaining that nobody else is here. Tell me who the office spark plug is, the person who, if there's going to be a party in the office, is the organizer.'

'Oh,' he said, 'Terry Itel.'

And I said, 'Can you set up a drink after work or something for you and me with Terry?' and he did.

I told Terry of our concern with the office local. It was an important organization but it had no life and no pep. Jim did his best with it, but he was from the older group and it needed some support from among the younger people. We said we had discussed all the people in the office to determine who could make something of this and that it was her. Well, Terry was intrigued with the idea, took it on, and we had the liveliest office local around. We had a good-size group at every meeting and the local held social events from time to time. For her part, Terry became a trade-union activist for the rest of her life. After English Electric closed, she divorced and moved to Toronto. Some years later, after David Archer's wife Doris died, Terry and David became a couple. Archer was president of the Ontario Federation of Labour.

In September 1960 we organized the civic workers in St Catharines. They had been in the old Trades and Labour Congress civic employees union but were decertified ten years earlier. Art Riseley and his colleagues from the plant local at English Electric – the company's closure had not yet been announced to be permanent – reached out to them and really led them into the Steelworkers. By that time, I had assumed new responsibility as area supervisor for the Niagara peninsula, one of six such positions created that year by Larry Sefton, the others being Toronto, Hamilton, Winnipeg, Sault Ste Marie, and Elliot Lake-Sudbury. We worked away at bargaining but arrived at a stalemate. With city council being difficult, we felt we needed to stir things up a bit so we asked for a public hearing before the full council so that we could explain the situation from our point of view. We prepared a brief and packed the council chamber with our members and supporters from the civic local and all the others as well.

There was a break in the meeting and probably the most conservative member of the city council, last name Jones, a well-known public figure and the owner of an excellent toy store, took me aside. He said, 'Lynn, couldn't you arrange a little wildcat strike for a couple of days? Then the people in town would know that you folks are serious and we can push the taxes up enough to look after you and we can settle this without further difficulty.' We never bothered with the strike – it seemed an unnecessary loss of two days' pay – and we knew Jones was interested in a settlement. In the end, we achieved it. I have always enjoyed telling that story as illustrative of some of the differences between bargaining in the public sector and in the private. I have never had the CEO of Stelco or US Steel or any of those companies ask me to arrange a little wildcat strike.

Also in 1960, one of the most embarrassing events in my life occurred. By then, the Steelworkers had become quite active politically in the peninsula and we had a strong leader there in Mel Swart. Mel was the backbone of the local CCF. Our people were very supportive, with George Marshall in particular leading the way. Mel was our perennial candidate – we ran him seven or eight times before he was elected. In 1960, however, there was a problem. Two federal by-elections were being held that year, one in Niagara Falls and one in Peterborough, and the 'New Party,' which would become part of the NDP the following year, could not run Mel in Niagara Falls because we were by then focused on electing him in Welland. We were running him both provincially and federally in the same riding and did not wish to complicate his identification any further. But we were fortunate to discover another fine person who was interested in becoming the candidate. Ed Mitchelson was the reeve of Stanford Township, in fact one of the most popular reeves it ever had. Word was that the Liberals had the terrible Judy LaMarsh, a local lawyer, as their candidate, and that she reputedly had a poor reputation around town and was not well liked. Putting all of this together, we saw a great opportunity.

We really went to work. We set up a canvassing organization, the likes of which Niagara Falls had never before seen. I went to the provincial office of the New Party in Toronto and pleaded for more money. I said, 'You know, there's no chance we can ever win in Peterborough because it is very conservative country, but we have a great opportunity in Niagara Falls.' I don't know to what extent the people there listened, but they gave me the impression that they were giving us more money than Peterborough, and they seemed to agree that if we were going to win one of these contests, it would be Niagara Falls, particularly in view of Ed's record of being elected reeve over and over in an area that made up a large part of the riding. It turned out, however, that his leadership was very much with individuals and small groups, and that making a public speech was not one of his strengths. When he moved out into the broader campaign, this became a serious difficulty. Of course, he could stand up and talk, but he was not comfortable or effective.

One of the Buffalo TV stations gave us time for an all-candidates debate. Also participating was Progressive Conservative Keith Lougheed, and there might have been a fourth, fringe candidate. Shockingly, at the beginning of the debate, Judy LaMarsh reached across, ripped papers out of Ed's hand, and said, 'Ed Mitchelson, if you did not have these papers in front of you, you wouldn't know what this New Party, or so called New Party, was all about.' Ed was dumbfounded. First of all, he was not given to glib chatter, but most of all he was a real gentleman. He simply did not know how to respond to LaMarsh's brash, rude attack. It was a terrible TV broadcast and I was in despair.

Finally, election day, 31 October 1960, arrived and some optimism had returned. I felt that at least we had a good get-out-the-vote organization, so maybe we could still pull it off. We knew where a good deal of our vote was, and we had canvassed the riding thoroughly, which had never been done before. However, the old Liberal machine simply oozed out of the woodwork. As soon as I arrived in the riding on election day and began working, I could see that Liberal workers were all over the place. My heart sank. Women were going in and out of the polling booths, talking to their inside person and being told, 'Mrs.

O'Flaherty hasn't voted yet, better see where she is.' They had young people driving cars for them. They had people in charge of different blocks and they seemed to know everybody.

Judy LaMarsh wiped us out, but that is not the end of the story. LaMarsh recorded 13,428 votes, the Progressive Conservative Keith Lougheed 8,309, and Ed 6,627. Meantime, Walter Pitman, our other New Party candidate, won in Peterborough where I had been so sure we had no chance. I didn't turn up at the provincial office for a little while after that.

But politics, while fascinating and important, was a sideline to my main work as a labour organizer, and on this front few cases were as challenging or absorbing than the Inco plant in Port Colborne. The campaign here, in 1962, was intimately tied to events at the larger Inco operation in Sudbury, events that stretched back several years and involved an epic struggle between two unions, the Steelworkers and Mine Mill.

Over the years, there had been contentious disputes within and between unions over allegations of communist leadership or other kinds of communist domination. This existed with particular intensity in communities such as Sudbury, where Mine Mill, one of those alleged to be communist-dominated, was strong on the local scene. Tension between the communist-dominated unions and the others reached a peak in 1947 and 1948, when a number of those unions were expelled by the CIO in the United States and the CCL in Canada. The expulsions triggered policy discussions concerning what should be done with the jurisdiction of these various unions. It was determined in the Canadian Congress of Labour and the CIO that the Steelworkers should assume responsibility for the hard-rock-mining jurisdiction and invite Mine Mill locals to join the Steelworkers and be active in organizing efforts in the mining camps where non-union mines existed. This led to a series of confrontations across North America at a time of general decline in the hard-rock-mining sector in the two economies, and the results did little to change the face of union representation in either country. It took some time to determine whether either union was gaining any particular advantage. The Steelworkers was much the larger union, though, having the steel jurisdiction along with its general activity across the labour movement to back it up.

Sudbury was much the largest base that Mine Mill had anywhere and undoubtedly the source of the principal support for the entire organization. But Mine Mill found itself in an untenable position in 1958. That year, Inco put an offer on the table that represented some improvements, but Mine Mill considered it inadequate. The problem was that Mine Mill was not well positioned to pressure the nickel industry, both because the economy was coming out of the most significant depression for some years and cutbacks were still the order of the day, and because of the union's alienation from the mainstream of the labour movement. Nonetheless, a strike ensued, at the end of which Mine Mill was forced to settle for little if anything more than what had been on the table prior to the work stoppage. At that point, a new slate of officers successfully challenged the existing leadership and took office in Local 598. Don Gillis, a Cape Bretoner out of the ranks of the Inco workers, headed the group and became president. Other new leaders included Don McNabb as vice-president of the local and Ray Poirier as financial secretary, both of whom were to become household names in Sudbury in the months and years of turmoil, struggle, and accomplishment that lay ahead.

After a great deal of examination, consultation with the elected local Mine Mill leadership and the workers, and discussion with the Steelworkers and the Canadian Labour Congress, it was decided that the Steelworkers should begin a campaign at Inco's Sudbury operations. At one level, the contest was really between groups both claiming to be socialists, one from a Marxist perspective, the other from the perspective of social democracy. The Steelworkers were supporters of the CCF, while Mine Mill supported the Labour Progressive Party, representatives of the communists at that time. But, more fundamentally, the struggle was really about workers' rights, and how best to defend and promote them.

The campaign – constant, vigorous, contentious, and sometimes threatening – intensified following a riot involving opposing Mine Mill forces at the Sudbury Arena on 10 September 1961. Eventually, the Steelworkers signed the required 50 per cent of members needed to apply for certification. After hearings, the Ontario Labour Relations Board announced that the Steelworkers had made their case and that a representation vote was to be held. The vote took place between 27 February and 1 March 1962, and the Steelworkers won by just 15 votes more than the required majority, with more than 14,000 cast. Because of various challenges, certification of the Steelworkers Local 6500 as bargaining agent did not take place until 15 October 1962.

A more cautious version of the Sudbury revolution took place in Port Colborne, home of Inco's nickel refinery. There, Jim Babirad, the president of Mine Mill Local 637, which represented the workers in the refinery, rebelled, too, and attached himself to the dissident group in Sudbury to a significant extent. Albert Desbiens relayed intelligence to the rest of us that Port Colborne's Inco workers were expressing an interest in the Steelworkers. However, in the early stages of our discussions with Babirad, he had not made a public commitment one way or the other. He worked with us and was very helpful but did not become the leader of the campaign as did Don Gillis, his counterpart in Sudbury. While Jim was certainly intelligent and quickly understood what was happening, he did not have the depth of trade-union experience that Don had and thus tended to proceed more cautiously.

Bill Longridge directed the Mine Mill effort. Then the secretary-treasurer of Mine Mill, Canada, he worked out of Toronto but came down to Port Colborne to manage the campaign. It was largely a campaign of argument, of point and counterpoint, of publicity pro and con, hurled back and forth by roving bands of organizers covering the pubs in town every night and distributing leaflets at the gate in the morning. It must have been a great time for owners of bars because they were much more crowded than usual with thirsty customers. Night after night, people went to their favourite places and debated the issues. And they did so peacefully. The police had come to both unions at the beginning of the Port Colborne contest, told us that they understood a campaign was going to take place, and while they had no problem with that they didn't want the reputation of the town to be besmirched by any difficulties. They said they intended to have officers around at our functions so people could see them. I don't know Mine Mill's position, but I supported the police presence. We didn't want anyone hurt and we wanted the decisions to be made on as objective and rational a basis as possible.

The co-chairmen of the organizing committee in Port Colborne were Doug Hart and Otto Urbanovics, both of whom went on to distinguished careers in the Steelworkers. They were co-chairmen because they were good friends, committed to the campaign, and rode to work together. Whether it was their idea or Albert Desbiens's or someone else's, they decided that they might as well be working on the campaign, planning and strategizing, while they were riding back and forth. They did an outstanding job. Otto was an immigrant who left Hungary to escape the communist leadership of the day. He had a deep and well-founded intellectual antipathy to communism and all it stood for. He and Doug were the leaders among a number of active younger workers deeply involved in the Port Colborne campaign. Doug's father-in-law, John Shedden, had been the full-time secretary of Local 637 back in 1948, when, for a brief period, the Steelworkers held the bargaining rights in Port Colborne. As the Mine Mill full-time secretary, John had been active in leading the move to the Steelworkers. When Mine Mill regained the certification, it expelled John and his closest colleagues for life from the union and made his life as difficult as possible around the plant for the rest of his time there. Not retiring for some years, he withstood it all most courageously and provided our campaign with much good advice.

Our office in Welland, which we had opened in July 1959, was on the other side of the Welland Canal, near the centre of town, but it was simply a little storefront office and had no place for meetings. Not far away, on King Street, there was a closed movie theatre. We made arrangements to rent it and use it as our meeting hall. It was available all the time and we made no attempt to convert any of the space into offices.

The campaign did not really begin until September 1961. Not many weeks into it, our committee had concluded that opinion was evenly divided and that some kind of catalyst was needed to bring about a decision, hopefully in our favour. It was decided at one of our committee meetings that there should be a debate between our leader and theirs. A substantial turnout was certain, interest would be high, and we all felt confident that Larry Sefton would prevail. We correctly anticipated that Mine Mill's representative of choice would be Harvey Murphy, its western vice-president, who was considered the best public speaker among their leaders. We began to set out what would be necessary to stage such a debate successfully. It first required Larry's agreement, of course, and we proceeded on that track first.

Larry was a remarkable trade-union leader. Hardened, experienced, and educated in trade unionism at a very young age as the recording secretary of the Mine Mill local in Kirkland Lake in northern Ontario, he had found himself tested in 1941 when his union had gone on strike against a local gold mine. It proved to be a classic mine walkout – no rush to settle on the company's part, with the gold sitting in the ground and gaining value just being there. The company, in effect, forced the workers onto the picket line. In the course of the three-month struggle, which ultimately failed to attain the objective of union recognition, the leaders of the union, including Larry, were blacklisted throughout the north. Many had come from southern Ontario to find work, and now they returned south, where, much to their chagrin, they discovered that the Steelworkers had been assigned the mining jurisdiction.

The Kirkland Lake strike was a watershed in the history of the Canadian labour movement. The idea that labour law in the United States would be more advanced than in Canada is a thought that would never occur to today's trade-union activist. That was, however, very much the situation in 1941, after Franklin Roosevelt, the New Deal, and the Wagner Act had done their job. What the Americans had, as they rushed into trade unionism in numbers not seen since the Knights of Labor, was a procedure for winning union recognition and a requirement that, once a union was formed, employers must negotiate in good faith. In Canada, in contrast, where industrial relations were being guided by Prime Minister William Lyon Mackenzie King, a former personnel consultant, the regime was one of conciliation and good-will meetings that more often than not produced nothing – which raised the temperature of working men and women in Canada by several degrees. Kirkland Lake made all of this clear. It also provided a great lesson in democratic politics by marking the point at which the direct political interests of the workers and the fledging CCF came together, resulting in a famous by-election victory by the CCF's Joe Noseworthy in York South in 1942 and a recruiting effort by Clare Gillis that established a trade-union base for the democratic left in Canada that remains vigorous today. A number of strong, determined, young unionists were at the heart of these developments, including the Sefton brothers, Larry and Bill, Jock Brodie, who later was the long-time president of Local 2900 in Toronto, and Pat Conroy, secretary-treasurer of the Canadian Congress of Labour.

And so the Kirkland Lake strike, hardly a success by normal standards, succeeded in raising the issue of recognition to national attention to a degree that required King, albeit in his halting and hesitant manner, to bring some measure of the American practice into Canadian industrial relations by such means as orders-in-council and other devices. Along the way, Larry Sefton experienced his baptism by fire in the trade-union movement. Although only twenty-two years of age at the peak of the crisis, he was chosen by the local union to lead the appeals for trade-union support all across Canada. The result was that he quickly became one of the most knowledgeable people in the labour movement concerning its 'on-the-ground condition.' With his sharp mind and observant nature, he also learned a great deal about what was working and what was not in the emerging field of industrial relations.

After the conclusion of the Kirkland Lake strike, Larry moved to Toronto, where his first job was at the Ronson cigarette-lighter manufacturing company in northwest Toronto (the street on which the company was located is now named Ronson Avenue and is the home of the District 6 headquarters office). Soon afterwards, he joined the staff of the Steelworkers, and in 1953 he succeeded John Mitchell as director of District 6, a post he held for twenty years. His accomplishments as director were remarkable, the district's membership growing over this period from 30,000 to 130,000. In general terms, one-third of the additional membership came as a result of organizing the unorganized, another one-third from people in other unions becoming Steelworker members as a result of mergers, raids, and such, and the final one-third from natural growth in the original enterprise. Larry was known across the international as the 'organizing director.'

With a leader like this, the Port Colborne troops in 1961 had good grounds for confidence. Larry came to Port Colborne to meet with the committee, the second such meeting with him. The first had been a gathering to discuss whether the Steelworkers would proceed with a campaign. I recall the essence of that meeting quite clearly. It was in our little office on Main Street, which was packed with committee members. Otto and Doug chaired the meeting, as usual, and they told Larry firmly at the start of the proceedings that they wanted assurances that the Steelworkers would be in the campaign for the long haul, that it would not be a superficial or fly-by-night kind of effort and that the union was really committed. When it came his turn to speak, Larry stressed that this was a difficult issue. It was expecting a great deal for the union to put everything on the line in another major confrontation with Mine Mill concurrent with the one in Sudbury. While there were some advantages in such an approach, it was no small matter to undertake. If they wanted a commitment from the Steelworkers, the union in turn had to have a serious commitment from them in order to embark on what would not be an easy battle. I don't recall any great shock being expressed at the meeting, though there was certainly surprise – including on the part of Doug, Otto, and Albert. After a full debate, a unanimous decision was made to proceed.

Now, on this second occasion, Larry had come down to Port Colborne to consider with the committee whether a challenge to a debate should be issued to Mine Mill. We decided to make the challenge and Mine Mill had little choice but to accept. It would be the major event of the campaign. We had meetings about the rules, which had to do with speaking order, time allotments, maintaining order, and tickets. There were elaborate arrangements with Mine Mill about the distribution of tickets for each union. Each group received the same number of reserved-seat tickets, but immediately each side started figuring out ways to obtain some of the other side's tickets in order to pack the crowd in their favour. It proved quite a struggle. Although they may have ended up with many of our tickets and we with theirs, the result was very much as was intended at the beginning. It was an evenly balanced audience, the cheers and shouts evenly divided. Every time I heard the other side cheer, my heart sank, and every time I heard our folks cheer, my heart rose. Most fascinating was the different approaches taken by these two smart, experienced, trade unionists in making their case.

Harvey was a person to whom the details told the story. He had his podium covered with newspaper clippings and articles and stories, the common theme of which was that Steelworkers were a terrible bunch of people. These were examples where we had failed or had trouble or whatever, and of course the stories involved Steelworker difficulties and Mine Mill successes. His presentation was quite a show. Picking away at these details gave a tone of authenticity to his message.

I don't recall us giving Larry a lot of advice and I think he had devoted considerable thought to how to approach the debate. Having come out of Mine Mill himself and knowing a great deal about how its leaders thought, he alone determined what his strategy should be. In the event, it was the polar opposite to Harvey's. He declined to get bogged down in detailed accusations about who did what to whom, because after a time the negativism becomes repetitious, confusing, and dull. Instead, he took the high road, emphasizing union principle, union democracy, union programs, and union accomplishments. At the end of the debate, both sides declared victory. It's difficult for me to be objective but I believe Larry made the more impressive presentation, in that it was so principled and sincere. It was not a whining litany of accusations but a serious presentation of real issues and achievements. Still, both performed with great style. It would have been difficult for a debate judge to decide who won because the two styles were so at odds. I think the ultimate evidence was that Larry did win, because we certainly won the campaign and that was the point of the entire exercise. I believe that people were attracted by his broader themes. And he had another thing going for him, too. There was deep suspicion of Mine Mill, a distrust that really went back to the 1958 strike in Sudbury. The Gillis/Babirad forces, Mine Mill's internal opposition, felt that whatever gains were claimed in that strike involved smoke and mirrors. In fact, they had been badly misled into the strike, without an appropriate evaluation of what leverage they might have and without resources to provide appropriate support. This view of events was the common opinion; even Mine Mill supporters were not very vigorous in their denials. As a result, Harvey's approach lacked credibility with many people, who were much more drawn to Larry's avoidance of propaganda or excessive claims or promises.

There was great enthusiasm after the meeting. Everyone marched off to their various pubs and claims began about who had won, though, as I said, the eventual result of the campaign – we carried the vote, 1,033 to 763, in December 1961 and were certified very early the following year – demonstrated that Larry had carried the day. Of course, all elements of a good campaign contribute to its ultimate success. In this case we had outstanding organizing committee participation and excellent leadership from Otto and Doug. We were all right there, so decision making was quick and communication easy, with literature prepared on the spot. Albert Desbiens made an enormous contribution. He was, in effect, our field leader, charismatic and tireless.

This vote in Port Colborne was the first of three votes, preceding those at Inco's operations in Thompson, Manitoba, and Sudbury. Therefore, if we won, it was critical to the Steelworkers that this vote be counted and the results made public immediately. Mine Mill, on the other hand, asked to have the vote held but not counted until Sudbury had voted. We went to the Labour Board for a decision and it came down on the side of an immediate count and immediate public notice of the result. The vote was counted and it was a decisive victory.

The story of Larry's involvement in the Port Colborne campaign illustrates why he was held in such esteem among Steelworkers and indeed throughout the labour movement. He had a great vision of what he wanted the union and the movement to accomplish – a decent life of opportunity and satisfaction for all people. He was eloquent on the necessity of struggle in some circumstances and on the necessity of being prepared, but his point was accomplishment, not struggle for its own sake. He also had a profound understanding of the importance of priorities and timing. That is why there was no hesitation about his two visits to Port Colborne; he understood quickly that the momentum of the campaign and the results of the debate were crucial. Larry was a doer, not a talker. But when the debate required a moving speech, when the committee needed inspiration or the company representatives were due a reality reminder, Larry could perform eloquently and effectively. At the same time, as a leader he was not given to precise, detailed instructions. We used to accuse him of speaking indirectly all the time, helping you set the scene yourself, analyse it, and figure out what had to be done. I am sure he felt that strategies and plans arrived at in that way were the ones most likely to enjoy a full effort and have the best chance of success. Larry often achieved that result in situations that appeared almost hopeless. He brought a deep compassion for people to his leadership, impatient on occasion with their frailties and weaknesses but always ready to try to build their knowledge and strengths.

For our new local in Port Colborne, we chose the number 6200 because 1962 was the year we were certified. We thought it would be a way of remembering when this most significant trade-union event took place. Not that our difficulties were over. We faced an awkward reality, in that now that we were certified we were required to bargain, regardless of what happened in Sudbury, and indeed we did give notice of our desire to begin negotiations. The company's position was that none of this should be happening because Port Colborne and Sudbury had always bargained together for essentially the same contract. Transportation access to the Welland Canal evidently was a major reason for locating the nickel refinery in Port Colborne, despite the fact that it really was an integral part of the Sudbury operation.

Obviously, the Steelworkers had no objection to integrated bargaining. In fact, we were in favour of it. But the law required, as did our public stance before the vote, that we accept and initiate action in pursuit of our responsibility to represent the people in Port Colborne. The company, of course, was playing a contradictory game, on the one hand arguing that we should be just waiting for Sudbury and on the other doing everything they could to delay proceedings in Sudbury. A year went by before we were able to begin the Sudbury negotiations. In the meantime, we went through the entire process in Port Colborne, holding negotiating meetings, presenting our proposals, arguing with the company's proposals, proceeding through the required conciliation process, taking a strike vote, and preparing to strike.

Of course, this was essentially a theoretical exercise. If it had a saving grace it was that we made it as effective an educational experience as we could. Our members, although frustrated to a considerable degree by the time that was passing, were sensible about it. In their heads and hearts they understood that nothing was going to happen until we could deal with Sudbury. Going through the drill was probably the best way to handle the situation. It certainly was a unique way of putting in time. We used a considerable amount of that time in positive ways, such as testing the water with Inco about proposals and relating the kind of issues we were arguing about to what we expected would ultimately be the critical decisions.

The availability of this new and enthusiastic group of members also provided an additional push to the organizing effort we had been attempting to put together around the peninsula, in order to build our union and the labour movement and to make our presence felt. We used the area council and organizing committee there to encourage our people as much as we could to pick up prospects around the peninsula and to advise the union about places where people seemed to be interested in organizing. One of our devices for this purpose was to talk to our people about their public conversations. These happened particularly in pubs, where union people are often heard talking to each other and complaining about a grievance that was lost, or an arbitration that was not as successful as had been hoped, or negotiations that were not as productive as they might have been. We would constantly remind our activists that non-union people who heard these conversations might be led to believe union labour relations are all bad news. In fact, workers without a union do not have the right even to file a grievance, to have issues settled by arbitration, to have a contract at all, much less the right to negotiate anything. The message was that we should be telling positive stories, so when people overheard us they would hear us talking about union successes. And if we were talking about problems we should put them into perspective. Years later, when Jimmy McGeehan from Philadelphia became our secretary treasurer, he encapsulated much the same idea in a slogan that he used all the time, which was, 'Say a good word about your union.' It was based on the notion that, unless we think about it consciously, we frequently tend to discuss problems and challenges rather than achievements, when we are talking union with friends while sitting around the table in a restaurant or bar. In my days in the peninsula, I don't know whether the attempt to tell a more positive story worked or not, but we certainly had good people available to help us on campaigns. They seemed to get a kick out of it and we tried to make sure that they had a good time and a positive experience.

There is no doubt that, as organizing proceeds, the very atmosphere seems to encourage good things to happen, however unrelated they may be. In 1962 that is what happened to us. The Elliot Lake uranium mines were then beginning to shut down. One of our leading rank-and-file activists there, the president of one of the locals, was Dick Hunter. As the place was closing, he and his colleagues, all enthusiastic Steelworkers, led an effort to find work for the people involved in other spots around Ontario where jobs were increasing. One of the results of this was the transfer of a number of workers to the new chemical plant in Port Maitland, a community a short distance from Dunnville. Dick was one of the transfers and he promptly organized the union and became president. This was all accomplished almost before we were aware that anything was going on.

Three organizing efforts in the Niagara peninsula, stretching from 1963 to 1965, are particularly worthy of note. The first, in 1963, was Ferranti Packard, an electrical equipment and transformer manufacturer in St Catharines. It had been the subject of many organizing efforts, some by us, some by the UE, and some by other unions, including the UAW. The principal activist in the plant was an energetic, strategic-thinking Irishman named Henry Duffy. He kept his ties with Ireland by regularly visiting the old country, and he used those visits for, among other things, keeping up to date with what was happening in the British labour movement. He was a sophisticated, knowledgeable trade unionist.

Over the years, various unions had all run very much the same kind of traditional campaign of bashing the Ferranti Packard company union, which in turn had fended off all comers. Doug Hart, co-chair of the organizing committee, became persuaded that a much more appropriate and effective strategy would be to have Henry become the elected president of the company union and then work towards affiliation or merger, and avoid altogether a head-on confrontation between our union and the company union. The strategy succeeded brilliantly, though it took a little time and required a complex mix of internal politics and outside promotion. Internal political activity brought Henry to the presidency of the company union. Outside promotion by the Steelworkers was then cast in a much more positive light than was customary in the attack-the-company-union approach. The campaign's success – we won certification on 1 April 1963, with 87 per cent of the vote – led to Henry becoming one of the best-known activists in the Steelworkers, as, under his leadership, the local won some excellent agreements and organized the office along the way. One of Henry's great accomplishments was to negotiate and continually improve the company incentive plan (a sophisticated piecework manufacturing system), eliminating its defects, refining its management, and making it much more productive. Some said in jest that only Henry understood it. I don't think that was true, but it certainly was true that he understood it. He made bargaining a major goal all the time and within that framework the incentive plan was crucial.

The second campaign also occurred in 1963. It involved Switson's, a vacuum-cleaner manufacturer in Welland that, with a workforce of about 300, produced for a number of companies under a variety of brand names. At the time, I had reduced my servicing load in order to have more organizing time, and the results at Switson's proved the wisdom of my decision. The workers there had been organized about ten years earlier by the UE, but the UE had been unable to get an agreement. We had got wind there was interest in the Steelworkers, so I asked Dan Russell, president of the area council, to focus on the place for a few weeks. We first sent him door knocking to see if some leaders could be found with whom to build an organizing committee.

Dan faithfully went knocking on doors, night after night, and he would come back with the same story. He had not found anyone willing to be a leader and serve on an organizing committee, but he had one or two more signed cards. This was frustrating. It seemed that it was almost impossible to make the number of calls Dan had and not find some potential leadership, but he insisted that nobody wanted to be on a committee or be a leader. Yet every night he signed up a couple of more cards, sometimes three. It was almost uncanny, but in due course we found ourselves with the place organized. The real miracle of the whole process was that the company, despite all the calls that Dan had been making, had not discovered anything was going on until it received notice from the Ontario Labour Relations Board that the Steelworkers had made an application for certification.

The company was locally owned. The president lived in the neighbouring town of Fonthill. When he learned what had happened, it was reported that he was, to say the least, very upset. He evidently could not imagine how this could have happened. It was approaching Christmas and, as usual, he put on the annual Christmas dinner, ostensibly for retirees but all the employees were invited. Once the notice from the board was up in the plant, the workers accepted it as if it was the certification itself and, indeed, we did receive an automatic certification in view of the large number who had signed up.

We had a bit of time before the Christmas dinner and in this new atmosphere were able to identify and develop some leadership. We knew the president used the dinner to make a speech to employees and we were certain, given the circumstances, that he would have something to say about the union. Having identified some leaders, we were able to be sure that some of them attended and arranged that Dan and I would meet them at the union hall after the dinner was over to get a report on what the president of the company had to say. As it turned out, the president did not disappoint. His essential message went as follows: 'The union just wants your money. They are after having your dues checked off. We did not let the UE do that and we will not let the Steelworkers do that, either. These unions also like to negotiate in back rooms away from the light of publicity or anything and we do not believe in that. Whatever goes on we are going to make sure everybody knows.'

Our people were quite excited when they came back to the office. 'What do you make of this?' they asked.

'Well,' I said, 'we are going to agree with him about everybody knowing what is going on before he changes his mind. We are going to interpret what he said to mean that the bargaining should take place in the plant and everybody should be invited to attend.' I told them I had been itching to have an opportunity like that for a long time.

We wrote a leaflet that night and distributed it at the gate the next morning saying that we were delighted to hear of the president's proposal that we bargain publicly. The leaflet went on to say that I would be calling him that day and would propose that we bargain once a week, at quitting time in the plant, and that everybody be invited to attend. The president agreed to our proposal. The first meetings were quite a novelty and everybody came. We had a table in the middle of the plant and the union committee sat on our side of the table with me in traditional style. He had some of the old-timers, mostly women, who I think had helped him defeat the UE, sitting on his side. I remember the substance of the first session well. We had proposals that I began to present, but the key part of the conversation was when the president said, 'Well, I know what you want, Mr. Williams, you just want dues. You want to take a lot of money from these people that isn't fair you should take. We stopped the UE from doing that and we're not going to let you do that, either.'

My response was something to the effect that, 'Of course, we want a dues shop. We have been given the responsibility by the government to represent your employees and that cannot be done for nothing. It costs money and if they want to have a local union they need some money, so of course we're asking for a check-off and we have it everywhere else.' But I added, 'It's difficult to just talk about that when we have many other matters we wish to discuss with you, for example, pensions. It's high time, now that your company has been here for some years and is so successful, that you had a pension plan. You have a great many fine people here who I'm sure would appreciate that and need that and would look forward to that.'

Well, it wasn't too long after introducing this proposal that a number of the elderly women who were supporting the president began nodding their heads in agreement. The pension was a pretty good idea.

And that was the approach I used in the bargaining. Every week I trotted out another issue and for a number of the subjects I brought people over from the national and district offices in Toronto. A result was that this group became as well educated a local union group as we had. At least proportionate to the amount of time they had been in the union, they knew a great deal about it. Over time, however, the process wound down a bit. People around the union were chastising me a little and saying I would never achieve a settlement that way. I said, 'You are right about that, but what an excellent education program it has been.' And I would ask them how often they had wished that all members could see exactly what takes place at a bargaining table.

Occasionally, I would take our members off to a corner of the plant for a caucus and we would discuss an issue and change a proposal. Yet it was difficult to progress very much, and as the novelty wore off and the crowds diminished in size we decided that it was time to put on some pressure, by applying for conciliation and taking a strike vote. By then, the local union was functioning well, with good meetings and some fine activists. We felt confident about moving things along.

The president of the company called me when he received his notice of the application for conciliation. By then we were coming to know each other quite well, and he asked, 'How does this conciliation procedure work?'

I explained that conciliation was necessary before we could take strike action, and that there was a group of government conciliation officers, one of whom would be assigned to our case. We both would be so advised. At that point, we would then be somewhat in his or her hands. I said that I knew most of the conciliators and, as soon as I knew who it was, I would explain to the person that we have been following a different and public procedure here.

The president asked, 'Well how would it normally work?' I explained: 'In the usual situation we would go to a hotel someplace and the officer would arrange for three meeting rooms, one for his use and one for each of the parties. The officer would sometimes visit each of them separately and sometimes bring them together, depending upon what seemed most useful in trying to find the basis for a settlement. The objective is to try to bring us together in an agreement.'

After a long moment of silence, he asked, 'Well, couldn't we go and meet in a hotel?'

And I said, 'Well, we would have a little explaining to do, because we made a big fuss about this public bargaining, but I think the people would be receptive if we put out a joint letter to everybody, saying that we think, in the interests of accomplishing something and making a serious attempt to achieve a collective agreement, we should not have these meetings in the plant but should go to a hotel. We should also affirm that we are both committed to keeping everyone informed.'

That is what we did and we achieved a settlement, including the dues shop. I still enjoy talking about this episode because I think it demonstrates the value of fresh, unconventional thinking. Despite some people around the union who looked at me and the process somewhat sideways, I not only enjoyed it very much, it was also very worthwhile. It helped establish an excellent local that made a most positive contribution to the union.

The final campaign on this list, and another in which I was deeply involved, was a second effort at Atlas, the focus this time being the office employees. After our last attempt there, in 1957, we had kept poking away at Atlas, and in the course of 1964 we heard that something was stirring among the officeworkers and that there was a committee of some kind. I immediately arranged for a couple of people to check with a few contacts and knock on some doors. Sure enough, there was a committee. We found out who was leading it and we found out he was organizing them into the UAW, not the Steelworkers.

This was still in the days when unions within the Canadian Labour Congress cooperated on basic jurisdictional situations, so I called Larry. He called George Burt, the Canadian director of the UAW, and raised the issue that this was clearly in the heart of our basic jurisdiction. George agreed to call off his person, Webb Cornwall, who headed up their white-collar activity at that time. George was to send Webb to see me and advise us on what he had accomplished. That meant that Webb brought Bill Summers, the Atlas worker who was leading their campaign, to meet me in my office. I have never seen an angrier young man than Bill Summers, because we had interfered. And I have never seen such an embarrassed person as Webb Cornwall. Webb's part of the meeting, before he turned things over to me, lasted just long enough for him to deliver his message from George Burt and to wish Bill and me well. Then he was gone.

Bill was angry because his campaign was off to a good start and he was feeling confident of success. I asked him why he hadn't come to the Steelworkers and he said, 'Well, you guys are losers. You have been fussing around with the plant all this time and you have not accomplished anything. I did not want to be associated with losers. It's tough enough.' There was more in that vein, which was somewhat indefensible from my point of view, but defensible in an objective way if you are the person trying to build a union. We had a long conversation stretching on into the night. I told him about the Steelworkers and the great record of organizing that we had, one of the best around. Finally, he said, 'I will not agree to help you. But I will do this. I will bring my organizing committee together for a meeting. If you can persuade them to go with you, I will come along, too. I will continue to lead them and I will be a good Steelworker, but you have to persuade them. I do not have my heart in it. I persuaded them to do what they're doing and it's going well. I don't believe that we should be changing. However, if you can persuade them, I will not interfere. I will go to the meeting and I will not argue with you. I will let you have a run at them. I know it's going to be tough because I know they like what they're doing.'

Bill set up the meeting. It was at Christmas time. These things always seemed to peak at Christmas when I was making promises to my family of one kind or another. In any event, this meeting was set up at 7:30 or 8:00 p.m. at the home of one of the committee members, not far from where I lived. We talked and talked and talked. I had decided I would not take a vote until I was sure I could win it. I took the vote as the sun was coming up, and I won.

Bill was absolutely as good as his word. He adapted to the new situation head-on and enthusiastically. I have never seen anybody work any harder in a campaign. He canvassed every night himself. He worked right through that Christmas vacation and I think he went out door knocking every night, except maybe Christmas Eve. It turned out that there were a number of interesting facets to the campaign. One was that the Atlas officeworkers were a brilliant group of young people. We learned that the Atlas hiring policy was to hire the top graduates from the high schools from around the peninsula who did not go on to college, which in those years was most of them. Another interesting thing about the campaign was what was pushing it more than anything else: a computer. This was an age when computers were monstrous and the company had placed this hulking monster right in the middle of the office, with a big glass wall around it, and air-conditioned the space it was in. People were terrified. This was the future and this gigantic machine was going to take their jobs. Ultimately, computers did eliminate many of the jobs, but in a very different way than was imagined at that time.

Our committee was on top of events and information all the time. I have never been in a campaign where we intercepted so many company messages. We were forever able to put out leaflets in the morning telling everybody what announcement the company was going to make. We knew that through the company's internal communication system and it drove the company crazy. It was a fun campaign, which was an important component in its success. But it was not that easy; there was a lot of work going on to support the house calls that a number of active members in the unit, as well as Bill, were making. The original committee was supplemented by the activists we added as the campaign progressed. We did not have to rely on people from other places. Of course, that's an ideal situation. Canvassers from within the group have the highest level of commitment and are by far the most effective. Nevertheless, it still took some work and once we were over the magic automatic certification line of 55 per cent, the committee was itchy to apply for certification. I had a fairly tough session with them and told them it was a mistake to apply with too tight a margin because there is always some slippage. They did not think there would be and I am not sure there was.

The committee and I negotiated with each other and finally reached an agreement. We would file an application as soon as they had twenty-five additional application cards signed, and we would do everything we could to facilitate finding those additional twenty-five members. I then asked them, 'If the company is trying to impress somebody these days how do they do it? Do they call a meeting?'

'Oh, slide shows,' the committee told me. This was at the beginning of the picture revolution, which has subsequently progressed from slide shows to Power Point to who knows what. Whenever the company had a promotion of importance, they put a slide show together on the subject.

So I said, 'Okay then, we are going to have a slide show. We will have a bean supper and you can invite all the best prospective but as yet unsigned members. I will prepare a slide show as the basis of our presentation to them and we will see how we do.' I prepared the slide show. I first went to a commercial artist in town to have him prepare a number of posters for which I developed the substance, such as a comparison of salaries in union-represented offices versus non-union offices, sample contract provisions, union benefits, and as many white-collar items as I could quickly put together. I took pictures of the posters and bought little slide holders. I have the slide show to this day.

We carried out the program exactly as planned. I must confess that we did not quite achieve our goal of twenty-five new members, but we came very close. The committee assembled a good group of prospects, a tribute to its level of influence. We applied and won an automatic certification. Out of that outstanding core group of committee members, Bill went on to become a Steelworkers staff person and was for a time assistant to the district director. Ivor Oram became a staff person in the Ontario Public Service Employees Union (OPSEU), ultimately serving as assistant to the president, and Wally Turk became long-term president of the local and his daughter later became an officer of the local as well.

The bargaining was almost as unique and as much fun as the organizing had been. Atlas had a new human-resources person, whom it had hired from a company in Pittsburgh, not to deal with us but to deal with the increasingly independent plant union. Since he was there, he dealt with us, too. I had had some conversations with him and had understood him to say that, since we were negotiating a first agreement and there were a variety of issues, we would not be constrained by the plant agreement. However, when we became involved in the critical stages of the negotiations, he adopted a very tough stance, saying he was tied by the plant agreement. There was no way the company would consider going past that line; the ultimate package could be spread around differently but could not in total be more than what the plant union had received. I was furious with what I considered a double-cross and I ran up and down him a few times without success. He concocted some rationale about me 'misinterpreting' our conversation. I was reluctant to test the local with a strike, although with the hindsight of experience it might have been the right thing to do. Indeed, it might have galvanized the whole situation with Atlas.

A number of the young officeworkers were from the accounting department. We did not have desktop computers yet, but they had quite advanced calculators. We decided that, if the plant package was the limit, we would need to be absolutely certain that we had received the absolute equivalent, and that we would achieve that certainty by computing the cost of every benefit to four decimals. We took the company package and made sure we received every decimal point that was there, one way or another. The committee enjoyed the exercise of making certain, the membership enjoyed the result, and the local was off to a good start.

The final piece of the story is that we had moved to Toronto by the time this agreement was finished. The certification had been received and the negotiations had begun in early 1965 and by the end of that year we were living in a townhouse in Toronto. I was actually in Sudbury dealing with the Inco situation – more on this later – but coming down to Welland for the Atlas bargaining sessions. It was Christmas Eve day when we settled. We had been in a hotel for a couple of days and the final negotiations had gone on all through the night of 23 December. One of the company negotiators and I each had to drive back to Toronto on Christmas Eve afternoon. We arranged to follow each other and honk horns occasionally and do whatever else we could to make sure the other person stayed awake. We made the two-hour trip to Toronto just fine. At this point the Williams family was living in a new development in the north end of Don Mills in Toronto and it was necessary that I drive up Don Mills Road. The Don Valley Parkway we use today did not exist then and there was still a level railway crossing on Don Mills Road, about a kilometre from home. As I approached the crossing, the gate came down and I stopped, the first car in line. I woke up with a parade of cars lined up behind me, a cacophony of horns honking at me, and a police officer banging on my window. I was dead to the world. The officer, of course, assumed I was drunk, it being Christmas Eve afternoon, and he hauled me out of the car. I assured him I was not drunk, proved it, and explained what I had been doing.

'Well you had better get home to bed,' he said.

'Well, I'm trying,' I replied. 'I will get there as soon as I can.' In the end he did not give me a ticket and I went home to bed.

I had discovered when we were able to have the number 6200 assigned to the local in Port Colborne that, if you chose a number ahead of where they were in the sequence, the international was quite willing to accommodate you by chartering you with the number of your choice. We had a little brain-storming session about what would be the neatest number for Atlas and we all agreed that number 7777 would be terrific. That is how the Atlas office group became Local 7777.

Beyond those three campaigns, there were other interesting situations. For example, in October 1961 there was a group of young people working in an aluminum operation near the Port Colborne refinery, beside the canal. It was a smelting-recycling operation. They melted aluminum in furnaces and then processed it further. A half a dozen of these young people turned up at our office in October 1961 and said they wanted to have a union. It was right in the middle of the peak activity in the Inco campaign in Port Colborne and I said, 'Gee, guys, I would sure like to help you but I am really tied up. If you can just hang on for a few days, we will arrange a meeting.' They were back the next day, urging that I go with them to see the plant and that then I would understand. When they turned up again the next day, I sat them down, showed them a card, told them about collecting a dollar and all the details of what they had to do to organize. Then I gave them some cards, told them to go to it, and wished them well. They were back the next day with 100 per cent of the plant signed up, forty-five or fifty people.

They asked what happened next, so I explained about the application to the board. They said, 'You must come and see our plant so you understand how badly we need the union.' They pursued this idea just as persistently as they had the organizing, so after a couple of days I said, 'Sure, let's go.' We hopped in the car and the moment I saw the plant I regretted that I had put them off at all. It certainly was understandable that they wanted to have a union. The plant was like something out of Charles Dickens. It was a beat-up old place, with holes in the roof, a bunch of little furnaces, and a dirt floor. When it rained, the rain came through these holes in the roof, falling right on the operators and the furnaces. It's a wonder the whole place up didn't blow up. The pollution was absolutely frightful, both in the plant and in the neighbourhood. It's the kind of place you would like to show people when they make remarks such as, 'Well unions were okay 100 years ago, but no one needs them anymore.'

The only place in my experience that was near its equal was one we discovered years later in Pittsburgh. It was an operation being carried out in one of our old can plants that involved ripping apart copy machines. They were recycling them or repairing them. The people who worked there had no benefits, no instructions concerning the chemicals to which they were being exposed, no protective gear or clothing, no holidays except Christmas and it was unpaid. The conditions were absolutely unbelievable. Once our organizers touched base with them and they caught a glimpse of what they could do with a union, they could not have been prevented from getting their union no matter what. It turned out to be something of a scandal. The company had some made-up name and at first claimed that a couple of Pittsburgh lawyers were owners of the plant. In fact, it turned out, as we probed further, to be a Xerox operation. What was particularly scandalous was that Xerox had a respected name in industrial-relations circles as one of the most progressive employers in the United States. It boasted about its worker-involvement programs in its plant in Rochester and was a regular participant in forums and conferences describing its systems as state of the art. Yet it was hiding this dreadful operation in Pittsburgh.

Back at Welland, there was one other experience there in which a union was almost self-organized. It was during my last year in the peninsula and concerned a small machine shop. I received a phone call one day from a fellow having a beer at the Legion, and he said he wanted to talk union and invited me over to have a beer with him. My visit turned out to be the campaign. He was the spark plug. I would take him cards, pick up cards, and join him for a beer. There were about one hundred employees and he did the whole thing. It was as slick as you could imagine.

I have often thought about these campaigns, and I am sure I am forgetting a number of others, and the variety of approaches involved. In many ways that is the critical element in campaigning: to find or create the approach that fits the circumstances and the people you're attempting to help organize. That sounds simple, but I have been to many organizing meetings where people made presentations that sounded like those of an insurance salesman. They did not do much to create a sense of ownership for the workers in the campaign. The presentations were somewhat as follows: Pay these dues and you receive these benefits. Which is almost like inviting some other insurance company/ union to come along and offer them a better deal. Whenever I have listened to such pitches, particularly in the light of these other experiences, it has always left me feeling uncomfortable.

One final episode in my peninsula days that should be mentioned involves not labour unions but higher education. Ed Mitchelson, a teacher and the New Party candidate in the 1960 Niagara Falls by-election, was a key activist in community development and we needed a university in the peninsula region. Our members' children had to leave home to go to the closest school, my alma mater, McMaster University in Hamilton, which did not always have the courses some students wanted. In particular, it was a difficult commute from towns that were farthest from Hamilton, such as Port Colborne.

Ed and Mel Swart discussed all this with me, I in turn took it up with our area council, and we decided we should encourage the labour movement to support the campaign for a new university. I joined the founding committee. Through the labour councils we decided that we should have a voluntary check-off for the cause, such as we had each year for the United Way, for a period of time. We felt that the establishment of a local university would be helpful for our people. To make a long story short, we raised $1.5 million from trade-union members for Brock University, in St Catharines, in a most unique project. I was on the university's board of directors of the university as long as I was in the peninsula. Labour still has a seat on the board, currently held by a member of the Canadian Auto Workers (CAW), so we in the labour movement have been part of Brock from the beginning. I expect that this might be the only time anywhere that the labour movement has contributed in such a way to a university. Others may reject the idea that unions should be involved with a university in this fashion, and I understand that argument, but I feel it is justifiable in this instance. Certainly, establishing Brock cost much more than $1.5 million, but $1.5 million is not an inconsiderable sum and it certainly gave our people a sense of ownership of the university and of it being an institution for their family. I'm sure it encouraged many young people and their parents. I can imagine the family discussions: 'We helped pay for it. We built it. Now we should use it.' When I was on the board, I used to check the percentage of enrolment that was local and it was always more than 50 per cent in those early years.

The years in the Niagara peninsula were one of the best periods of my life. Because of the decentralized way the labour movement works, and our having such a big district geographically, nobody was looking over my shoulder. Being an area supervisor, as the title was then, made me feel like I was running my own little union most of the time. As long as I was not altering policy and doing things I shouldn't, I was free to act a good deal on my own initiative. There is always far more to be done in the labour movement than is ever possible, so there is always

a big wish list of ideas. When I pursued the public-bargaining opportunity at Switson's, for instance, there was never a word of complaint
from Larry. I told him the story when it was over and he enjoyed it
immensely. He was always there for help, never for interference.

The Williams family was also enjoying being Steelworkers. We were
feeling quite prosperous, with my larger salary and a nice new home,
and, to top it off, we had a beautiful new daughter too, Barbara. My
memories of the Welland years are precious.

7

SUDBURY

Not all my work in the late 1950s and the first half of the 1960s was confined to the Niagara peninsula. In 1963 Inco finally announced that, with certification of the Port Colborne and Sudbury locals now in place, it was ready to enter into negotiations for a collective agreement. I moved north for a time to participate in the talks.

My personal participation in the events in Sudbury leading to the certification of the Steelworkers in October 1962 had been minimal. I was more occupied with the concurrent campaign at the Inco plant in Port Colborne. The two locals, however, were quite close, in view of the fact that the Port Colborne refinery was really, in effect, a department of the Sudbury operation. There were fairly frequent visits back and forth by committees of one kind or another, and there was also considerable mutual support, the people from Port Colborne encouraging those in Sudbury and Gillis and his colleagues encouraging Babirad and his people. All of this mutual support was helpful to us in both locations. Indeed, the victory in Port Colborne had been particularly significant to winning in Sudbury, given that we won in Sudbury by such a razor-thin margin. If Mine Mill had retained Port Colborne, I expect we would have lost enough momentum to deny us the victory in Sudbury.

I have vivid memories of my time in Sudbury, one of which concerns the town's bars. At the time, there were Steelworker bars and Mine Mill bars in the city and not many where the workers mixed. There was always a concern that, if there was too much mixing in the bars, real trouble could ensue. Ken Levack, who later served as my assistant when I was District 6 director, thought I was 'either crazy or fearless' because I would walk into the Coulson Hotel, which was a Mine

Mill hotel in Sudbury. 'I wouldn't go within ten miles of that place,' Ken recalled in 2008. 'But Lynn would go in there, talk to them and he usually convinced somebody. He's a very persuasive guy. You couldn't scare him. He could have been scared but he sure didn't let you know.'

The first Sudbury/Port Colborne negotiations were an incredibly formal, military-like operation. Inco was furious that we had taken over bargaining rights. In its view, it had exercised its authority most effectively in the strike of 1958 and had Mine Mill members exactly where it wanted them – cowed, undisciplined, and demoralized. A new, fresh union coming onto the scene was clearly not what the company would have chosen.

The negotiations were held initially in the company's headquarters in Copper Cliff, part of Sudbury, before moving in the summer of 1963 to Toronto. The company's committee members marched in every day in the order in which they were seated. They always sat in the same seats and, in the initial rounds of the talks, only the lawyer was permitted to speak on behalf of the company, even when we asked questions of particular members of the committee, who were mostly operations people. Later in the negotiations, things weren't much better: before any company committee member could respond to our questions, the lawyer first had to know the proposed answer by means of an exchange of notes. Only then might he permit the committee member to speak. We made an issue out of the formality of the proceedings, which made any exchange and understanding as difficult to achieve as possible.

Leading our team as chairman was Larry Sefton. Over the next months, he treated us to an impressive display of leadership in bargaining with a major, powerful, and difficult company. The other team, of course, was experienced as well, although in dealing with Mine Mill the company had surely enjoyed a more one-sided power relationship. From the Second World War on, the accusations of communist influence in Mine Mill and the union's reaction to it, the union's expulsion from the house of labour on both sides of the border, and the internal stresses and strains brought about by attempting in the early stages to follow Soviet foreign policy greatly sapped its energy and weakened its solidarity. The result often was a retreat to maintaining the status quo, rather than pushing for ground-breaking new issues or even playing serious catch-up with the broader labour movement in collective-bargaining improvements.

The bargaining with Inco was challenging, to say the least. The company, while furious we had won the bargaining rights, was also emboldened because of the narrowness of our victory. In addition, it tried to exploit a tug of war between the two unions, Mine Mill and us, over the kind of collective agreement we would negotiate. For our part, we presented a full range of contract proposals. We had been gathering suggestions throughout the campaign, in both Port Colborne and Sudbury, and efforts had been made to review and keep track of these ideas as an important part of our preparation for bargaining.

The company's bargaining objectives were quickly evident – to move backwards from the Mine Mill agreement by, for example, using the argument that the sympathies of the workers were so evenly divided between the two unions that we were not entitled to a compulsory check-off of dues from everyone. It was also evident immediately that this bargaining would go through all the steps, by which I mean top-flight conciliation, mobilization of the membership, and probably a strike vote before a settlement could emerge. In the negotiations, our strategy was to hang on to the check-off and to achieve some positive changes to the Mine Mill contract. I thought this was absolutely essential. In the internal debate that raged around this point, some thought that maintaining the Mine Mill agreement, while we furthered the process of building the membership, was a reasonable expectation. Larry was always patient in listening, but he was decisive in his recommendations once he determined the appropriate direction.

In the end, we achieved improvements in four important articles in the contract language, with the key one the health and safety clause, which had not been changed for years and was a hot-button issue in the Sudbury area. The clause addressed the problem of pollution, a serious concern in Sudbury and all neighbouring communities, and, of course, it held special importance for workers in an industry where occupational injuries and fatalities were all too common. In addition, wages were put on a par with the rest of the steel industry, and improvements were made in pension, early-retirement, and sickness and accident benefits. Inco workers had moved into the modern era of collective bargaining.

Many people deserve credit for this achievement: Terry Mancini, Gib Gilchrist, Ken Valentine, Don Gillis, Don McNabb, Tony Soden, Homer Seguin, Ron Macdonald, Mickey McGuire, David Campbell, John Fera, Murray Cotterill, Frank Drea, Ray Poirier, and Albert Desbiens. May those who have been named stand on behalf of themselves and all the others.

Following the settling of the contract, I returned to the Niagara peninsula and thereafter had little to do with Sudbury. That wasn't true of the union as a whole, though. Mine Mill and Steelworkers disagreements continued quite vigorously, both at Inco and at Falconbridge, which was still very much an issue in that about 3,000 workers there remained with Mine Mill. Also, the margin of victory in Sudbury had been so small that everyone in the Steelworkers had an eye on developments in the town.

As for Mine Mill, it had suffered considerable loss of membership through changes in the mining industry, which are constant, and through its battle with the Steelworkers, which had been raging for years. Its last major source of dues income was the Sudbury base. Since it could maintain this by winning certification back, that was its goal. The foundation for such an approach was to encourage as large a group of Mine Mill workers as possible in the Sudbury operation to remain outside Local 6500 and maintain their own organization. They were required to pay dues to Local 6500 under the dues check-off but were not required to become members. The law in Ontario was that an application for regaining bargaining rights could be made at the end of two years. This meant, in the case of Sudbury, that although the current agreement ran for three years, Mine Mill could begin raiding at the end of two, which is what it did.

It was during these events that a special opportunity came my way in 1964. An opening became available at a seminar of the then newly established International Institute for Labour Studies, part of the International Labour Organization, in Geneva, Switzerland. Larry Sefton had become aware of a spot being held for the AFL-CIO that was not going to be used and could be made available to one of us. He indicated that I would likely be interested, which I immediately confirmed. It involved attending the program in Geneva for three months. I could not believe my good fortune. My experiences at this seminar would deepen my understanding of a host of issues affecting workers and also broaden my horizons considerably, awakening me to the challenges confronting the labour movement – and the forces shaping its future – internationally.

The seminar was the institute's premier program, bringing together labour, management, and government figures to consider social programs such as unemployment insurance, workers' compensation, health care, and health and safety as they existed in developed countries and might be applied in the developing ones. The 1960s had been labelled 'the development decade' in the expectation that a development trajectory could be established for Third World countries by the end of the ten-year period. It turned out to be much more complicated than that, but we met in Geneva in a very optimistic atmosphere.

The program consisted of two groups, one French-speaking and the other English. Each had a facilitator who worked with us and arranged for a steady stream of ILO and other experts to meet with us. We met in the mornings, had the afternoons for private study, and were expected to produce a paper by the end of the three months (I chose Sweden's social programs as my subject). Most of the participants were from developing countries in Africa and Asia, but there were also some delegates from Soviet bloc countries and a sprinkling from the West.

The program took place during the spring, March to May, and we quickly learned to enjoy the weather while working. Afternoon private study could begin with discussions at an outdoor pub across the street from our building. There was a participant from New Zealand, an employer representative, who shared my enthusiasm for seeing Europe. We determined to travel every weekend, which evolved into our becoming travel organizers many weekends for groups of members who chose to see Europe with us.

One of the delegates was the director of education for the Ghanaian Trade Union Congress. A pattern developed of his going after me first thing every morning about the evils of Western society. I agreed with him in many ways, but he described things in a rather extreme way. Over the three months we became good friends. Another participant, a labour official from Nigeria, read *Time* magazine every week cover to cover and asked me to explain the violence of American society. One of the most dedicated people in the group was a trade-union official from the Philippines.

Our facilitator was an Egyptian economist, Dr Faragh, an intelligent, well-informed person with whom we were all impressed. He was also scheduled to give one of our most important lectures on a Tuesday morning following a long weekend. My New Zealand friend and I decided to travel to Marseilles, do the Mediterranean coast, and come back on the train from Nice. The plan worked fine except that we missed the train. I was determined that we not embarrass Faragh or ourselves by missing his lecture, so we decided to keep the car we had rented and drive across the Alps through the night. We played tag all night with a couple of young men in a little Peugot whom we passed going up every mountain, because their little engine had little power, but who passed us on the way back down because they drove the switchbacks with much more dash and style than I had the courage to muster.

Following Geneva, the focus returned to Port Colborne. Our overall strategy there was to use the success at Inco and the publicity it generated to mount an active organizing effort across the peninsula. Larry Sefton appointed Doug Hart as a temporary representative in the peninsula and we made him a full-time organizer. By now, too, the area council, which had become more active during this period, had a pattern established of a meeting every three or four months for a day, with a real program and a committed effort at developing union spirit. It provided education programs, organized social programs, and built solidarity among the activists. The council did some great work with its volunteer organizing effort as campaigns developed.

One day, Larry called me to Toronto for a meeting, the purpose of which was to invite me to transfer to the district office and join the staff he had working with him. To say I was elated at the prospect is a huge understatement. The opening appealed immensely to me, principally, of course, for the opportunity to work closely with Larry. Another draw was Larry's small but talented and effective staff. Larry's assistant, Mike Fenwick, was a great reader and raconteur with a host of exciting stories about his days as a radical activist during the Depression and his experiences in the early days of the Steelworkers. Then there was Bert Gargrave. Bert had been a CCF member of Parliament out of British Columbia but had been defeated, which is difficult to understand because he was a terrific politician. He then came full time into the labour movement, with which he had close ties and much experience. Mike was the administrator and Bert the principal negotiator and presenter of arbitrations. Bert was the major troubleshooter in this area and the next in line for troubleshooting and special projects was to be me.

At this same time, I was hearing through our Port Colborne people at Inco, who spent a lot of time in Sudbury because we were all under the same agreement, that there was considerable divisiveness up north. Mine Mill was making headway in its campaign to regain the bargaining rights. I reported these concerns to Larry periodically and always indicated my willingness to go up there to help.

Meantime, after receiving Larry's offer, I announced to the family at the supper table the next day that I was being transferred and we would be moving. Much to my surprise, the whole family burst into tears. My wife's tears did not flow as much as the children's, but there were some. All the tears were a tribute to how happily and contentedly the family had settled into the peninsula. The kids had grown up in Welland. We had had a great life there. It was home. We had a new house. For the first time, we had a second car. For the only time in our married life, Audrey had an aunt and uncle close by, indeed a favourite aunt and uncle. Audrey was the oldest of a family of three and when the other two came along, Uncle Marc and Aunt Pat's was where she had gone for vacations and special visits. (As it happened, Marc was an auditor for the Unemployment Insurance Commission and in that capacity visited many of the plants where we represented the people. We would talk about these companies and he would let me know what was happening in them if he picked up stories. Nothing confidential, but he would share general information that might not otherwise come to my attention.) Tears aside, the target for our family move was the late summer of 1965, so we could arrive in Toronto during the summer and our children could begin at their new schools in the fall.

We were now two years into the Inco agreement, Mine Mill was active, and we were increasingly worried that things did not seem to be going so well for us. In Local 6200 in Port Colborne, where our connections were close, the sense of the situation was that they were trying to operate as a normal local union and do good work while attempting to ignore a Mine Mill campaign that, nevertheless, was significant and strong.

Then, one day in the spring of 1965, Larry called and said, 'I want you to go to Sudbury.'

'That's wonderful, there's no place I want more to be,' I said. 'In a couple of weeks I'll have things in shape to leave here and I'll be there.'

'I want you to go to Sudbury,' he said.

'I heard, I am happy to go, there are some things I really must look after first,' I replied.

'I want you to go to Sudbury,' he said.

'You want me to go to Sudbury, when, right now?' I asked.

He said, 'Yes!'

So I went right away. In truth, I was there most of 1965. I had an office there and one in the district office. The family did get moved to Toronto without me, thanks to my father-in-law and my brother-in-law, because I had to be in Sudbury when moving day came around.

The Steelworker area supervisor in Sudbury was my old friend Terry Mancini. It seemed to me that Terry was trying to apply the good things he had learned in Sault Ste Marie with Local 2251 to the Sudbury situation. It was a worthy objective, but the Sudbury scene was enormously volatile and had many different elements. It required a continuing campaign atmosphere for a considerable time as we worked through a variety of complications. Only with these behind us could we settle down to the careful and appropriate administration of a well-organized large local union.

In those days, Sudbury was an exciting place. Frank Drea, formerly a labour reporter with the *Toronto Telegram* and later an Ontario Progressive Conservative cabinet member, was our full-time public-relations person in Sudbury. Murray Cotterrill, our PR director, came in fairly regularly to assess, supervise, contribute ideas, and help with the work. We had, in fact, a steady stream of visitors. We were certainly pursuing the advantages of incumbency, being active in representing members with grievances and arbitrations and in inspecting for and correcting health and safety hazards.

Terry and Gib Gilchrist and the staff were then searching for alternatives to the hopelessly inadequate temporary Cedar Street office and operation. Mine Mill's constant argument during the campaign was that we were carpetbaggers, operating out of rented space that frequently featured smashed windows. Our people all said that a solution that had been on their minds for months was the Legion Hall. It was a fine facility, relatively new, having been built after the Second World War, and was the pride of the Legion. I learned quickly that it was suffering hard financial times. With suburban legions drawing members away from the downtown one, it was no longer able to sustain itself. Every time a new one cropped up in a nearby suburban or exurban community, it nearly always took a core of founding membership away from the Sudbury lodge.

Looking for somebody to take me over to the Legion Hall and show me around, I found Elmer McVey, who was delighted to be host and guide. He was one of our long-time stalwarts in Sudbury, an NDP and Steelworkers supporter long before this campaign. The majority of the board members of the Legion supported Mine Mill and the last people in the world they wanted to have the building was the Steelworkers. Not to be deterred, Elmer and I did our personal tour. It was a magnificent building and precisely what we needed to change our carpetbaggers' image. In the heart of the city and on a nice lot at a major intersection, it was a pleasantly designed building of red brick and stone. More important, it was a large building and featured a huge auditorium, so it suited our purposes better than any conceivable alternative and did so with a minimum of renovation. Over the years, there had been considerable renovations, but none had changed the building in any fundamental way. The Mine Mill-dominated board had attempted a variety of measures to avoid it falling into Steel-workers' hands, including offering it to the city for $1. As the head-quarters for Local 6500 and a base for our campaign, it was perfect. The executive board of the Legion, losing more members to outlying legions every month, was becoming more desperate. People around town were saying to them that they might as well sell it to the Steel-workers, an argument unwittingly reinforced by Mine Mill's attacks on our union for being rich and uncaring. Meanwhile, our interest was increasing by the day. Finally, the Legion board devised a scheme whereby they authorized their agents to sell it to whomever they could, without requiring any signatures from board members. We bought it immediately.

That was a key step for us in 1965 and we held a grand opening, planned skilfully by Gib Gilchrist, which was well advertised and drew a great crowd. The building immediately became the symbol of perma-nence we were seeking. It was obvious that the Steelworkers would not invest all this money in a major building in the city, doing the commu-nity as well as itself a great service, unless we were serious about being a permanent part of the place. That was how we put the carpetbagger accusations to permanent rest.

The building operating as a Legion had not needed as much office space as the union would, but it was adequate for our purposes, at least in the beginning, and contained more than enough room for conver-sion to the office space that would be required. Local union offices were installed on the second floor and the international offices on the top floor. There also was a magnificent basement, part of which was a bev-erage room that we continued to use, while the rest waited to be devel-oped. This space required a little remodelling to provide an office for me and offices for the organizing crew that we brought into town. And so all of the staff involved in the Inco campaign were brought into one location, which resulted in a much more united effort. There are always crises and issues in a campaign and dealing with them efficiently and effectively is always easier when the people involved are working in reasonable proximity.

There is really no substitute for communication in these matters. That was particularly true in such a campaign as this, where the opposition was vigorous and the community sharply divided. Stories flew, partly because they were relevant and partly because everybody was inter-ested in them. Building our communication capacity, in turn, meant that we had to look around the district for some full-time regular staff

and other help. Our objective was to have one really good person working with each Inco property, of which there were fifteen or sixteen at
the time. Once those people were found, I discussed their assignment
with them. The fundamental point I made went something like this. I
was sure that in their time as local union leaders, which virtually all of
them had been prior to receiving staff assignments, they all had strong
opinions about what their staff representative should do in working
with their local union, what he should not do, what was done well and
what was not, and matters of that kind. I asked them to let their past
experience be their guide, do what their staff person had done or what
they thought he should have done, and we would be all right.

And we were. The Steelworkers repelled the Mine Mill attack, winning a better than 2,000-vote majority out of what was then a 15,000-per-
son bargaining unit. There seemed to be general relief in town that the
unrest and division of the years since 1958 were finally put to rest and
we could finally concentrate on negotiating the best possible agreement. Fifteen bargaining committee members were elected from Local
6500. I was privileged to be chairman and Terry Mancini, Gib Gilchrist,
Maurice Keck, and Ken Valentine served with me.

Negotiations continued all spring and summer but were made very
frustrating by the slow, nit-picking style of the company. Finally, on
the morning of 15 July, all of Inco was shut down. Upon reaching a
procedural agreement that the union would permit staff to enter the
premises without the issuance of passes, negotiations resumed. It was
very difficult, however, to negotiate in these circumstances, as the company kept trying to use the alleged illegality of the strike against us.
Eventually, we decided that the wisest strategy was to return to work
while making clear our right to resume the strike if necessary. This
resulted in a memorandum of agreement and, after a second vote, contract ratification. The contract provided five weeks of extended vacation for every employee with five or more years of service, an hourly
wage increase of fifty-four cents per hour, and further recognition of
the role of health and safety committees, among other highlights.

In closing this story, I wish to note that my experiences in Sudbury
prompted me to give some thought to a matter I had largely ignored
until then – the power of big locals. These locals have often been difficult entities. Being large sometimes leads them to estimate their power
quite generously in terms of their expectations and assessment of their
influence. From time to time, one or another holds an independent
view in matters such as internal union politics, frequently related to the

ambitions of various local union leaders. On the other hand, a number of large local unions, well led and well focused on union objectives, provides their members an opportunity for exciting, progressive, and effective trade-union action on many fronts.

Traditionally, our dues structure provided a basic 50–50 split between the international, national, and districts on the one hand and the locals on the other, after 7 per cent was taken off the top for the strike and defence fund. This has been modified in various ways over the years, but the heart of it has remained the same. The result is that big locals have big incomes, but this along with their greater depth of human resources is what makes them such potentially effective organizations. Wealth, of course, is an invitation to pursue broader objectives in terms of constructive activity or wasteful activity. While the vast majority of large locals pursue the former, from time to time it is necessary to deal with the latter. Still, the potential power for good that large locals hold makes whatever efforts are required in support of positive programs and activities well worthwhile.

A further advantage of the Steelworkers structure is that locals are not expected to do all of their own servicing, as is the case with many locals in other unions. Large locals pay for more of the servicing than smaller locals, but the Steelworkers tradition has been to have a large international staff that service all of the local unions. The existence of the big locals and the resources they provided, until the restructuring of the mining and steel industries in the 1980s, made it possible for us to maintain for a long time the structure of a great many field representatives servicing, as we used to boast, small locals and large ones all to the same standard.

At the time it was established, Local 6500 in Sudbury was the largest in Canada and one of the two or three largest in the entire international union. Yet, at the same time, I thought that Local 6500, like other large locals, functioned with much too narrow a base of leadership. The constitution of the Steelworkers requires a thirteen-person executive board and three committees: health and safety, civil rights, and organizing. However, these are minimums. There are no constitutional restrictions on the number of committees or the number of members on the committees. In my travels around the union, I observed that most middle- and large-sized locals would have some additional committees – political action and recreation were common. It had become my view that the locals and the union would be better served with a much larger group of activists and people with responsibilities and titles – lots of committees, assistant stewards or committeemen, assistant health and safety representatives. Theoretically, the best possible local union would be one in which every member had a responsibility and carried it out. In organizing campaigns, large and small, we often come close to achieving such levels of participation, but involvement falls off when the local becomes more settled and established. Literature and communication devices of all kinds are part of every effective organizing campaign and should be a significant part of the daily life of every active local union. The more involved every member is, the stronger the union. The stronger the union, the more we are able to meet the needs of our members and achieve our objectives.

Based on these beliefs, I took a couple of initiatives in Sudbury and was supported widely. These were popular ideas so it wasn't as if I had to foment a crusade. I simply proposed that we go down the path of lots of committees with unlimited membership. There were a great many first-class leaders in Local 6500. They were interested in leadership from day one and involved in all the things that help leadership evolve, such as volunteering, campaigning, nominating, and being an activist. The people I sought out were another sort – those whom I thought displayed considerable talent but appeared to be walking away from being active. The reasoning of those who were reluctant frequently went something like this: they were good Steelworkers and good union supporters and when the union was in a crisis and they were needed, they would be there. However, in terms of their personal interests and their limited spare time, they would choose to use what time they had in other pursuits or causes.

I am pleased to say that I was able to change the minds of many of these individuals. And the result was a much stronger Local 6500. This initiative in Sudbury taught me some things, too. Particularly in recent years, what seems to be a lack of interest in the union is not. People across both countries in our union and in many other unions as well have a capacity to come together. They will support a position and exercise a high level of solidarity far beyond what their behaviour might suggest during a quiet period. Misreading this has led companies to act in a way they come to regret. Many companies have misinterpreted disinterest, sometimes fed by rumours from company people that are wildly inaccurate, as evidence that the union is much weaker and less united than is actually the case – as quickly becomes apparent in a crisis.

On the same subject of committee activity, I wish to quote the testimony of a good friend, Leo Gerard, the current Steelworkers president, who was growing up in Lively, just outside Sudbury, when our campaign there was in full swing. Leo says that he was struck by what I was able to achieve in what became his home local, 6500, 'which I think is one of the best locals in the Steelworkers union.' He echoes my view that 'we needed lots of involvement and lots of activism and lots of activities, so they created committee after committee after committee on everything you could imagine. There was no limit to the number people who could be on a committee. So I remember from the early days when you'd go to an education committee you would have 45 people in a room. Go to health and safety and there'd be 80 people in a room. Go to a stewards meeting and there'd be 200 people in a room ... Now lots were at the same meetings and some weren't, but they're all involved. So this local union was doing things all the time. That's how I grew up.'

A few more words about Leo. When I was sent to Sudbury by Larry Sefton to lead the Steelworkers' organizing raid against Mine Mill, a teenage Leo remembers overhearing his father, uncle, and other Mine Mill supporters meeting in the Gerard family basement.

'All I could ever hear was that "God damned Williams ..." I was sixteen years old before I realized Lynn's first name wasn't God Damn,' Leo jokes.

Leo went to work for Inco and when he decided to become a shop steward for the Steelworkers, his father kicked him out of the house. 'There were not going to be any Steelworkers in his house,' says Leo. 'I never went back. I got married, so I got my own place. The separation only lasted three or four months, and my mother breached the divide [inviting her son and his new bride for Christmas].'

During that visit, Leo walked into the living room and told his dad, 'Look, you always told me that the union was made up of the members and all I'm doing is doing what you taught me. It doesn't matter what it's called.' 'He just said, "Well, don't screw up." That was it. It was over.'

'My dad was bitter because he loved his union,' says Leo. He says he remembers me telling him, 'If you can be as loyal to your union as your dad was to his, you'll do fine.'

Years later, Leo and his brother campaigned for me when I was running first for international secretary and then for international president. I returned the favour in 1985, travelling to Sudbury to campaign for Leo as District 6 director, handing out leaflets with his father and brother and talking with them. After Leo won the election, I swore him in as District 6 director. Leo recalled the day this way: 'My dad said to me, "I'm really proud of you." So I took my Steelworker lapel pin off and I put it in my dad's hand and I said. "If you're really proud, you'll wear this today." And he put it on. That was almost a twenty-year evolution, from 1965 roughly to '85. My dad died two years later. My dad is one of my heroes. His name was Wilfrid. That's why I put the "W" (second initial) in my name. It's not my real name. I put the "W" in for my dad.'

8

DIRECTOR, DISTRICT 6

The years immediately following my transfer to the district office in 1965 passed as quickly as any time I have known. In the beginning, I was busy mostly with campaigning and bargaining at Inco in Sudbury. In fact, from the summer of 1965 until the summer of 1966, I really lived in Sudbury, finding it possible far too seldom to be back in Toronto for a weekend, or even more rarely for a day or two of working at the office. After we had defeated Mine Mill for the second time, much more decisively than the first, and reached a new agreement with Inco, it was clear that Local 6500 could operate effectively without my direct, day-to-day involvement. The range of my activities then began to broaden significantly, although Inco continued to be one of my major responsibilities.

Throughout this period, I was fortunate indeed to be able to work alongside Larry Sefton, who had earned recognition as 'the organizing director' because of the outstanding record of District 6 in that regard. Tucked in among all of the more dramatic events was a most successful organizing project in Toronto that combined a volunteer organizing committee with a structured program of continuous home canvassing. Created by Wally Ross and administered for many years by Otto Urbanovics, this project was steady, well organized, and focused but not flamboyant or excessive. It produced a steady stream of certifications and provided a training ground for very successful staff representatives such as Lucky Rao and Brando Paris.

The genesis of the project was the high level of immigration, mainly from Italy but from Portugal as well, that found its way into the metal shops of west-central Toronto, where the immigrants would begin the typical struggle in their new country at often dirty, miserable, and always low-wage jobs. The Steelworkers labelled the area an industrial ghetto and established a volunteer organizing committee to cope with the challenges it presented. Wally Ross, my friend and colleague from the Eaton drive and from Kitimat, was asked to lead the effort. The system he established was based around a committee supper and a home-canvassing program one night a week. The union provided supper and paid a driving allowance for the use of a car. During the week, by using a city directory that indicated occupations, the committee prepared index cards for persons whose job identification indicated a metal shop. The cards were arranged into convenient routes to maximize the efficiency of the canvassing night. If any canvasser found a really good lead, canvassing would then be focused on that shop, with the person who found the lead directing the activity. If it came to be a real campaign and there was need for a little extra full-time help to finish it up or to work towards winning a vote, the person who found the lead would normally be given the short-term, full-time assignment. Wally was succeeded as administrator of the program by Otto Urbanovics. It was an incredible success, producing at least a certification every month for years on end. A number of its graduates went on to successful careers as staff representatives. It was the beginning in many ways of the Steelworkers' commitment to the multicultural city that Toronto has become. And later, under the leadership of Don Montgomery and John Fitzpatrick, it contributed a great deal to the energetic labour centre that the new district headquarters became and has remained.

In my own case, three or four areas were of particular interest during my first years at the district office. One was the beginning of regional conferences across the district. Larry had always been reluctant to have a district conference because of his concern that it might be perceived as competitive with the national policy conference. The idea of the regional conference was to focus on the particular circumstances of each province and territory that fell under District 6's jurisdiction. The format was to begin with a report from the director; then, depending on where we were and the circumstances at the time, a guest or two might make presentations, after which we would move into a free-wheeling open discussion. Larry was always interested in new technology, and so we used tape recorders to record all these conferences. It was useful to have this material at hand and to know exactly what commitments had been made in the discussions. Admittedly, we never did find an efficient way to index the tapes so as to facilitate the location of items with relative ease. But the format and process produced many ideas and improvements, the most important result being that, through the conferences, our members gained a sense that the union was paying attention to their situation and making whatever policy adjustments were required.

We had some interesting people of our own and from the outside involved. Jim Russell was one of the original and most effective organizers in the union, but a person with little regard for the constraints of time. He always had some organizing contact, old or new, to visit with along the way. For instance, he arrived at a 1968 conference in Lethbridge, Alberta, with the conference delegates' kits just in time for adjournment. It was at that same conference that we had a wild political discussion with a most hospitable but very right-wing owner of the hotel we were using. He lived in the penthouse suite, which had the largest and best-stocked living-room bar I have ever seen, and he invited the leadership in for a few refreshments one evening. I doubt there were any conversions that night, but by early morning every political argument imaginable, from the left and from the right, had been worked over, noisily if not thoroughly. In a different vein, we learned in Manitoba how useful it can be for working people when a premier like Ed Schreyer and a union leader such as Len Stevens bring the programs of the NDP and the labour movement together.

My principal task during these years was troubleshooting, mostly in collective-bargaining situations where last-ditch attempts were needed to avoid a strike or where fresh attempts were required to settle existing strikes. This was fascinating work – varied, close to our members, nearly always providing a backroom look at the companies in question while also illuminating the way they treated their workers. I quickly developed a rule of thumb. If the union's bargaining committee was upset, anxious, or at odds with itself, I was likely to meet a management negotiating committee that had not demonstrated an interest in imaginative problem solving. On the other hand, if I met a committee that was digging hard at its material, searching for the best arguments to use and the best support for them, I expected to meet a management team that was well prepared, utilizing facts and figures and not simply playing a power game. I came to know a significant number of our activists quite well because the nature of the negotiating procedures would often leave a committee free, with many hours available for our own internal discussions. These were great opportunities to come to know each other as friends and colleagues. Many of these friendships endured and provided great support in the political battles of later years.

Another responsibility of mine might be called special projects, such as educational functions, including our biannual staff seminars, or the orientation program for staff of District 50, a creation of the mineworkers that had subsequently become an independent union and eventually merged with us. In addition, it could include speechwriting for the director, frequently in the context of developing a conference of some kind.

I also served, during most of this period, on the provincial council of the NDP, in a role somewhat akin to that of the representative to the council from District 6. I never lost interest in the political side of our movement and learned over and over again how inextricably tied together we were. To be sure, it was not all clear sailing. The most important issues of that time – and the ones that generated the most tension – were the provincial leadership and the emergence of the Waffle.

Donald MacDonald was the leader of the CCF and then the NDP in Ontario from November 1953 to June 1970. He led the party through some difficult times without ever losing his energy, his commitment, his willingness to work, or his optimism. I remember one election from which we emerged with only three members in the legislature. Donald made it sound, as he toured the province discussing the future, like a victory. By the time he reviewed all our new second-place finishes and our strong thirds, he left his audiences almost poised for a real win the next time out. When the legislature met, he was a whirlwind of questions, announcements, and activity. By the late 1960s, he had become, in many ways, Mr Ontario.

At the same time, there was some restlessness in the party, a feeling of concern about the future and the possible need for change. Younger leadership was emerging, in which the talents of Stephen Lewis, David's son, were particularly apparent and exciting. These new pressures first emerged at the provincial convention in 1968 when Jim Renwick challenged Donald's leadership. We supported Donald. I was privileged to make one of his nomination speeches at the event and the challenge to him was eventually defeated, but the damage to his leadership had been done. When Stephen himself challenged in 1970, Donald chose to resign rather than participate in a very divisive contest.

Concurrently, the Waffle was emerging in the party. This was a group of people in the NDP who believed that the party should adopt a significantly more left-wing style, approach, and policy. Two university professors, James Laxer and Mel Watkins, led it. What was different about them was not that they were pushing for a more leftist program – there has always been a range of opinions within the NDP and so there always should be – but that they established a fully organized and financed group for this purpose. To many of us, this was in effect establishing a party within a party, designed to devote its energies and finances to attacking the party while we were attempting to promote it and to win power. We also thought they were far from correct in their analysis of where voters would be with regard to a more radical program, so we urged them, if they were so confident, to put their convictions to the test and organize themselves into a party of their own.

Naturally, these developments created deep concerns within the party. There were attempts by many of the leaders to find a formula to bridge the gap. There was much wringing of hands. Larry, our leader, stood firm, strong and unequivocal. In his opinion, unity was essential. To divide the fledgling party in two, one part dedicated to using its organizing talents and its resources to attacking the leaders of the party while the other attempted to present the party to the electorate with a winning policy and program, was to court disaster.

The drama of this conflict played itself out in Ontario at a series of provincial council meetings. At one stage, Stephen Lewis, then leader of the party, came to see Larry while we were in negotiations and 'holed up,' as we described it, at the Royal York hotel. It was a tough meeting. Larry made it clear where the Steelworkers stood and that there would be no change in that position. Subsequently, there were two council meetings that turned out to be crucial, one at the UAW hall in Oshawa, east of Toronto, and the second at the Steelworkers hall in Orillia, an hour north of Toronto. The highlight of the Oshawa meeting was a brilliant speech delivered by Stephen, which he stayed up all night to write and presented with the oratorical sensitivity that is so uniquely his. It resulted in a clear decision to deal with the question of the Waffle at the next council meeting, to be held in Orillia three months later. I'll never forget, as I left the hall in Oshawa, Mel Watkins screaming at me, 'What makes you think you are better than me?' Of course, I didn't think that at all. It didn't occur to me that his positions were anything but sincere and well intentioned. I simply thought they were wrong and would be enormously destructive if they succeeded. I am sure that I also thought, correctly or not, that I knew a little more about what the reactions of working people, our key constituency, would be to the ideas that he and Laxer were promoting.

The Orillia meeting was decisive: parties within the party were not acceptable. The Waffle, standing alone, did not remain part of the political scene for long. To the best of my recollection, none of the other provincial sections dealt with the issue as firmly as we did in Ontario, with the result that some individuals around the country would for some years describe themselves as Waffle, but they were few in number, without organization, hardly a party within, or outside, the majority.

A couple of years later, my own career reached a turning point. By the early 1970s, Larry Sefton, seriously ill with lung cancer, was turning his mind to the issue of succession. At our 1972 convention in Las Vegas, already too sick to make more than a brief appearance in his role as secretary of the constitution committee, he called for personal interviews of each of the people on the staff who had reason to be considered or to consider themselves possible candidates to succeed him. He also urged each of these putative candidates to support me as his successor. For some, this required a heart-wrenching decision to set aside their own dreams, but after a few hours virtually everyone had accepted Larry's recommendation. Then the idea developed that, since Larry had been elected all those times without opposition, I should be in the same position.

In the Steelworkers, a qualified candidate for leadership must meet tests such as length of membership, citizenship, and work in the jurisdiction, and must receive a certain number of nominations from local unions. The number of nominations required is in relation to the size of the district. In terms of the actual procedure followed for the election of officers and directors, the Steelworkers' approach – a union-wide referendum – is unique in the labour movement in the way it is done and almost unique regardless of the system used. Only a tiny number of unions use a referendum of any kind for such positions, instead choosing officers and directors at a convention where activists can influence the outcome. The Steelworkers' approach is more democratic. Our union's officers and directors are elected by a referendum vote of all the union's members in the case of the officers, of all the union's members in Canada in the case of the Canadian national director, and of all the members in the district in the case of the district directors. The elections are conducted in each local union on the same day, under common election provisions. At the practical level, the referendum requires much more vigorous and expensive campaigning than does a convention election. Candidates must move around the union, make speeches, present ideas and proposals, answer questions, and, most important, present a vision. Local unions conduct the election by secret ballot. There are procedures required across the union, such as nominations at certain times and, as mentioned, by a required number of local unions, related to the size of the district.

In fact, Larry Sefton was the director of District 6 for twenty years and never had an election, nor had his predecessor, the first director, John Mitchell. Since Larry, however, we have had as many or more directors than any other district and a number of elections. What accounts for the change? I think the answer lies squarely in Larry's success as director. Because he did such outstanding work in building the district, no one thought to challenge him or, if someone did consider a challenge, they realized quickly what a hopeless venture that would be. He also did exceptional work in encouraging participation and developing leaders, so many people were interested in succeeding him.

In my case, an election was necessary since there was another candidate, Harry Greenwood from Local 1005 in Hamilton. My supporters initially tried to overwhelm his candidacy by preventing him from winning sufficient nominations. I felt the atmosphere becoming uncomfortable, so I called my principal supporters together and urged that we ease up. I took the position that, if I could not win an election, I did not deserve to be a candidate and that an election would be a healthy event in the life of the union. It was a good decision.

During the campaign, an incident occurred from which I gained particular, but ill-deserved, satisfaction. It happened while I was campaigning in Thompson, Manitoba, among the members of Local 6166, employed for the most part as miners or surface workers by Inco, a fairly muscular group. My opponent, Greenwood, was a tradesman at Stelco and somewhat disparagingly described me as a pencil pusher. Since this was in 1972, and I had not worked in a plant since 1947 but rather as an organizer and staff representative, the description was not entirely inaccurate – though, of course, I did not acknowledge that at the time. Greenwood had been campaigning in Thompson just ahead of me and his supporters were anxious to expose me as the pencil pusher I was. The method they chose was to provoke an arm-wrestling contest at the Legion. I was busy trying to think up an effective line to use after my defeat, but I gave it my best shot and somehow, unbelievably, I won. I don't recall there being much fuss about it but word must have spread among Greenwood supporters – at least I have no memory of being challenged again, although I would not likely have been so lucky on another occasion.

On election day, 13 February 1972, I won quite comfortably. Everyone agreed that the contest had been well and fairly conducted in all its aspects. It gave me, as a new leader, following in the footsteps of a giant, a moral authority that would not have been achievable, at least not as directly or as quickly, in any other way.

A few events and issues stand out in my memory of my term as director. One concerns Larry Sefton, who died in May 1973, the year following my election; he was much too young, just fifty-six years of age. He was the most significant trade-union leader in my life. He gave me work in the Steelworkers, invited me to work directly in his office, and went to extraordinary lengths to support and promote me as the person who should be his successor as director of District 6. I learned more from my association with him – working together, socializing, planning, philosophizing, evaluating – than I can begin to remember. To this day, insights will occur to me that I suddenly realize came from him.

One aspect of Larry's contribution to the labour movement, and to Canadian society generally, that is not widely known was his steadfast environmentalism. Interestingly, he was concerned about the fate of the environment long before the cause became fashionable. Given his pioneering concern for the environment, it was fitting that our union would publish its first convention-endorsed environmental paper in 1990, two years before the first Earth Summit in Rio de Janeiro would spark the beginning of widespread interest in the issue. And that interest should come naturally to our members. As Ron Bloom, special assistant to the Steelworkers' international president, puts it, 'Who suffers the most from factory pollution? The guy in the factory. Who lives in the community where the water's polluted? The workers live in that community. The bosses don't live in that community. The bosses live on the hill. The workers live down in the valley. So if there's runoff, guess where it goes? It goes in the workers' yard.' After Larry's death, members, locals, and other friends donated to the creation of Larry Sefton Park on Bay Street, directly adjacent Toronto's city hall. The park has become a regular site for labour events, such as the annual Workers' Day of Mourning.

My stint in the director's chair had a rather seamless beginning. During the final months of Larry's term, as his illness worsened, I had assumed more and more of his responsibilities, attending board meetings, dealing with staff issues, and the like. In this I had the good fortune that Mike Fenwick continued with his duties as assistant, a position in which he had provided outstanding service throughout Larry's tenure. Mike was a man of many talents – writer, administrator, storyteller, political analyst, thinker – and it was an education to be his associate. He had been an activist on the left during the Depression and participated in the 'On to Ottawa Trek' of 1935 – an event that led to the Regina Riot of 1935, in which the RCMP charged the crowd of unemployed workers to arrest the ringleaders, leaving one policeman killed and several protesters, policemen, and citizens injured. Many of Mike's best stories involved this period. He was a great reader and shared the ideas he discovered in books. For example, as an early Marshall McLuhan fan, he led in building a staff seminar around McLuhan's ideas. Larry was strongly of the view that staff seminars should not be used for nuts and bolts, that such matters could and should be learned along the way and with local training programs. Instead, staff seminars were to concentrate on big-picture ideas. Mike enthusiastically supported this position and was most effective in its implementation. It was a blessing that he continued to work with me during Larry's illness and well into 1973, when I appointed Ken Levack to succeed him. Ken had great people skills, a wonderful sense of humour, and outstanding talent at steering the two sides of a bargaining table in the direction of understanding and agreement.

As Larry's successor, I tried to build on what he had accomplished rather than strike out in a new direction. In this respect, I placed a high value on staff. I remember on one occasion using my speech time at the staff seminar banquet to go around the room and, in a sense, 'introduce' myself to each of the roughly seventy staff. In some cases they were new and it was a real introduction, in others it was a matter of telling stories about old hands. Afterwards, a number came up to me and said they had no idea I knew that much about them. My response was that I thought of little else. This concern with staff never left me. In as decentralized an organization as the Steelworkers, staff are usually the representation of our international union to most of our members. When it comes to moving the organization to meet changing times, or to attempting to change the culture of the union, they are absolutely critical.

Besides Mike Fenwick, some other staff members deserve special mention. After the *Toronto Telegram*, the city's second evening newspaper at the time, had ceased publishing in 1971 after years of difficulties, the Steelworkers hired two of its labour reporters, both of whom made very useful contributions, one of short duration, the other much longer, in labour public relations. The first was Frank Drea, an earlier Steelworker who had worked with us in the Sudbury campaign. He did highly creative work but became interested in Conservative Party politics in Ontario, was elected as an MPP, and became a cabinet minister. The other was Marc Zwelling. After years of analysis and discussion, Larry Sefton had been persuaded that District 6 should have its own public-relations person and was attracted to Marc's abundance of skills and talents and his independence. I was the principal beneficiary, as Marc worked in the district most constructively throughout my term. Later, he would move on to the National Office, and, later still, he would establish his own public-relations firm. He has served and continues to serve the labour movement with impressive creativity and great skill.

Meanwhile, in Canada, the breaking up of some of the international unions was at its peak as I assumed the directorship. We had lost the Kitimat local to a homegrown so-called Canadian union in 1972, while another small Canadian union, the Canadian Association of Industrial, Mechanical, and Allied Workers, was raiding us with some success, particularly in British Columbia. We had been monitoring and active on this issue for some years. Larry and our leadership generally took the position that it made little sense, as one viewed the world around us, to be breaking up international unions. The word globalization was not yet in use. Instead, we talked about phenomena such as internationalism and the global village, from the point of view that that was the direction in which we were headed and, should we break up our internationals, we would soon enough be trying to figure out ways to recreate them. We also felt strongly that the Steelworkers had developed a model that worked very well, making it possible for our members to enjoy the advantages of both systems. The mechanisms of our own districts, our own national office, and our own Canadian policy conference enabled us to deal with Canadian issues as we chose, while we also enjoyed the benefits of the strength of the international union and the opportunity to engage there in the broader discussions of issues facing the labour movements in both our countries. At the same time, Larry, in his work on the Executive Council of the Canadian Labour Congress, was sensitive to the reality that there were a number of international unions that had not developed structures in Canada that met the needs of workers in two countries in the same union. As a result, he was a leader in the development of standards that affiliates would be required to meet, standards that today are set out in the CLC constitution.

Raids in this period were always viewed as being tied to the nationalism issue. The reality was usually much more complicated, related in most cases to issues that were of long standing. Thus, halting and defeating the raids very much involved dealing with these underlying concerns, while also engaging in the public discourse around Canadian unionism. The most critical spot was Local 480 in Trail, British Columbia. Local 480 had come to the Steelworkers as a result of the merger with Mine Mill, subsequent to our second win in Sudbury when it was clear that we were established as the union at Inco, meaning the last major location for Mine Mill had disappeared. The merger in Trail was successful and in Local 480, despite years of fierce defence against the Steelworkers, the leadership quickly became integrated into our union. However, experience with and appreciation of a union in the membership can take long to develop. Before that was accomplished sufficiently in Trail, a local Canadian union launched a raid.

The law in British Columbia was accommodating to such developments. In most jurisdictions, for example, if a three-year agreement had been negotiated, the agreement was not open for a raid by another union until, at the earliest, the last two months of the second year. In British Columbia, under the new NDP government of David Barrett, the agreement was open every year during the last two months, including the first year. This meant that it was much easier for an opposition group to keep issues alive, and more difficult for leadership to resolve issues before the raiding season arrived. In meetings with Labour Minister Bill King and his senior officials, I protested this aspect of the law as it was being developed, but without result. I think that, generally speaking, the leadership of the labour movement in British Columbia liked this feature of the law, felt little or no vulnerability, and saw me as representing a more conservative and cautious eastern view. From my perspective, it was a more realistic view that provided greater stability and a greater opportunity to develop sound, effective collective-bargaining relationships.

In any event, in Trail we were able through legal deficiencies on the raider's part to prevent a vote at the end of the first year and by the second we had resolved the difficulties. As a result, we have had a strong, well-led local union there ever since. Included among those involved was Ken Georgetti, the son of a key leader and now the president of the CLC.

On the national stage, the debate regarding Canadian versus international unionism required appearing on radio and television and in other forums to discuss the issue. Such discussions were not as easy then as they are today. At that time, the argument that one needed to be an internationalist as well as a nationalist was felt by many to be somehow less than patriotic. Now that the reality of globalization is fully upon us, more and more workers understand that effective international solidarity has become absolutely essential and increasingly is the basis for resolving some of our most difficult collective-bargaining struggles.

In terms of our own structure, I had a growing concern that some elements needed an updating, especially our national policy conference. The Canadian versus international debate meant that our Canadian structures were being examined constantly by friend and foe alike. Traditionally, the conference had been held for two or three days immediately preceding the congress conventions, first those of the Canadian Congress of Labour and later those of the Canadian Labour Congress. As the CLC grew, its agenda became more crowded and the number of contentious issues increased. Bill Mahoney, the national director of the Steelworkers, and Larry, the senior district director, were both on the congress executive. This meant that increasingly they would be called out of our sessions to deal with congress issues, leaving us somewhat leaderless and leaving the delegates with the feeling that their leaders were not paying attention. This situation became most critical at the final conference Larry attended, when there was serious difficulty with sustaining an effective focus on the agenda while he and Mahoney, the leaders whose attention the delegates sought, were tied up in congress meetings.

At the first opportunity I proposed that we give up the idea of meeting before the CLC convention, that we establish a separate date and location for our conference, that we invest some energy and creativity into its style and content, and that we fully engage the districts in its planning and preparation so that ownership of the event was fully shared. These ideas were quickly accepted and fit in well with another of my major concerns, the necessity of a much greater focus on occupational health and safety.

The Sudbury experience had been especially meaningful to me in developing a deeper understanding of the impact and importance of this issue, and the need for the union to provide leadership. I drew upon this experience in 1974, when a wildcat strike occurred at the uranium mine in Elliot Lake, Ontario. Many workers there had been diagnosed with cancer and silicosis attributed to radioactivity from the uranium, and the strike gave us a golden opportunity to raise the profile of the issue, beginning in the mining industry, by focusing the publicity away from the wildcat itself and towards the health- and life-threatening aspects of working in the uranium mines. We called for an investigation.

Our efforts were greatly enhanced by the number and quality of staff and activists who were knowledgeable and vigorous in this arena. Gib

Gilchrist was the senior person in charge, ably supported by Homer Seguin and Paul Falkowski, rank-and-filers from Local 6500. In addition, there was from the earlier days in Mine Mill an activist named John Gagnon who devoted himself in particular to the cancer-causing impact of the pollution at Inco's Sudbury operation; and John Lennie of Local 1005 at Stelco in Hamilton, who worked through the mechanism of the Ontario Workmen's Compensation Board. He knew the issue of health and safety as well or better than anyone in the province.

All of these people were part of the health and safety network in the union, activists who made the cause of health and safety their cause, who found in it, in most cases, their principal focus and who in this way made an enormous contribution to their fellow workers. The union also always enjoyed outstanding staff leadership in this area at different levels – in the Canadian national office, in the international headquarters in Pittsburgh, and in a number of the districts as well. Mike Wright, the long-time head of the Safety and Health Department in Pittsburgh, would be one of those appointed by the international labour movement to investigate the Bhopal disaster in India. And, to this day, Andy King has provided thoughtful leadership in the national office.

Our hard work bore fruit. Public interest in the issues behind the Elliot Lake strike, along with prodding from the union, resulted in the government's creation of a royal commission led by Professor James Ham, an engineering professor from the University of Toronto, to investigate health and safety conditions in the mining industry in Ontario. One of the first and critically important suggestions he accepted was that he go on the road, visiting and hearing submissions in the mining communities themselves, rather than holding hearings in Toronto, which was a trip that was extraordinarily difficult, and indeed impossible, for many injured and handicapped miners.

The Ham Commission began its hearings in June 1975. Our people prepared submissions. Ken Valentine, one of our Sudbury staff representatives and a health and safety activist in his own right, followed the commission from location to location, serving as our principal examiner of company witnesses. The hearings concluded in July 1976 and Ham issued his report before the end of that year. This report, which set the stage for improved legislation in Canada for years to come, contained 117 recommendations. Not surprisingly, many were targeted specifically at uranium mining. But there were many others with ramifications for health and safety in a broad range of industries. Among the recommendations were:

- that the Mines Inspection Branch of the Occupational Health and Safety Authority consult with industry and labour in the preparation of codes of practice in mines to address prevention and confinement of dust and the provision of ventilation in workers' breathing zones;
- that the branch establish requirements for measuring dust in mines and workers' exposure to it;
- that the workers be entitled to rehabilitative compensation for exceptional exposure to environmental hazards in the workplace, via amendments to the Workmen's Compensation Act;
- that uranium mines install monitoring systems in their ventilation systems to check air quality and flow in reference to dust, radiation, or other contaminants.
- that the Occupational Health and Safety Authority consult with the Workmen's Compensation Board, industry, and labour, and review reporting procedures for injuries and accidents;
- that a joint labour-management health and safety committee be established at each mine and plant with a membership consisting of equal numbers of representatives from each of the two parties;
- that government, industry, and labour make it a high priority to develop standardized and accredited training for workers in mines and plants;
- that, if, after consulting his immediate supervisor, a worker believed that a job he has been assigned involves unreasonable risks, the situation be assessed by a senior supervisor, with a worker auditor acting as an observer; and
- that mining companies establish occupational health surveillance.

There were also several recommendations on the appointment of worker auditors to report on health and safety in all workplaces 'in underground, open pit, reduction plant, and shop and surface operations.' The worker auditors were to be paid regular wages while carrying out these duties. They were to be appointed for three years through the union, or in a vote by workers in non-union workplaces. They would be empowered to participate in probes of fatal accidents and serious injuries, and to cross-examine witnesses at inquests stemming from fatal accidents.

In Ontario, the Ham Report led to the passing of Bill 70, which, in turn, was followed by the passage of the Occupational Health and Safety Act. The Ontario Ministry of Labour describes the main features of this act, which came into force on 1 October 1979, as follows:

- Responsibility for health and safety issues is shared by workers and employers.
- Workers have four basic rights: to help identify and resolve health and safety concerns; to be informed of hazards they may face, complemented by safety training on equipment and processes and the implementation of the Workplace Hazardous Materials Information System (WHMIS); to refuse work they believe compromises their health and safety; and to stop, via the authority of joint health and safety committees, work that is dangerous.
- Employers have the responsibility of taking reasonable precautions in workplace health and safety, as well as specific issues such as protective equipment for employees, worker education, and working with toxic substances and dangerous machinery. Workers are charged with the responsibility of working safely and following the act's regulations.
- In cases where health and safety issues are not addressed or the act is not being followed, inspectors can investigate and initiate prosecutions, if necessary.

Concerns about the national policy conference, its location and substance, and the emphasis on health and safety all came together in the planning for and execution of the next policy conference, which took place in the midst of the Ham Commission on 8–9 May 1975. It was decided that this conference would be held at the Royal York Hotel in Toronto, on a date unrelated to the CLC convention, and that health and safety would be its theme and 'Stop the Slaughter' its slogan. We invited Dr Irving Selikoff from Mount Sinai Hospital in New York, famous for his pioneering work in identifying the hazards associated with asbestos fibre. It was one of the most moving presentations I have heard and it brought our conference to its feet again and again. Our new approach to conferences had more than proven its worth with this beginning.

My term as director also coincided with a contentious time in the political life of the union. An insurgency was under way in District 31, the other district with about the same membership as District 6. It was located in Chicago and northwest Indiana, the heart of the American steel industry in terms of tons produced and also in terms of the numbers of workers employed in the vast old integrated mills. Two candidates vied for election as district director. One was Sam Evett, who had been the assistant to director Joe Germano, the latter a powerhouse both in the union and in Democratic Party politics. The leader of the insurgency was a staff representative named Ed Sadlowski, a second-generation Steelworker of somewhat radical reputation, with significant financial support from the intellectual leaders of the progressive movements in Boston and similarly the film and theatre artists in California. The division between the two groups was largely around positions of support or opposition to the war in Vietnam and an internal issue regarding the method of ratification of collective agreements in our major industries. These were the days of industry-wide bargaining in steel, one bargaining procedure covering all the companies and all the locals. Those in Sadlowski's camp criticized the long-time practice of ratification of agreements by the union's industry conference, in effect by the local union presidents, rather than by the membership, which was the more customary union practice. This ratification procedure was liked by established union leaders – it required companies to bargain with the most solid, best-informed union leaders.

In any event, Evett won the election and Sadlowski challenged under the Labor Department's rules. The very extensive departmental investigation revealed infractions by some locals in the conduct of the election, but most of these were technical in nature. Nevertheless, the Sadlowski campaign was effective in painting a false picture of widespread, sinister election abuse and laying it at Sam Evett's doorstep. Sadlowski won the second election in 1973 with an overwhelming margin.

During my term as director of District 6, the grape boycott organized by César Chávez was at its peak. Don Taylor, the assistant to the national director, had been the most active and involved Steelworker leader in Canada in support of the struggle of the United Farmworkers. I thought the district should increase its support in this regard as much as possible. Our people in Toronto were responsive. The then new Larry Sefton building at 25 Cecil Street was the centre of much activity, as was Toronto's new Nathan Phillips Square, home of city hall, where the autoworkers and ourselves, and a host of other unions, frequently rallied in support of the cause. The Farmworkers' Marshall Ganz, now a professor of public policy at the Kennedy School of Government at Harvard University, and Jessica Goveya, who died a couple of years ago after retiring as a representative of the New Jersey AFL-CIO, were outstanding facilitator-organizers who had been sent to Toronto to work with the labour movement on the boycott. In subsequent years, I frequently remarked to César that the Farmworkers' boycott effort and its related activities did much more for us and our labour movement than we accomplished for them. It moved us out into the streets. It brought us all together in a great cause. It became a family activity in many cases as we kept vigils and walked picket lines and distributed literature together. Many had the privilege to go to California, to participate directly in activities at the working sites. They inevitably returned home full of inspired enthusiasm, and urged us on to a higher level.

During this period, Dennis McDermott, Canadian director of the UAW, and I worked together frequently and became good friends. Among other concerns, we felt that David Archer, who had given long and wise leadership in the labour movement, should turn over the presidency of the Ontario Federation of Labour to a younger person. David was not open to persuasion. We successfully supported Cliff Pilkey in the ensuing election and did our part in ensuring that David received appropriate recognition for his many years of service.

I had assumed Larry's chair on the Executive Council of the Canadian Labour Congress and by this time in my life I had seen a good deal of the labour movement, had been reasonably close to the work of the congress, and was excited, to say the least, about serving on the council. Among the first major issues facing the congress at that time was the choice of president. The two executive vice-presidents, Bill Dodge and Joe Morris, were both candidates and good friends. I knew Bill somewhat better. Because of my experience on the Eaton drive, I had retained an interest in white-collar organizing, an area in which Bill had been providing leadership in the congress. Coincidentally, Bill was also a good friend of Eileen Tallman Sufrin, the head of the Eaton campaign. Bill expected that I would support him.

However, the attack on us as an 'international' union, rather than a purely 'Canadian' one, was then reaching a crescendo. I was more and more persuaded that cutting up our international unions, just as the world was rushing to internationalize, would be a classic case of fighting yesterday's war just as tomorrow's battle was rising in our face. Bill had a somewhat national focus. Joe, on the other hand, had devoted much of his trade-union experience to the international scene, both in the international labour movement and through the international activity of his own union, the International Woodworkers of America. He was also a world-renowned labour leader in the work of the ILO. I supported Joe.

Another major issue was facing us simultaneously. Canadian Prime Minister Pierre Trudeau was expressing frequent concern about inflation, while also ruminating about wage and price controls as the only effective response. The labour movement vigorously opposed controls, believing that collective bargaining could handle the problems. Conversely, employers favoured Trudeau's position. Joe Morris, drawing upon his European ILO and ICFTU experience, presented a proposal for a tripartite mechanism as the fundamental procedure by which Canada could deal with rapidly changing economic circumstances. The proposal gave both labour and business a real voice in the economic leadership of the country. This was to be accomplished by means of the participative control mechanisms involved and also by joint mechanisms designed to ensure that everyone had access to the same facts and information, and to the same understanding of and rationale for the various policies and proposals.

The executive quickly endorsed the proposal. It immediately put a dramatic new face on the discussion within the congress and with the government and employers. The reaction in the congress was positive, the left and other traditional opponents of the leadership being somewhat stunned by the audacity of it all. However, the prime minister's reaction was profoundly disappointing. I had hoped and expected that, as a former member of the CCF, Trudeau would embrace the basic approach of our proposal, if not all its details, and thereby put Canada in the forefront of modern political-economic policy. Instead, his response was disappointingly traditional – no vision, no interest in participating in a grand, societal effort, nothing to my mind remotely representative of his progressive public reputation.

The result of the government's rejection of this opportunity to provide real leadership, and to contribute to the leading edge of social and economic progress, was that the labour movement moved to the second program the congress had presented in its document: a national day of protest in which we would 'shut the country down for a day' in a European-style, informal, shutdown strike. This issue had been under discussion for months, pushed largely by the UAW and elements in the public-sector unions. Bill Mahoney, our national director, and I were both on the CLC council. Bill thought the idea of trying to shut the country down was madness and said so at every opportunity. I had many reservations, too, but the idea clearly represented the wishes of the membership. It was also my view that, if the shutdown day happened and we didn't support it, if it appeared to be less effective than it could have been, our union would never hear the end of it. My senior colleagues in the district and I decided we would give it our best effort and we did.

where such events are commonplace. European laws are much different, generally a great deal more progressive with respect to the right to demonstrate, and governments and employers view such events as significant indications of workers' concerns that must be addressed, one way or another. That said, since October 1976, taking to the streets and demonstrating our concerns has been much more important in the life of the Canadian labour movement. We have learned how to do it in ways more appropriate to and effective in a North American environment. Demonstrations have been key events in relation to a variety of issues, particularly ones involving free trade and the exporting of jobs. Such was the case, for instance, in Seattle in 1999, Quebec City in 2001, and Miami in 2003, where trade unions joined with other progressive economic and political organizations to voice their concerns.

Another CLC issue I became deeply involved with, in this case as chairman of the constitution committee, concerned the question of representation at conventions. The constitution provided for representation from each union's central leadership and from each local union. As a result of wide variations in local union structures, the number of delegates from a particular union could be wildly in excess of that from another union with the same number of members but a different structure.

The building-trades unions, by and large, were those most affected by this inequity and we set about in our committee to devise a new system. When we presented our recommendations on this issue to the convention, Grace Hartmann, then president of the Canadian Union of Public Employees (CUPE), took the floor and condemned the committee recommendations as being unfair and undemocratic. I could hardly believe my ears; she had been a member of the committee and had worked on and voted for every single recommendation. When I confronted her with this incredible contradiction, her explanation was that the CUPE caucus had voted against the recommendations and she was bound by its decision, to which I somewhat bitterly replied that she might have let me know what she intended to do during the debate. In any event, CUPE's decision doomed the vote and an opportunity for decent progress along the path to democratic reform was lost.

As my term as director of District 6 moved along, the politics within the Steelworkers was becoming more intense, almost by the day. President I.W. Abel was in his final term, which would come to an end on 1 June 1977. Secretary-Treasurer Walter J. Burke would be retiring at the same time. Ed Sadlowski, having won the re-run election to become director of District 31, the largest membership district in the United States, was an announced candidate for the presidency of the union. Within the rest of the international executive board, all of whom generally were supporters of the administration, there was considerable confusion as to who Abel's successor should be.

The referendum election system, since every member has a vote, opens itself up to some degree of influence from outside. In this case, various elements in the Democratic Party in the United States were keeping a close eye on the election. Abel and Burke had always been stalwart supporters of the party, including the government and its policies in Vietnam. At the Democratic Party convention, Abel had seconded the nomination of Henry ('Scoop') Jackson, a supporter of the war. Sadlowski, on the other hand, had come home from Vietnam opposed to the war, and those within the Democratic Party who shared that view were understandably interested in seeing him become president of one of America's premier labour organizations, the United Steelworkers of America.

I watched this with interest, while becoming familiar with international executive board procedures. I also was becoming better acquainted with the direction of American foreign policy, which I discovered to be an increasing concern of most of my American colleagues on the board. Friends in Canada used to ask me what being on the 'top board' was like. My response was always that it was much like any other union meeting; we spent time learning what was happening, discussing what to do, and planning how to move ahead, with all this including ideas that were variously great, good, bad, and bizarre.

A few years earlier, at the Atlantic City convention in 1974, a group of us from our district had been having a drink when Stu Cooke, then an assistant in the district office, asked me who I thought should be Abel's successor. I replied without hesitation that it should be Lloyd McBride, adding that he was much the smartest director around the board table. Stu asked, in his pointed way, if I had done anything about it. I acknowledged I hadn't, quickly adding that we could do something about it right now if I called Lloyd and we went to see him. Despite the lateness of the hour, we decided I should call. Lloyd was already in bed but, when I explained our mission, he invited us up. We met with him and urged our point of view. He did not agree immediately, but for us, that was the beginning of the campaign.

Not too long after, Lloyd came to me and said he would like me to be on the ticket as candidate for vice-president in 1977. This presented me with a quandary. I was comfortably established in a position I had never expected to hold as director of District 6. My family was enjoying life in Toronto, Audrey and I had a home in which we expected to live the rest of our lives, and I took great satisfaction from working with the Steelworkers and the Canadian Labour Congress. Canada was my country, life was good, and the challenges were great.

At the time, many of us had been thinking about the national versus international union issue and about which route represented the best interests of our members and working people in Canada. Larry and I had talked about the inevitability of a more international world economy, of greater interrelatedness, of the desperate needs of the Third World, of the tensions of living next to a superpower, and of the great advantage of having a trade-union structure that could deal with these realities. These were key social, political, and economic issues with significant impact on the concerns and future of the labour movement. When we discussed these matters, as we frequently did, we counted our blessings for the way the Steelworkers union was structured and how its policies and procedures had evolved. We had independence with regard to national concerns, we enjoyed international solidarity and support in struggles within the North American community, and we had a steadily expanding role in the world labour movement. One major improvement we felt we could make would be to have a Canadian voice among the top officers so we would be involved in a policy role at every level.

Larry would have been ideal for such a role. He was highly respected throughout the union. He had played a key role in the CLC in establishing standards of service and autonomy for Canadian sections of international unions. He was a person of many interests and with a great deal of understanding of a wide range of human concerns. He had an instinctive sense of the importance of finding the best strategies and defining the appropriate priorities in building a people's movement.

But Larry was gone and here was an opportunity staring me in the face. I had much to think about as 1977, the last year of my term as District 6 director, opened.

With my big brother, Ross, in front of the parsonage in Aylmer, Ont.
(Author's Collection)

Here, some of my family are gathered at my grandparents' home in New Hamburg, Ont. Back row, left to right: Uncle Bob Bradley; my mother, Emma Williams; my brother, Ross; my grandmother Eva Williams; and my grandfather Daniel Williams. Front, left to right: cousin Bruce Bradley; my sister, Carol; and me. (Author's Collection)

My father, Waldemar, started his high school studies in Summerland, BC, as a young adult. This photograph was taken in 1907. (Author's Collection)

In my navy uniform, January 1945. (Author's Collection)

A meeting of the Canadian Congress of Labour committee responsible for the Eaton campaign, 1948–52. From left: Charlie Millard, Canadian director, United Steelworkers; Eileen Tallman Sufrin, campaign director; Tommy MacLachlan, Canadian director, Retail, Wholesale and Department Store Union; Fred Dowling, committee chairman and Canadian director, United Packing House Workers; counsel David Lewis; George Burt, Canadian director, United Auto Workers; and Pat Conroy, CCL secretary-treasurer. (Author's Collection)

Eileen Tallman Sufrin in our office during the Eaton campaign, with charts in the background outlining the campaign's structure, objectives, and progress. (Photo by Gilbert A. Milne, Toronto. Author's Collection)

Eaton drive staff. From left: the author, Jack Jolly, Marjorie Gow, Henry
Weisbach, Olive Chester, Wally Ross, Eileen Talman Sufrin, and Ernie Arnold.
(Author's Collection)

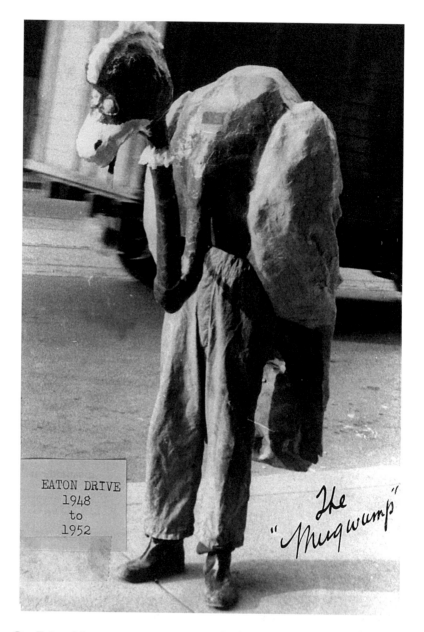

EATON DRIVE
1948
to
1952

The "Mugwump"

Our Eaton drive mugwump, representing those workers who couldn't make
up their minds. (Author's Collection)

Lynn WILLIAMS, pictured here with his wife and family, knows the problems of a rapidly expanding suburban community. He's living through them.

AND he shares the hopes we all have, for a life of opportunity and security for our children.

It is his conviction – and he will so represent us at Queen's Park – that the function of government is to use the vast resources of our Province – not for the private gain of a few corporations – but to help provide education, medical care, pensions and other absolutely essential needs of all our people.

on October 18th

Elect LYNN **WILLIAMS**

Audrey, David, Judy and Lynn

A copy of the 'vote at' card that was distributed throughout the riding of York West in a 1956 by-election. (Author's Collection)

The best-known portrait of Larry Sefton. (Photo by Joseph Schweld, Toronto)

Taken at the first meeting following the merger agreement between the Mine Mill and Smelter Workers and the Steelworkers, 29 April 1967. From left: Harvey Murphy, vice-president, Mine Mill Canada; Larry Sefton, director, District 6, Steelworkers; Bill Berezowski; Mine Mill staff representative; Ray Stevenson, Mine Mill, public relations; Pen Baskin, B.C. area supervisor, Steelworkers; Joseph Molony, international vice-president, Steelworkers; Nelson Thibeault, Mine Mill staff representative; Jim Keuhl, Steelworkers staff representative; Albert Desbiens, Steelworkers staff representative. (Author's Collection)

Marching in a Labour Day Parade, Toronto, 1970s. (Author's Collection)

★ McBride ★ Williams ★ McKee ★ Odorcich ★ Lynch

THE McBRIDE TEAM   FOR A BETTER STEELWORKERS UNION

PRINTED IN U.S.A.

Campaign photograph of the McBride team in the 1977 Steelworkers election.
(Author's Collection)

Ed Broadbent, leader of the federal NDP, speaking at an event held in my honour when I left Toronto to become secretary of the international union. Left to right: Audrey Williams, Ken Levack, Ed Broadbent, Lynn Williams, and Shirley Carr. (Author's Collection)

Clément Godbout (left) and Jean Gérin-Lajoie (right) welcome me to a
District 5 conference. (Author's Collection)

I am flanked by Lane Kirkland and Shirley Carr at my swearing-in as
president of the Steelworkers. (Photo by Walter E. Eiseman.
Courtesy of Visual Perceptions, Pittsburgh [8614-C-13])

An official portrait of me taken during my tenure as president of the
Steelworkers. (Photo by Jonas, © 1990)

To support workers during the 1980s shutdowns in the Mon valley,
Pennsylvania, we utilized operations such as the Rainbow Kitchen, which I
am visiting here with Lane Kirkland and Tom Donahue (far right).
(Photo by Walt Eiseman, VPI)

Leo Gerard, left with a megaphone, joined with me and Gérard Docquier, Leon Lynch, Ken Neumann, and Harry Hynd in marching in support of Local 1005 at Stelco, Hamilton, during the 1990 Steelworkers convention in Toronto. (Photo by Tom Fitzpatrick, VPI)

I can't recall what 'wisdom' I was imparting here, but I managed to hold the attention of, at back row from left, Ed Ball, Harry Lester, Tom Streigel, and Bernie Hostein; and, front row from left, Lou Thomas, Dick Davis, Leon Lynch, and Bob Guadiana. To my right is Harry Guenther and to my left with his back to the camera is Dave Foster. (Photo by Gary Hubbard, USWA)

In support of the Ravenswood strikers. Left to right: Dan Stidham, USW Local 5668 President representing the 1,700 workers locked out by Ravenswood Aluminum Co. in West Virginia, from November 1990 to June 1992; Harry Lester, Director, USW then District 29 in Michigan; retired USW President Lynn Williams; and Jim Bowen, Director, USW then District 23 in West Virginia. (Author's Collection)

Speaking at Ravenswood. (Photo by Gary Hubbard, USWA)

César Chavez of the United Farmworkers, champion of the grape boycott, visited the Steelworkers often and found great support among us for his cause. Left to right: Tony Rainaldi, Ed Ball, César Chavez, and J.T. Smith. (Photo by Tom Fitzpatrick, VPI)

My wife, Audrey, enjoying a happy moment with Jim Smith, left, and
George Becker, right. (Author's Collection)

Touring the Edgar Thompson works along with local union president Don Thomas. As part of the settlement of the 1986 lockout, U.S. Steel guaranteed that Pittsburgh's last integrated steel mill would remain open. (Photo by Gary Hubbard, USWA)

To Lynn Williams —
with warm best wishes,
Ted Kennedy '85

Two Steelworker colleagues, Sam Dawson (far left) and legislative director
Jack Sheehan (at my right), with the author and Senator Ted Kennedy in 1985.
(Photo by Robert Knudsen, Annandale, Va)

Working for Michael Dukakis, the Democratic Party presidential candidate in 1988, was important to our union. Here we are meeting as Jesse Jackson looks on. (Photo by Tom Fitzpatrick, VPI)

Testifying in Washington was a key part of my mandate, as I am doing here accompanied by Jack Sheehan. (Photo by Tom Fitzpatrick, VPI)

The UAW had the event timed nicely with its 'Big Three' and related auto-parts bargaining, and it was in the open period in virtually all of its agreements, during which it could strike legally. For the UAW locals, it was simply a matter of walking out, parading, and walking back, without fear of personal or institutional penalties. We were in exactly the opposite position. The overwhelming majority of our people, if they shut down their plants, would do so in a time frame that meant they would be engaged in illegal walkouts. Since public employers in North America do not, for the most part, handle their employee relations in the tough, hard-nosed way so many private corporations do, shutting down most public operations for a day was not perceived to be nearly as risky as doing it in the private sector.

The National Day of Protest was slated for 14 October 1976. We spent the preceding few weeks meeting with our locals and urging their participation. We notified the companies of our intention, asking them to respect the democratic right of protest. I attended two meetings of the shop stewards at Local 2251, the local that represented the workers at Algoma Steel in Sault Ste Marie, and two general membership meetings. The members were shocked to hear their director promoting, in effect, an illegal strike because we had an agreement in place. In the end, members of the local participated in the parade in the Sault and in the rally, but they kept the plant operating as well.

Generally speaking, our people were at the top of the heap, along with the Auto Workers, in the percentage participating. Of course, for the most part, the Auto Workers did not walk out in defiance of their collective agreements. Participation from the rest of the labour movement, however, was not nearly at the level that had been hoped, or expected. Then came the great difficulty that accompanies all such single-day events: what to do the next day. What I did was go to work on all the trouble spots to avoid paying fines or the loss of anyone's employment. For many subsequent years, I boasted in speeches that we paid only one fine and lost no jobs. However, on one occasion an activist came up to me at the end of a meeting and said, 'Lynn, you have forgotten about the three brothers who were fired in our plant.' Indeed, I had. I apologized and from then on revised my remarks. I believe that we found them other work but, regrettably, not back at their former plant.

To the best of my knowledge, the idea of such a national one-day work stoppage has not been seriously proposed since. In retrospect, the 1976 event was a remarkable accomplishment in view of the circumstances and made clear how different our situation was from that in Europe,

A family gathering. Audrey and I on the dock at the cottage in July 1998. Brian and Barbara are on the left, David and Judy on the right. (Author's Collection)

Visiting with Jack Layton, leader of the federal NDP. (Author's Collection)

Governor General Michaëlle Jean and I have our picture taken together after I was presented with the Order of Canada in 2005. (Author's Collection)

9

ON TO PITTSBURGH

There is no hanging on to one elected position while you run for another in the Steelworkers system. You run for one, and you make it or not. If I were to run for the post of vice-president, it meant really putting my future on the line – risking the loss of a fine position that I thoroughly enjoyed for an unknown future. On the other hand, this was an opportunity to take the Canadian experience in our union into the highest councils of the union, thereby ensuring that Canadian concerns were recognized and, more important, furthering the broadest possible kind of solidarity in our organization.

I consulted widely around the union, with close colleagues at home, of course, and with President Abel, Lloyd McBride, and Bernie Kleiman, our general counsel. Kleiman was already a good friend, one who was destined to become my best friend in the travails that lay ahead. Another friend I approached was the late Bert McNamara, director of District 32 in Wisconsin, a good friend of Larry's and a person of wide experience who had served as a labour attaché in India. He and I discussed my candidacy for almost an entire night during a union golf tournament in West Virginia. I also sought out a variety of senior staff, in particular those who were widely travelled in the union and were knowledgeable about the key leaders in various districts and well versed in union politics.

One director sought me out with advice of a different kind. Roy Stevens was our director in New England, and he flew up to Toronto from Boston and took me to lunch to advise me that the idea of a Canadian running for international office was a very bad one. His argument was essentially about American politics. He said he knew a good deal about Canadian politics because he listened to the CBC on his short-wave radio and, therefore, understood how different we were. He pointed out how important politics were to the American labour movement and that, in his opinion, a Canadian, or at least this Canadian, could not come to understand all of this well enough to represent the union's needs adequately. I thought his argument so outrageous that I did not bother making a number of points as effectively as I might have, such as listing for him the large number of Canadians who have enjoyed very successful political and politically related careers in the United States.

I was fortunate that there were no serious family complications. Audrey was ready for an adventure. Our two oldest children, Judy and David, were finished university and beginning careers in western Canada, in teaching and engineering, respectively. Our third, Barbara, was about to begin university. I did try to tempt her with the promise of a horse if she came with us, but her boyfriend, Chris, later her husband, had more influence and she remained home in Ontario. Our fourth, Brian, who was ten and heading into Grade 5, was no bundle of enthusiasm about the project but he did become quite interested in the election as he came to understand what was involved.

I decided to take the plunge, advised Lloyd of my decision, and was congratulated by President Abel as we gathered before the next board meeting. This was prior to any public announcement. Our team, which now included Frank McKee, the candidate for treasurer, had decided it was to be known as McBride, Williams, and McKee. As word spread, some members of the board congratulated us. Others were noticeably silent. It was not long before complications of one kind or another set in. The first complication was that a decent man, John E. Johns, one of two vice-presidents, and a long-time friend and trusted colleague of President Abel's from the days when they were local union leaders together in their home local in Canton, Ohio, also wanted to be president. There was also a long-serving, well-respected, and well-liked director from District 9 in eastern Pennsylvania, Bill Moran, who had always expected to be an officer before his time was finished. And in the wings was Joe Odorcich, director of one of the more famous districts in the union, District 15, which represented, in militant fashion, our members in what had been the heart of the steel industry in the Mon valley south of Pittsburgh. Odorcich had been a staff representative for years, and while he had not been a director for long, he had quickly established himself as competent, hard working, and strong.

These were about as complicated political considerations as could be imagined within a group of close colleagues. They resulted in what seemed to be endless meetings with various individuals and board members, and especially with President Abel, seeking his support. He was considered by everyone to have the decisive influence, if he chose to exercise it, in determining who would be on the administration slate. We remained confident that Abel was really on our side; his support certainly was critical from my point of view if a Canadian breakthrough was to be achieved. At the same time, we recognized that loyalty was a key value for Abel and that he and Johns had never been divided along the way. Everyone thought the world of Johns, but at the same time there was almost total agreement that he was not a strong enough personality to give the union the leadership it required.

Meanwhile, Ed Sadlowski's campaign was building considerable momentum within the traditional opposition circles in the union, which were a mix of some left politics and some traditional disgruntlement over dues and similar issues. The most popular anti-administration argument in basic steel circles was the same one that Sadlowski had emphasized in his run for the directorship of District 31 – ratification of contracts by the membership, rather than by local union presidents. The Abel administration vigorously supported the existing ratification procedure and we on the McBride team did as well. It was an easy position to support. Ratification by union presidents was the practice followed by the three other major industry groupings of that time other than steel – non-ferrous, aluminum, and can (the remaining members of the union, a substantial and increasing majority, used the system of membership ratification). The system meant that companies were bargaining with the strongest activist group in the union, the elected local union presidents. It encouraged companies to forget about campaigning among members in an attempt to weaken support for the bargaining program, and focus instead on the bargaining. On the union side, it encouraged the presidents to be focused as well, since they were the ultimate decision makers and had to present themselves accordingly to their members.

Nevertheless, the ratification issue was a potent one that the Sadlowski campaign exploited to the fullest. His campaign also benefited enormously from considerable media attention and support. He was viewed as a young, progressive voice challenging an aging conservative establishment leadership. Most of this was encouraged by and a reflection of the views of the anti-Vietnam War group within the Democratic Party. This group saw in the Sadlowski candidacy the possibility of bringing an important major union over to their side. At one point, a talented young anti-war, Democratic activist, Ed James, now a labour lawyer in Washington, D.C., was manager of the Sadlowski campaign. Another most important side to the relationship between this group and the Sadlowski campaign was in the area of fundraising. We ultimately were able to establish that significant sums of money were raised in California and in Boston. This demonstrated how vulnerable our referendum system was to the influence of outside money, which might not necessarily be from people with any concern about the labour movement for its own sake.

Two people did outstanding work for our campaign in ferreting out where the outside money was coming from, labour attorney Bruce Miller from Detroit and Paul Feldman, a labour movement activist who then was employed in our public-relations department. Both were noted for their intelligence, tenacity, and understanding of the movement. Indeed, Feldman's commitment was such that he did all his investigative work as a volunteer on his own time. Jim English, later the union's secretary-treasure (now retired), played a role in sorting out how the union would deal with the outside-funds issue and other related problems after the election was over. English explains: 'I was the union's neutral attorney and I was responsible for making sure the election was conducted properly, and post-election meetings within the union revealed a general belief that this [outside funding] wasn't a good thing, and there were discussions about whether that was something that could be remedied.' The union later adopted a rule barring outsider contributions to union election campaigns. Sadlowski then sued to block the rule and the case ultimately reached the U.S. Supreme Court. That court found that the rule served a legitimate union purpose and did so reasonably.

Meanwhile, after months of off-and-on crises with regard to whom the slate was to include, the basics of a Johns slate included him for president and director Bill Moran for secretary-treasurer. But, with the Sadlowski campaign gaining momentum, a summit meeting was held, including all the board members in support of a single administration slate. At this meeting, after much review by the principals, Johns volunteered to step aside for Lloyd if room could be made for Moran. It was ultimately agreed that the group would recommend an increase in the number of officers to five and the line-up would be Lloyd McBride, president, Lynn Williams, vice-president (administration), Leon Lynch, vice-president (human affairs), Bill Moran, secretary, and Frank McKee, treasurer. Leon Lynch was an incumbent.

Our slate was indebted to Johns for his gracious and unselfish act. He had waited a long time for the opportunity to be president of the Steelworkers, but he recognized it was not to be. The other unresolved issue of fundamental importance was the appointment of a campaign manager. The new people on the slate were all district directors. This meant that when we met we were able to focus on decisions and move things along, but then we would go home, become immersed in our districts, and little would happen. We desperately needed a manager.

The situation came to a head when we held our first rally in Pittsburgh, in the Homestead local union hall on the city's south side. As we drove along the main business street in the area, it might well have been Sadlowski Street because his posters were on every post and other spots as well. In front of his headquarters, there appeared to be a larger crowd on the sidewalk than there was at our rally. My heart sank. Was I giving up my directorship for as uncertain an adventure as this appeared to be? All I could think of was the need for a campaign and, therefore, the need for a campaign manager. We had no other real option. Continuing to lead our districts while campaigning was essential to maintaining our voting base.

At our evaluation/planning meeting at the end of the Homestead event, I proposed that we ask George Becker to become our campaign manager. The idea was quickly adopted and immediately I felt better. It now felt like a campaign was under way, because we all knew we had just taken a critically important step forward. George was keen for the job and all the formalities were looked after in record time. One could feel tangible change; for the first time, we now had events planned and schedules organized.

Once the politics of the team were resolved and Becker was installed as the campaign manager, campaigning began in earnest. As it turned out, the crises were not quite finished. We were only a few weeks into campaigning with our new structure when tragedy struck. Bill Moran fell over dead in an airport on his way to the funeral of another director. Moran was a good man, a pioneer in winning health-care provisions in collective agreements and in the promotion of non-profit Blue Cross and Blue Shield organizations as the best way to meet the health-care needs of members in the United States.

We needed to adjust the ticket. Lloyd called us together and there was quick agreement to bring in Joe Odorcich. Shortly thereafter, I called Joe to suggest we trade places, that I would prefer to be secretary and that I expected he would prefer to be vice-president. It was quickly done. It is my opinion that this exchange had implications in Joe's mind that it did not have in mine, not that I was any more forthcoming at the time than he was. He said he was pleased to change because he didn't like taking minutes. In fact, we had never had a secretary's position before. It had always been combined with the treasurer's position, and, in any event, we both knew that it would essentially be up to Lloyd as to how responsibilities were divided among the officers. For me, two considerations were at work: first, as the only Canadian on the board, I would be the vice-president for Canada in fact if not in name, with responsibility for Canadian affairs; second, while I was happy to handle matters Canadian, I also wanted to be involved in the broader life of the union – something that I could accomplish through the job of secretary. In short, holding the secretary's position rather than the vice-presidency suited my interests perfectly. With Joe, other calculations may have been at work. The vice-president's responsibilities involve assisting the president. However, in the by-laws concerning the local unions, the vice-president automatically succeeds the president should the latter for any reason vacate the office, and I think Joe felt something similar applied to the international. If that speculation were accurate, perhaps in Joe's mind he felt that, in offering to switch, I was almost offering to support him should such a situation arise.

The campaign was a massive undertaking. There were members and local unions in every state of the union except North Dakota and in every province and every territory in Canada. Given the referendum election, it was necessary to 'show the flag' around the union as widely as possible, although it was clearly impossible to visit every one of roughly 6,000 active local unions. We used all the devices we could imagine – rallies, workplace leaflet distributions, media interviews, appearances at meetings and conferences, public events, and special luncheon or breakfast gatherings with key supporters and/or influential opinion makers. Public-relations efforts were particularly critical because Sadlowski and his slate were so far ahead from the outset. With his support from political friends from outside the union, most noticeably in New England and California, his budget, judged by what he financed, seemed much larger than ours. Of course, we were not without advantages. We had all worked our way up through the ranks of the staff and most through the ranks of a local union prior to being on staff. We all enjoyed good support in our own districts and were well known and had good reputations among the activists across much of the union.

I believed we were in a close and tough struggle. My enthusiasm for the referendum approach was reinforced since it provided for, and indeed required, continuing campaign contact with the membership and enabled more and more of them to make their own face-to-face judgment of the candidates. I very much liked, and urged everyone to adopt, a campaign philosophy attributed to John F. Kennedy – that you run all-out from the beginning of the campaign until the last poll was closed.

Towards the end of the campaign, with the election on the second Tuesday of February and so many critical votes in the northern states and in Canada, the weather became an issue. To this day, I am not sure if it was colder in the wind at Burns Harbor in northwest Indiana or at the pitheads in Sudbury. It persuaded me that we needed a more sensible date and that we should recommend a change at the earliest opportunity, which we did.

There were many debates, formal and informal, at gates, picnics, and family gatherings, in bars, restaurants, and meeting halls. Two events are particularly clear in my mind. One was the day Sadlowski and I both turned up, leaflets in hand, early in the morning at the gates of Northwestern Steel in Sterling, Illinois. There is something about a gate exchange that invites a level of candour rarely approached or duplicated in any other setting. I learned a great deal that morning in terms of Ed's anger, his ambitions, and his feelings about the union during a vigorous debate with him.

The other occasion was the nominating meeting at Local 3199 at Great Lakes Steel in Detroit, to which each side had been invited to send a representative. The first sign that things were a little different was that, after we had had a pleasant dinner, the district director, Charlie Youn-glove, dropped me off a few blocks from the union hall, making it clear he did not wish to be seen driving a McBride team member around and that he had no intention of attending the meeting. I pondered the implications of this briefly, but the meeting was at hand and it soon took on a life of its own.

The Sadlowski representative at the meeting was the candidate for vice-president (administration), Marvin Weinstock, an experienced staff representative from Youngstown. The local president was Floyd Chambers, who immediately called us together to agree upon the rules of engagement for the meeting. As I remember, there were to be two fifteen-minute opening presentations, followed by alternating five-minute rebuttals. We tossed a coin to determine speaking order, with the result that I was to speak first. We then moved from the president's office to the hall, where it took about two seconds to sense that it was

Sadlowski's meeting. The audience listened to me with reasonable politeness, not too much booing, but welcomed Weinstock with roaring enthusiasm. Weinstock's presentation was both his major policy outline and his rebuttal of my remarks. After the cheering died down, a member rose and made a motion to the effect that, since they all knew what they were going to do regardless of what was said, they should proceed with the vote immediately. The chairman appeared about to accept the motion, but I rose and started shouting 'point of order' as loudly as I could. There was much noisy protesting, but order was restored. I repeated the rules of the debate, described a couple of the distortions and inaccuracies in Weinstock's remarks, and claimed that an immediate vote would deny me and the McBride team our democratic right to correct such allegations. The chairman ruled in my favour and I proceeded with my rebuttal.

I don't believe I changed a vote, but I won considerable respect. The meeting organizers divided the house; almost everyone moved to the Sadlowski side, a sturdy dozen or so to mine. I shook the hands of my new supporters most ostentatiously. I then asked permission to speak briefly again and thanked everyone for their attendance and participation. After adjournment, a group of some size from both sides remained to shake hands, most memorably a fellow named Sam, one of the health and safety activists, who had been quite outspoken on Sadlowski's behalf during the meeting. But he came up to congratulate me on my determined stand. From then on, for some years until his retirement, Sam made a point to come to speak with me any time we were at the same convention or event. What he so clearly demonstrated was the inherent fairness of our people, occasionally forgotten in the heat of debate but quickly restored.

The campaign became a blur of travel, rallies, meetings, fast food, press conferences, hotels, short nights, early mornings, and long days, but the more I participated the more enthusiastic and determined I became about the referendum. The level of communication between members and leaders, the opportunity to find out what leaders think and for the members to express their views, could not be achieved in any other way that could match the effectiveness of the referendum process. George Becker and the campaign team he had pulled together were thorough beyond belief in facilitating that process, scheduling the events for maximum impact by the most efficient and economical means.

As the campaign progressed, Lloyd became more and more confident, finally almost eliminating the final weeks of his campaign schedule, though, as was typical of the man, he made no attempt to force such views on the rest of us. For my part, I stuck with the Kennedy program, campaigning right to the end. The campaign concluded on election day in February 1977, with the McBride team winning: McBride with 328,861 votes to Sadlowski's 249,281; myself with 341,281 votes to 220,731 for Ignacio (Nash) Rodriguez; Frank McKee with 316,466 votes to 242,191 for Andy Kmec; Joe Odorcich with 324,419 votes to 231,848 for Marvin Weinstock; and Leon Lynch with 303,958 votes to Oliver Montgomery's 251,782.

There was some fallout from the 1977 election. Because of the wide diversity of responsibility across all the local unions, there had been, quite naturally, some slip-ups, some mistakes in procedure. Deliberate? Accidental? It's difficult to tell, but an internal union report, after hearings on protests, recounts, and re-votes, and reviewing any other matters that could affect the final result, was issued on 28 April. It concluded that, in the main, the election had been fair and that whatever irregularities that had occurred were not numerous or significant enough to overturn the results. But that wasn't the end of the matter. In a post-election investigation, the U.S. Department of Labor was asked to probe balloting in Canada. The U.S. officials replied that they could not, and, says Jim English, 'at some point made noises that if they couldn't investigate the election in Canada then they would simply not consider the reported Canadian vote in determining whether there were violations that were sufficient to overturn the election. From the point of view of a union that's an international union, that's a pretty challenging kind of a position for the government to take.' Ultimately, concerns about the election in Canada were addressed by an independent report whose findings were accepted by the U.S. Department of Labor. The election results stood.

The installation was held on 1 June 1977 at Linden Hall, the recently purchased and newly renovated Steelworkers education centre on the Youghiogheny River, near Dawson, Pennsylvania, about fifty-five kilometres south of Pittsburgh. The day was hot and muggy, with a storm threatening, but we were fortunate that the bad weather held off until after the ceremonies. In his address in passing the torch to Lloyd, outgoing President Abel asked union members from time to time to 'stop and retrace the steps that we've traveled, so that there won't come the day that we need to relive the past because we have forgotten it.' He paid special tribute to retiring Secretary-Treasurer Walter Burke, noting that on his watch the Steelworkers' net worth had grown from $11 million to $45 million and its pension fund from $20 million to $95 million. He went on to announce that the board had decided to rename the education centre the Walter J. Burke Education Center. Burke was surprised and touched, replying: 'Those of you who have known me for many years know that back as far as the days of Clinton Golden, who was one of our earlier pioneering officers, and in some respects many years ahead of his time, Clint and I used to talk about labor education. And those of you from my old district and whom I have had the opportunity to meet in the last 12 years know that labor education has been at the top of my personal priority list.' Then, as he was about to swear in Lloyd as his successor, 'Abe,' as he was commonly known, expressed his confidence that we would 'continue carrying this union on the high plane it has been traveling these many years, and continue down the road of progress under the great leadership of Lloyd McBride and his associates.'

In assuming the presidency, Lloyd saluted our team and then, turning to his predecessor, added: 'I say to I.W. Abel: The legacy that is now mine will be continued. That legacy was perhaps best expressed by our founding and first President, Phil Murray, when he told our first Constitutional Convention in 1942 that he wanted our union to be built "upon the basis of love for the union rather than for the man. If you hew to the pursuit of a philosophy of that description, your organization will endure. Men will come and men will go but the union will live forever."' Lloyd also urged our members to unite after the bitter battles of the recent election and took a strong stand against those intent on continuing the hostilities:

Unfortunately, there are some among us who are still casting stones. There are still a few who give personal political advantage precedence over the welfare of our members. I say to them what I have said many times before: Good trade unionists and good Steelworkers do not smear their union in public; they do not engage in radical, bull-horn tactics designed to embarrass their union. Such tactics only give aid and comfort to our opponents and enemies.

Our recent election also sent out a message loud and clear – a message from Pittsburgh to those outsiders, those professional meddlers, who interfered in our private business and attempted to take over this union for their own personal and political purposes. That message to the outsiders was this: This union is not for sale; it is not for rent; it is not for lease. It

is for Steelworkers, to be run by Steelworkers for the benefit of Steelworkers. And that's the way your new officers intend to keep it.

The principal speaker at the installation was George Meany, president of the AFL-CIO, who saluted Abe for his success as determined by
'the only measuring rod that I know in assessing the value of a trade
union ... what has the union done to improve the conditions of life and
welfare of the general membership of the union ... And on that score I
want to say to you that Abe has come through ... You have better contracts, you have better conditions on the job, and you have assumed a
position of high responsibility in your industry as a whole.' Meany also
addressed the tendency evolving even then of U.S. companies exporting jobs to Third World nations. 'That's the question of the preservation
of American jobs, Steelworkers' jobs, shoe workers' jobs, pottery workers' jobs, jobs of every type from unfair, cheap ... competition. That's
the only reason an American corporation goes abroad. You talk about
shoes, ladies' shoes. Ladies are getting shoes with American labels on
them made by an American manufacturer, using American machine
tools, American know-how, American technique, but using 60-cents-
an-hour labor from Taiwan or Hong Kong.'
    The installation ceremony attracted a good crowd, largely composed
of activist members who had supported the McBride team. But there
were also some opposition supporters from District 31, where Jim Bal-
anoff, a Sadlowski supporter and former president of the 18,000-mem-
ber Local 1010 at Inland Steel in East Chicago, had been elected director,
and a few from other districts. There were a number of company officials from steel and other jurisdictions in which we were privileged to
represent the workers and also some national, state, and local political
officials.
    All of this was a new experience for me. I had never before attended
an installation, including my own as director. I discovered that most
directors had invited groups of supporters to their installations. Larry,
possibly because he had never been opposed and therefore there had
been no election, never did. Abe had chastised me somewhat four years
earlier when I had been absent from my installation.
    Work officially began the next day. It had never been my habit to be
in the office first thing in the morning, except on those days on which
leaflet demonstrations, early breakfast meetings, or some other specific
event was on the schedule. My preference was to work late, particularly
in view of the fact that our district included three time zones, which

resulted in many late calls in the east. On this festive occasion, not yet having a home in Pittsburgh but living in a hotel, there had been considerable revelry the night before. When I arrived at the office at about 9:30 the next morning, there was a note on my office door: Job vacancy, good hours, decent pay, comfortable office. That was Lloyd's good-natured way of making his expectations clear and I never subsequently failed to be there by 9 a.m.

I noticed quickly that this was a somewhat general cultural difference between Canadian and American work habits. The U.S. style was much more into breakfast meetings, early mornings, and early quitting times, if the day's work was 'done.' Another noticeable difference was the willingness to schedule events during the two summer months. As I often explained, in Canada summer is something of a 'religion,' and one doesn't interfere with the good stretch of weather except when it is unavoidably necessary.

Another matter I was concerned with in the beginning was more symbolic than tangible, but, as the future played out, it was in the end of some importance. The other officers had all been in and around Pittsburgh during the weeks preceding the installation, while I had not. By the time I arrived, the available corner offices had all been claimed, by the president of course. The former secretary-treasurer's office went to treasurer Frank McKee, and the former vice-president's (administration) went to vice-president Joe Odorcich. I discussed the matter with Lloyd, suggesting that, as the holder of a new office, and the first officer elected from Canada, I, too, should have a corner office, if only for purposes of perception. Lloyd immediately agreed and we proceeded to create a suite of offices where the boardroom had been, with an office for Maxine Carter, my secretary, one for George Becker, my assistant, and one for me, along with a conference room.

Lloyd shook up whatever complacency there may have been among the headquarters' department heads by requesting their resignations so he could make his own appointments, either by reappointing the incumbent or by making a new appointment. Such an idea had never surfaced before, particularly when, as in this case, the successor was perceived to represent a continuation of the essential approaches and spirit of his predecessor. Nor did the idea come up again. I think that in this instance Lloyd was reflecting some of the tension between the regions and headquarters, particularly the idea that some senior staff felt themselves to be above the fray in a contest such as that between Lloyd and Sadlowski.

As we settled into our positions, circumstances were reasonably good, with most of our major industries active and our membership at a reasonably traditional level of about 1.25 million. This encouraged us to take an early focus on improving internal efficiencies and morale. One of the ideas was that each officer would drop in unannounced at a general membership meeting of a local union. Lloyd and I managed two such visits, one together and one separately, before we became too busy. To the best of my recollection, the others did not do it at all. The local Lloyd and I visited together was Local 1211 at Aliquippa, part of the Pittsburgh metropolitan area, then representing a thriving steel plant of approximately 12,000 members. The eyes of those at the meeting popped when Lloyd walked into the room, but the reception was warm, the questions friendly, and the local executive was quick to arrange a special meeting to follow immediately after the membership meeting adjourned. At this meeting the questions were more pointed, around such items as issues for next negotiations, contract ratification, and contracting out. Lloyd handled it well, demonstrating the confidence that comes from years of experience as a district director.

The local I visited alone was Local 1256 at Duquesne, south of Pittsburgh. It was a great experience, with lots of questions that included campaign issues and the past and the future. At the end, I was invited to join the beer-drinking group at a favourite watering hole. I accepted with alacrity and enthusiasm, always having believed that one needed to engage in open, informal conversations before one really understood the needs and concerns of our members.

One issue concerned me that night. After we had begun focusing on the move to the United States, Audrey and I discovered much to our shock that Greater Pittsburgh had no unified school structure and contained 132 separate municipalities, which, although there had been some mergers of public-school systems, still had 88 systems of varying quality. Toronto, with its single, unified system, left us quite unprepared for this situation. The education of our youngest child, Brian, was at stake. We asked everyone we met which municipalities had the best schools and were advised almost universally of the same four or five. Mt Lebanon, a suburb on the south side, was on every list. It was one of the older, somewhat more prestigious suburbs. Housing prices were reasonable and it was closest to downtown.

So we bought a home in Mt Lebanon. I knew the day would come when I would be asked where we would be living and hoped Mt

Lebanon would not be considered too luxurious. I became more convinced as we headed toward the bar in Duquesne that this would be the night the question was asked. I was right. In reply, I told the group what we had done, explained why, and then asked where they lived. I discovered that, almost to a person, the dozen or so people around the table lived in fancier homes and suburbs than us, and that they chose such places as a result of the same desire to have the best possible education for their children. It was a great relief to learn this about our new home.

Over the next few years, my personal mission, in addition to carrying out my officer responsibilities, was to become better acquainted with the American labour movement. Not only is the Canadian movement much smaller, but, having grown up in it, I knew most of the players personally and almost certainly knew who most of the rest were. I knew them from raising money from them, knew the heroes among them, and had watched their careers grow and flourish. This was in sharp contrast to my slight knowledge of union leaders in the United States, other than Steelworkers. Given the vastness of the country, there were many with whom I was acquainted but not in the way I was in Canada. I had a great deal of catching up to do. As one proceeds with programs and activities and faces crises, knowing the players on the other side of the table is critically important, but so is knowing the supporters on your own side of the table. It is helpful to have a sympathetic, friendly, understanding relationship with as many people around the movement as possible.

With the United States being one rather blank slate for me in the beginning, I devoted myself to filling it up as quickly as I could. I accepted speaking invitations whenever they arrived, attended conferences that came to my attention, and continued to expose myself to all useful information, education, or discussions I could find. Soon I developed a high regard for the labour movement in the United States for a least three major reasons. The first is that it operates in a much more hostile environment than any other labour movement in an advanced country, and even many labour movements in the developing world. This has required it to be extraordinarily tough, persistent, and imaginative if it is to survive. The second is the willingness of so many workers to strike for extraordinarily long periods of time when that is what must be done. For large numbers of workers, particularly in industries such as steel, copper, and metal mining where we represent many people, they are not living in a world of demonstrations and short strikes but in one of long and difficult struggles. Finally, in its daily trade-union work, the American movement is much more engaged in political and legislative activity than is the Canadian, despite the fact that the latter takes great pride in having its own political party. The reality is that the U.S. legislative system is without party discipline, and, therefore, with independent voting by each member of Congress, the need to lobby, inform, and attract Congress to our way of thinking requires a much more vigorous, continuing effort than is the case in Canada.

Given the controversy surrounding the election results, we introduced the idea of an outside committee to supervise the international election procedures and be the final body at which appeals of earlier decisions on complaints could be decided. We succeeded in winning the appropriate constitutional authority for such a move and appointed a distinguished committee, chaired by W. Willard Wirtz, who had been secretary of labor in the Lyndon Johnson administration, and also including Eric Springer, the leading civil rights lawyer in Pittsburgh, and David Lewis, the retired leader of the New Democratic Party in Canada.[1] The committee, known as the Campaign Conduct Administrative Committee (CCAC), has virtually eliminated Department of Labor complaints and investigations of our international elections. Its first chair, Wirtz, contended that to be seen to be fair, his committee needed not only the authority to enforce the prohibition against the use of outsider funds but also the power to enforce the prohibition against the use of union funds in elections. English relates:

> So the executive board gave the committee that authority and that worked out well because what it meant was that in the future if you had a local that published something in the newspaper that was deemed to be advancing the candidacy of one of the candidates, the CCAC could say now in your next issue you have to run something for the other side so that you offset the effect.
>
> Since they [the CCAC] were established in the late '70s, if they've had 500 cases, and I'm sure they've probably had [that many], 499 of them would have been cases that related to union funds and one at most related to outsider funds.

---

1 In recent years, Springer has become the chairman, replacing Wirtz. The member from Canada is now Thomas Berger, a former labour lawyer, former leader of the New Democratic Party in British Columbia, and former chief justice of the Supreme Court in that same province.

There were some complaints in the beginning from candidates who were seeking special consideration and failed to receive it. Then it all settled down, almost miraculously, as our people realized the committee was strong in its resolve but absolutely fair-minded in its decisions. I believe the success of the committee was the result of the quality of its membership.

I had hoped that the success of this endeavour would encourage the union to establish a similar outside group as the final authority on internal union discipline disputes, as the UAW has. I came to believe, however, that the CCAC example so permeated the union's executive board, and so encouraged those of its members who serve on the discipline committees to emulate the CCAC's fair-minded and objective approach, that there was no need for a new body. During my time in Pittsburgh, criticism of the union's discipline procedures was very rare.

Coincidental with the settling in of the McBride administration was an attempt to win bargaining rights at the Newport News shipyard in Virginia, then represented by an inadequate 'company/independent union.' This 17,000-employee yard was too important a prize to be ignored. Wages and benefits at Newport, and in the shipbuilding industry generally, were far too low in comparison with industry in general. Still, there was some hesitation in our group before the progressive, pro-activist camp carried the day. Lloyd authorized and participated in an all-out campaign, one that had moments of high drama. Because of threats that had been received, Lloyd was 'wired' while leading one rally. Nothing untoward happened, but it made for some tense moments.

The challenge of developing a fully effective local at Newport News had been great. Not only was the workforce large and about evenly split between blacks and whites, but Virginia was a 'right-to-work' state where mandatory dues collection was not allowed. In my view, we established too small a committee and far too limited a structure of union representatives, such as shop stewards and health and safety committee members, to lead and represent workers to maximum effect in such a large, diverse, and demanding operation. Further complicating union work was the fact the workers lived all over in a host of different communities, so many of the active organization people spent their spare time in the communities where they lived, rather than the one in which they worked. In the end, though, we carried the day. Despite continuing challenges, the local has steadily improved its effectiveness in terms of its solidarity, training, and education, and has become a critically important flagship in the labour movement in Virginia. The various district directors who have been responsible for its development have all worked conscientiously with local union officers to develop the local into the significant force for progress it has become.

Within the union, George Becker, now my assistant, and I began reviewing the work of the various departments that came under the secretary's office in Lloyd's new administration. One of the first issues we addressed was confusion in our membership mailing list, a subject about which we had heard many complaints during the election. Our list at this time was managed by our printer, Cornelius Printing of Indianapolis, since the list's primary use was for the mailing of *Steelabor*, our monthly paper. Cornelius Printing has a history in the labour movement worthy of its own book. In the early days, it was one of the few businesses that would work for the CIO, even when it was not paid immediately and, in some cases, never, because it supported the cause of working people. The company worked for us for many years – for two generations of the family – and made a contribution to the development of our union that can never be acknowledged adequately.

The crucial persons in the system were our local union financial secretaries, who were responsible for maintaining local unions' mailing/membership lists and forwarding address changes to the union. The financial secretaries in turn were dependent on members to notify them of changes of address. The whole system was a nightmare to try to improve, and I found it one of the most difficult, frustrating administrative tasks I ever faced. The first person on my complaint list was President Emeritus I.W. Abel, who had suddenly stopped receiving his *Steelabor*. We moved right away on his case and soon he was receiving two copies of *Steelabor* a month!

At the time the union had approximately 5,000 locals. Our basic structure called for each plant, office, or mine to have its own local union, and in the case of some of the larger steel plants there would be a number of locals based on some set of functional, geographical, or historical considerations. This was particularly true in Bethlehem Steel. Apart from some large locals where some of the officers would be full time, on leave of absence from their plant jobs for the duration of their term or terms, the other and the vast majority of financial secretaries were volunteers or received modest honoraria for their work. Most tried conscientiously to keep the mailing system up to date, but the number of moves people make and the slowness with which they advise of the change are high hurdles to overcome. There were so many opportunities for slippage, and not simply between the member and the financial secretary. For example, if George Becker was on a list and a new address was sent in, but the name used was G. Becker, the mailing list very likely would end up with two Beckers, George and G., where there had earlier been one.

We began by improving the forms. We made what were called check-proof lists available and these were exactly as the mailing list had them. This put the financial secretary into the heart of the system. She or he could check and change the addresses directly and send them in. We arranged to have a change form available in *Steelabor* itself that members could send directly. We urged the negotiation of lists with companies on the theory that workers would be most concerned that their employer had the correct address. That was not always so. In any case, over the years, the process of change continued. As a cost-saving measure, we reduced the number of *Steelabor* issues published each year, and, for similar reasons, we moved the mailing operation into a centralized effort managed by the AFL-CIO.

In the area of education, we had the newly purchased and renovated Linden Hall as an asset. The establishment of this educational centre had been a long-time goal of President Abel, Secretary-Treasurer Walter Burke, and Burke's administrative assistant, Larry Spitz. Its location on a 300-hectare site on a mostly sweeping bend in the Youghiogheny River – a tributary of the Monongahela, which in turn flows into Pittsburgh to join the Allegheny River in becoming the Ohio River – is magnificent. The site was first developed in the late 1800s by a Pennsylvania coal baron named Philip Cochran, who built a summer cottage on it. He died as a relatively young man in 1901, leaving a vast fortune to his wife, Sarah, and their son. She travelled extensively in the early 1900s and, while in England, conceived of building a Tudor mansion on the property, which was completed in 1913. After her death it went through various functions, including serving as a seminary and a casino, and eventually, in the hands of various owners over the years, a golf course was added. When purchased by the Steelworkers, it was being run as a golf course, and the former cottage, known as the White House, served as the clubhouse and restaurant and contained a fine old panelled bar. The Steelworkers discovered that the cost of using the mansion for classrooms, with respect to meeting safety and other regulations, would be quite extensive and would also interfere with the historical integrity of the building. As a result, it was restored as a showpiece and the White House was taken down, although some of its glass and panelling was preserved and used. A new conference centre including classrooms, a dining room, bedrooms, a kitchen, and a bar was built where the White House had been.

This was all accomplished at the end of a relatively prosperous time in the union. No one was anticipating the difficulties that lay ahead. One of my concerns regarding Linden Hall was that our membership was spread across two vast countries, and although many would have reasonable access to the centre, a great many would not. When I raised this concern with Abe, his reply, in the optimistic spirit of the times, was that we would build more centres. It is a remarkable property, back in the hills off the main roads yet less than sixty kilometres from Pittsburgh. Our members take great pride in the place, including showing off the mansion as an interesting example of rich living at the beginning of the 1900s, complete with a built-in vacuum system and a bowling alley in the basement.

Education programs have a noble history in the United Steelworkers. These programs have developed and evolved in an enormous number of directions, but they have always been very much at the core of the union, a tradition that Philip Murray, our founding president, introduced and that has been carried on enthusiastically ever since. Murray believed profoundly that knowledge brought strength and understanding and, indeed, was crucial to the union's success. One illustration of the early commitment of the union to education was when Clinton Golden, one of the first vice-presidents, was chosen by Harvard University to be the first head of the prestigious Harvard Trade Union program. In the United States, as well, the union made full use of the labour education centres in many of the state universities across the country. These centres had been established after the labour movement pointed out the magnificent services, such as county agents or consultants, provided by such schools to the agriculture sector. There was no such development in Canada as far as universities were concerned, but the union had the same commitment to education. The first education director in Canada was Howard Conquergood, who, as I've related, provided me the fellowship at the Y in Hamilton. His first initiative was weekend schools, mainly instructed by staff representatives, which were buttressed with summer schools.

The McBride team's ascension to office coincided with the retirement of George Butsika as education director and his replacement by John Carney, a long-time staff representative in the department. Butsika had been preceded by Fred Hoehler, one of the most outstanding labour educators in the United States, who, after a couple of years with the Steelworkers, was hired away by the AFL-CIO to establish the George Meany Center in Washington, D.C. His most important contributions, among many, were to bring coordinators from each district into the process and to establish a significant staff training program. Carney, our new director, was, as were his predecessors, a true labour intellectual. He had a particular interest in developing a leadership program for rank-and-file activists that would be substantive and challenging, as well as directing all the existing items on the curriculum. Carney fashioned a wonderful program that helped to produce many future leaders.

Public relations was another activity for which our office was responsible. When the McBride administration took over, our officers were not speaking to John Moody of the *Pittsburgh Post-Gazette*, the only labour reporter in town. One result of ignoring Moody was that he picked up all his information from the dissidents in town who received great publicity, enjoyed it, and were not shy about seeking more. We were all determined to change the situation and had proceeded a good distance in that direction during the campaign by having no prohibition on speaking with Moody. Our initial efforts, in addition to restoring relations with him, were devoted to making sure our story was told. We worked hard to ensure that all the officers, especially Lloyd, were available for press interviews, to seek opportunities to meet editorial boards, and to pursue and accept invitations for radio and TV appearances.

Moody, who started covering labour at the Associated Press in the mid-1950s before taking over the same beat for the *Post-Gazette*, has his own memories of conflicts with Steelworker officials. He says that Jim Griffin, who was assistant to former president Abel, wouldn't talk to him. One day, Moody was waiting outside a meeting when Griffin came out and the reporter asked what was going on. Griffin told the reporter it was no use telling him because he'd never get it right. 'I said, "Well you'll never know until you try,"' Moody recalls. 'He said, "Okay, here goes. U.S. Steel has welched on its promise."' The *Post-Gazette* ran the story prominently. Griffin, who was the former director of District 26 and had chaired negotiations with U.S. Steel through the early 1970s, responded by telling Moody, 'From this day on, you can call me any time.'

Moody had an interesting way of accommodating his contacts after a hard day at the bargaining table. One bargaining session he remembers was in Washington (he thinks it was with the coal workers). He had rented a room in the hotel near the suite where the talks were taking place and stocked it with a bottle of whisky. The union chiefs came out of the negotiating room and walked right into Moody's room, leaving the rest of the press outside. While they had a drink of his whisky, Moody recalls, 'I listened and then started to type. They weren't drinking a lot. They just wanted a place to get away from everybody. I got the story.'

Moody was still marching to his own drummer on his last day on the job. Jim McKay, now on the communications staff of the Steelworkers, was a *Post-Gazette* reporter when Moody retired. Moody had taken McKay under his wing and given him his book of contacts from three decades on the labour beat. It was invaluable because it contained the names and phone numbers of innumerable people, from the rank and file on the plant floor to the highest echelons of steel management and our union's 12th floor executive offices. McKay was with Moody when his mentor was leaving the *Post-Gazette* newsroom for the last time. It was a Friday and the business editor called out to Moody that he'd see him Monday. 'Moody said, "No, I'm retiring,"' recounts McKay. 'When the business editor asked him who was going to take over the labour beat, Moody pointed at me and said, "He is." The business editor shot back, "You can't pick your successor." Moody replied, "I just did." Then he walked out the door.'

At the time, we were much preoccupied with the great discrepancy between the amount of publicity accorded the UAW and the much lesser amount received by Steelworkers – a reflection of the industries in which the unions had developed. The UAW represents workers in an industry that markets to the general public, so it is very interested in the public's opinion. When bargaining is under way, the company people are just as interested in being seen in those newspaper pictures, ties undone, shirts rumpled, having been bargaining hard all night to achieve a settlement, as are the union leaders. On both sides of the table there is a shared interest in how they are perceived. The steel industry, on the other hand, does not sell to the general public but to other industries, so traditionally there had been much less interest in daily publicity, and much more in controlled, positive institutional information. Thus, the traditional slogan of company and union alike was that 'we don't bargain in the newspapers' and agreements to that effect were often sought at the beginning of negotiations. The union favoured this approach because its leaders often felt that the media were not very sympathetic to them. More and more of us, however, in all unions, had come to see the importance of the media in a new light, realizing that increasingly in today's society if you do not have an effective presence in the media, for many purposes you do not really exist.

In the area of public relations, one of the most interesting projects we carried out was to broadcast a session of our 1978 international convention, held in Atlantic City, New Jersey, via satellite to eighteen strategically located union halls around the United States and Canada, where significant numbers of our members could gather to listen. We arranged with locals at each location to prepare a social event for that evening, developed around what would be a special session of the convention on the subject of political action. When it came to the day of the broadcast, we amended the convention schedule to meet through lunch and then adjourn early in the afternoon. This was partly to give the delegates a break because they were coming back in the evening, but also because we needed the time to have all the gear set up and tested before broadcast time. The event came off magnificently. Many who watched the broadcast told me later that it gave them a totally different conception of the convention. It wasn't simply party time, as many imagined. Serious and important discussions took place.

Two things particularly impressed me. The first was that it appeared a totally different convention in that the delegates, knowing they were going to be on TV, had gone back to their rooms, showered, and dressed in their best clothes. The second notable feature was the quality of the speeches – I did not notice even one speaker at any microphone completely without notes, and many had written their speeches. The quality of the speeches was much higher than it would have been had we simply held the debate in the usual way. The event was a morale booster, particularly in the convention hall but noticeably, too, according to those who were keeping track, at locations that attracted a substantial turnout, which most did. We were all pleased. Bob Maurer, head of the public-relations firm in Washington that we principally used, and his people had done all the technical work. And, apart from about sixty seconds at the beginning when Lloyd's microphone did not work as it should have, it went off without a complication. Our daughter, Barbara, who had just graduated from the

Newhouse School of Communications with her MSc degree, came with us to the convention and was intrigued with the whole event.

It was all part of an effort to inspire, involve, and mobilize our members more effectively. The need to mobilize our membership was crucial, both as a very old-fashioned idea and as a very new one. This was so because we had just gone through a generation in which the labour movement was strong, relatively cohesive, and, despite the tearing away at the fabric of industrial relations by some outlaw firms, still accepted by most employers as legitimate and reasonably credible representatives of their employees. This acceptance was never complete, however, and strong challenges were coming, so our strategy was to emphasize membership education and mobilization, thereby making the union an informed and united force, without weak spots that employers could exploit.

As well, we paid much attention to the reporting of settlements, especially in the larger units. Back in my district, we had been moving to the preparation of attractive and detailed brochures covering all items in a settlement in a well-presented, clear, 'coffee table' document that could be studied by the membership. Concurrently, we had slowed the rush to decision making so members had plenty of time to digest a proposed settlement, both in terms of what it accomplished and in terms of what it did not. We introduced these same ideas in the international, and many colleagues contributed to their improvement, so that they came to be a permanent part of the process. It was in such ways that the various portfolios that Lloyd had assigned to the officers enabled each of us to exercise influence and learn what was happening far beyond the confines of our own department.

Apart from organizing and bargaining, the public-relations area was in many ways one of the most challenging and difficult. It was very sensitive, everyone had ideas about it, and every negative story was one the public-relations people should have 'done something about.' We had a number of good people, who each took a turn at running it, who each brought their own skill sets to the task. Ray Pasnick was good at newspaper-style products, Russ Gibbons was an excellent writer and historian, Gary Hubbard sought to cover all bases in as up-to-date a fashion as possible, and Frank Romano was accomplished with film and music. We also used outside firms to good effect. In the early years with Lloyd, Bob Maurer and his people were helpful, both with us and with the AFL-CIO.

Disappointingly, Lloyd's breakdown of roles was without specifics in terms of collective bargaining, except that Frank McKee, the treasurer, who had been chairman of the non-ferrous industry conference, continued in that capacity. Tradition established the president as the person in charge of 'big steel' negotiations, with the assistance of the other officers. How much or how little the other officers were involved very much depended on the leadership style and the practicalities involved from the vantage point of the president. Basic steel was the traditional core of the president's leadership contribution and of how his term in office would be judged.

One steel project that did come the way of the secretary's office early on was the development of an orientation program for new members, and more specifically orientation films, one for each company where these new members worked. This was a project close to my heart. It had always seemed to me that first impressions of the union gained by new employees were exceedingly important and often far too negative: too frequently, first contact was a notice of a dues deduction out of their paycheques. I had been impressed with the way I had joined the union when I went to work at John Inglis in Toronto. A compulsory check-off had not yet been negotiated, but a check-off arrangement had been made. The procedure was that the new employee's final interview, before the hiring procedure was complete, was with the local union president. The union chief welcomed the new hire, presented the person a copy of the contract and a brief rundown on the accomplishments of the union, answered questions, and requested that the new employee sign a voluntary check-off. Not many, if any, refused. Of course, a compulsory check-off is better, but there is no reason not to tie an orientation program to it.

The details of this project fell to Richard (Dick) Davis, an extraordinarily competent union professional who had come to us in the merger with District 50. My favourite comment about Dick was that there was no labour movement job he had not done, nor one that he hadn't done very well indeed. At this time, the major difficulty in preparing the films was that circumstances were changing for the worse at an almost unprecedented rate as whole sections of the U.S. steel industry collapsed. This collapse quickly spread to other parts of the manufacturing economy. Dealing with it became the major preoccupation for all of us, and in such circumstances there were few new employees for orientation.

The signs of difficulties ahead developed very quickly with a surge of imported steel from all over the world. The basic background to the problem was the expectation, supported by most experts, that there would be a shortage of steel in the world in the 1980s. This prediction rested on the assumption that the rate of growth of the world economy would continue at the pace of the early 1970s, so it would be difficult for steel capacity to keep up. The message the U.S. steel industry took was that the present state of technology could be continued for a while and modernization would take place at a measured pace. Assuming high levels of demand, this is a most profitable way to function. The change the prediction missed, however, was the energy crisis of 1979. The resulting high energy costs caused the rate of growth of the world economy to slow dramatically. Suddenly, instead of a shortage, there was excess capacity for steel production in the world of 200 or 300 million tons. The American market was the largest and most open market of them all and steel flooded into the United States. To make matters worse, the other advanced economies were resistant to imports. European countries talked about high import and export percentages, but their figures included trade within the European Economic Community (EEC, forerunner of the EU). Imports into the EEC from outside its borders were held at about 10 per cent of the market and in Japan at about 2 per cent. By contrast, in the United States, the numbers were in the high 20 per-cent to the low 30 per-cent range.

An additional factor was the more advanced technological state of the industry among the major competitors, mostly as a consequence of the bombing of industrial targets during the Second World War. Damaged or destroyed facilities in Europe and Japan were replaced with the latest technologies. Consider the percentage of steel that was continuously cast – the most efficient mode of production, since it eliminates the need for the repeated heating and cooling of the traditional method – in various countries. William R. Hogan of Fordham University has written that, from 1980 to 1990, the percentage of steel continuously cast increased from 39 to 90 per cent in the EEC, from 60 to 94 per cent in Japan, from 20 to 67 per cent in the United States, and from 39 to 84 per cent in the entire Western world. In the same ten-year period in the Third World, continuously cast steel (as a percentage of overall production) grew from 32 to 96 per cent in South Korea, from 34 to 58 per cent in Brazil, and from 56 to 96 per cent in Taiwan.[2]

---

2 William R. Hogan, *Capital Investment in Steel: A World Plan for the 1990s* (Lexington, Ky.: Lexington Books 1992).

The response of the industry to the changed environment was to shut down facilities, push for employment reduction in the continuing plants, and begin to pressure for concessions. Shockwaves ran through the steel towns whenever a facility closed. Steel plants are enormous, complex industrial behemoths. They have the appearance of such size and power and solidness that, in the late 1970s and early 1980s, one expected that they would be there forever. When they suddenly appeared to be as vulnerable as sandcastles rather than as formidable as medieval fortresses, people were shattered. As the crisis developed, people felt that somebody should do something more effective and felt let down by what many perceived to be the failure of all the major players – the industry, government, and the union. As for the union leadership, we devoted our attention to little else. Lloyd had a much clearer perception than the rest of us that we were really facing quite a different situation in the industry, rather than simply a serious, but nevertheless traditional, cyclical slowdown.

When the crisis hit, the industrial-relations processes in the industry adhered to the traditional structure of coordinated bargaining involving several companies, with U.S. Steel leading the way. Our members were at this time the highest-paid steelworkers in the world, largely as the result of something called the Experimental Negotiating Agreement (ENA), which was, in fact, a mechanism for using arbitration instead of the traditional right to strike. This idea had first been raised by U.S. Steel with President Abel in the 1969 negotiations, and Abel in turn had presented the idea to the International Executive Board (IEB), where it was hotly debated. I recall Larry discussing with me the reasons why we should not give up the right to strike and asking me to prepare a paper, based on our discussion, for his use in opposing the idea on the board. He did this and it contributed to the idea disappearing for the time being. However, J. Bruce Johnston, vice-president of U.S. Steel, and Abe saw value in the idea and both put some of their creative people to work on it. The 1969 proposal had been barebones, without criteria or structure. A new proposal began to emerge that picked up on the 3 per cent productivity guarantee that was then included in some contracts. There were some 'sacred cow' provisions that were not to be touched, such as management's rights, union security, cost of living, and local working conditions. Arbitration was to be conducted by a five-person board, one of whom would be appointed by each party and the remaining three by agreement of both parties.

The proposal was aimed at the marketing opportunity traditional strike-threat bargaining created for steel imports. At each round of bargaining, as the deadline approached and the possibility of an industry shutdown emerged, steel customers began shopping around for imports. Frequently, the results would be a settlement, no strike, stockpiles of steel, and layoffs until demand and supply sorted themselves out again. As one of our leaders once remarked, 'Our members are unemployed under the best agreement we ever had!'

ENA was in place for three agreements – 1973, 1977, and 1980. Under it, individual locals could strike their plant over 'local working conditions,' a defined term not including contract issues. With one exception involving incentive yields on the iron ore range, few locals chose to exercise this right. Its presence, however, did serve as an escape valve for strike pressures in a local and certainly increased the agreement's acceptability.

As the crisis became more severe, as more operations and plants shut down, the company cry for concessions grew more and more intense. The high wages produced by recent agreements, in concert with an inflationary economy, began to be described as excessive and non-competitive, and Johnston and his colleagues started talking about $40,000-a-year steelworkers. This number was readily picked up by the media and caused many in the middle class to become less sympathetic towards steelworkers than they should have been and to have less understanding of the implications for them than they should have had. The number was presented for the most part quite dishonestly, in that it was only rarely mentioned that it included the cost of all benefits – pensions, health care, vacations, Social Security, and so on – as well as wages. Most people in middle-class occupations were quite unaware of their benefit costs and simply related their salaries to the $40,000 figure, whereas, in those years particularly, the cost of their benefit packages would have added most significantly to an annual figure.

As outlined earlier, in the steel sector, bargaining was the union president's personal responsibility. He was to direct the 'top table' of the union side and, in protracted negotiations, could be involved for months at a time. Obviously, he was still required to pay attention to his overall responsibilities in the union, but his major commitment was to be to the negotiations. The idea was that this set the pace for everything else. In the early 1980s, there was a perception that the other officers were also significantly involved. In Lloyd's way of handling things, this was not the case. We were there for meetings, and certainly we were consulted, but we had little serious presence at the table. During his presidency there was only one issue in which I participated to a significant degree, although I used the secretarial responsibilities of my office to ensure that I was well informed about what was happening. In the 1980 negotiations I was intrigued to learn that Labor Management Participation Teams (LMPTs) – an early attempt at worker participation in the management of industrial enterprises – were being seriously proposed by the industry. My enthusiasm for the idea led me to invite myself into this part of the process. The value of LMPTs, however, was apparent to others too, and a number of people in the inner circle of Lloyd's advisers, in particular Sam Camens and Ed Ayoub, picked up on it immediately.

During the early 1980s, Lloyd's closest advisers in contract negotiations were: Bernie Kleiman, who, as general counsel, had been in the heart of steel bargaining from 1965 on and would continue to be for many years to come; Ed Ayoub, the union's chief economist; Carl Frankel, associate general counsel; Jim Smith, research director; Sam Camens, assistant to the president; and vice-president Joe Odorcich, who had been called to fill in for the president in the 1980 negotiations when Lloyd became ill. Joe was the only one of the officers who had had direct experience in basic steel negotiations in the United States. I had, of course, been involved in basic steel in Canada, but we did not have the same elaborate coordinating arrangement as existed in the United States. We did 'pattern' bargaining with the two largest companies, Stelco and Algoma, and negotiated with the rest to have them keep up as well as they could.

The contract at U.S. Steel did not expire until 1982, but the pressure was on for early bargaining. Johnston was a brilliant man, skilled in argument and debate, with a retentive and curious mind. My most frequent comment about him, and not infrequently to him, was that his talents and style would have been magnificent in a courtroom but were too abrasive and confrontational for effective industrial relations. His basic bargaining approach was always: 'If I give something I receive something in return.' This was first evident in a number of sessions Johnston held with Lloyd, principally focused on the state of the industry, as best it was understood by the industry. This resulted in the idea that a meeting of the union's executive board be held at Linden Hall and that Johnston and colleagues be invited to present their views concerning the state and the future of the industry. The meeting was a serious affair, with Johnston cross-examined vigorously by board members. The result was greater concern on the part of board members but

Harris Wofford campaigning for the Senate in 1991. We had a great
relationship with him. (Photo by Gary Hubbard, USWA)

no dramatic conversions to Johnston's catastrophic views of the future. There was in fact a great deal of internal tension around the analysis of exactly what kind of circumstances we were confronting. In the entire senior leadership group, Lloyd was virtually alone in the belief that we were facing an entirely new situation in steel, while all the rest of us were inclined to the view that this was another cyclical downturn in the traditional style of the industry, more serious than most but from which, in due course, we would recover. Lloyd, of course, turned out to be correct, although he did not share the totally calamitous opinions of Johnston. Ed Ayoub, our chief economist, represented a different mix of opinions but was also convinced that we were in the midst of a new and markedly different kind of crisis. He had some theories for an approach to compromise that never received the hearing they probably deserved.

This activity and consultation culminated in the coordinating companies sending a letter to the union in May 1982 proposing discussions and in Lloyd calling together a meeting of the Basic Steel Industry Conference (BSIC), consisting of local union presidents, for the purposes of reviewing the companies' letter and examining the situation in the industry. The session, however, quickly turned into a bargaining round. It was all too quick. The local union leadership did not have an opportunity to consider the situation adequately or become accustomed to Lloyd's direct and plain-spoken approach as their chief negotiator.

U.S. Steel had recently purchased Marathon Oil in a move that carried with it nothing but bad vibrations. From a worker's point of view, it was money that they had earned for the company and that should have been used for modernization and other competitive enhancements in steel, not to enter what seemed to be an alternative business, a way of saying goodbye to steel. It was a strategy that seemed patently self-serving for David M. Roderick and his colleagues in upper management, widely regarded as the bean counters who had taken over, people without real roots in or commitment to steel.

Johnston and George Moore, a retired industrial-relations executive from Bethlehem Steel whom Johnston had brought in to work with him, also simply asked for too much. They missed the boat with Lloyd. He was at least as concerned about the industry as any of the players from either side and significantly more than most. He was more than willing to make some concessions, believing them to be absolutely essential. He attempted a last-ditch offer, embodying a cost-of-living allowance (COLA) clause that depended on profit levels. This could have provided considerable savings to the companies, and, from their perspective, had the added advantage of making the union back away, of its own volition, from its commitment to the existing COLA clause. Nonetheless, the talks were probably the shortest on record. They began on 8 July and were concluded, without an agreement, on 12 July 1982.

Lloyd seemed to take it well, although I am certain he must have been terribly disappointed, not only in a personal sense of having failed the first time he was out there on his own, but also because there was simply no doubt about his concern about the state of the industry. Yet, as the general prospects of the industry continued to worsen, he didn't give up. The union's 1982 convention was coming along shortly and that would be the next significant gathering of the principal players on the union side of this drama. Lloyd was receiving a number of concerned communications from local union presidents and other activists in the basic steel locals. They were, for the most part, promoting reconsideration one way or another, wondering if the action had been somewhat hasty, concerned about whether enough time had been taken for examination of the situation and exploration of how it might be approached. Lloyd's thinking emerged at the convention when it was announced that he was holding a breakfast meeting of the basic steel delegates. It would include the members of the IEB, as well as the members of the BSIC who were present at the convention, for the purpose of discussing the situation in the industry. There was a different atmosphere at this meeting. The level of concern was clearly higher as the deterioration in the industry proceeded, with layoffs, shutdowns every day, and supplementary unemployment benefit (SUB) funds running out. Lloyd decided there was a consensus that favoured further conversations with the industry, and after the convention he moved in this direction.

The general situation in the industry had worsened considerably since the last attempt at bargaining. I remember that the union was besieged with crises all over the industry. A telling number has remained seared into my memory ever since: we lost 250,000 dues-paying members through layoffs or shutdowns in the four months from September through to the end of 1982. That number exceeded the total membership of a great many individual unions in the AFL-CIO. It was a disaster for the individual members, and also for the union and the steel communities. In terms of the latter, this was particularly true in northwest Indiana and Chicago, in the Mon valley, in Buffalo and Cleveland, in Ontario and California – everywhere there was a steel town.

Besides U.S. Steel, there was a great deal of other bargaining continuing at the same time – with other steel companies that were not part of the coordinated system, with companies across the manufacturing sector, and with many other industries and businesses where we were privileged to represent the employees. For example, as the turmoil in the steel industry increased, with a mix of concession demands, threatened and threatening bankruptcies, and plant shutdowns of various kinds, and with varying projections of what the final result might be, Wheeling-Pittsburgh became the scene for the development of some new initiatives. One was the idea of employee ownership.

This idea had first been raised in Youngstown, Ohio, when the major U.S. Steel facility there was closed. Lloyd had rejected the idea as impractical in that situation, but had also asked Jim Smith to explore the possibility of it being useful in some situations. Jim found his way to Lazard Freres, an investment bank, where the one Wall Street person known to all of us as a Democrat and a progressive, Felix Rohatyn, was a partner. It was under his aegis that Jim found Eugene 'Gene' Keilin and his associates, Ron Bloom and Josh Gotbaum, who were interested in employee ownership. Once word had spread that we were exploring this approach, everyone who saw their plant collapsing turned to the possibility of employee ownership. Clearly, however, many were beyond saving and would not have been viable had the workers been willing to work even for nothing. The route to opening the door to employee ownership meant facing a tough feasibility study as a starting point. If this hurdle could be overcome, then questions of financing had to be arranged. In some cases, the proposed enterprises were, in fact, spinoffs from larger corporations where the employees had received severance pay, portions of which were usually used as an investment from the workers. At the peak of our activity we would have eighteen employee-owned enterprises in the United States and one in Canada.

Wheeling-Pittsburgh was a pioneer in this area. In April 1982 Jim Smith and Paul Rusen had negotiated an agreement with Wheeling-Pittsburgh that reduced its employment costs to about the level the coordinating companies already were at, but also introduced for the first time what we came to call investment bargaining, the provision of stock to employees to compensate for any concessions they might be making. Jim was an enthusiastic promoter of Employee Stock Ownership Plans (ESOPs) in circumstances where an otherwise to be shuttered company was found to be viable enough to function as an employee-owned enterprise. I used to tease him that the long-suppressed entrepreneurial business genes in his heritage – members of his family were mostly very successful businessmen in Texas – were finding an outlet in helping create employee-owned enterprises that brought the two elements of his nature, business genes and a social conscience, together.

Wheeling-Pittsburgh had been in difficulty before the 1982 agreement, and its problems continued in the years that followed. In many ways, these problems had been compounded by the attempts of its CEO to lead the company into significant modernization efforts, the need for which was a constant refrain from the critics of the industry. But, regardless of whether you affix the blame to the company overreaching or to the times becoming dramatically worse, Wheeling-Pittsburgh became one of the first to face Chapter 11 proceedings, in 1985. For all these reasons, we proceeded very carefully. Paul Rusen was the chairman of our committee on the company. Jim Smith worked very closely with him and our top leadership group paid careful attention to what was going on. All our efforts were directed to having as much voice and influence as we could and making our case as carefully and thoroughly as we could.

The bankruptcy judge was unable to bring about an agreement on the terms of a new collective agreement, and the company rejected the existing agreement in the bankruptcy process. The judge then issued his decision as to what those terms should be, adopting each and every proposal advanced by the company. We were astounded at the severity of its terms, and at his utter failure to give any weight to the facts and arguments we had presented. What to do? We knew that, if we simply accepted this decision, its precedent-setting impact would be devastating. We also knew there was one thing we could do, although virtually nobody ever did it in the face of Chapter 11. We could strike. We decided that it was the only recourse that made any sense, and we struck. We also appealed the judge's decision on the grounds that he had used the wrong legal standard for rejecting the agreement. Though it came too late and had no practical effect on the ultimate settlement at Wheeling-Pittsburgh, our later legal victory in the Court of Appeals did impose a tougher set of requirements on companies seeking to reject labour contracts in the bankruptcy process, thereby establishing a valuable precedent.

Our actions had an impact all right. One member of the Wheeling-Pittsburgh board, the CEO of Iron City Brewing, immediately commented to the effect that the conflict showed how ridiculous these union people were, striking in the face of Chapter 11. A day or so later, he was back in the newspaper complaining about the boycott we had organized. I have always wished in my heart of hearts that we could make such a claim but the simple truth was that the boycott organized itself. In any event, everything was ultimately resolved. The ultimate fallout from the strike was the resignation of Dennis Carney, the CEO, and another board member, the head of Iron City Brewing, and the company survived to face many more crises in its future.

One of the basic elements in our approach to the continuing crisis in the steel industry was to attempt to preserve as much capacity as possible, while struggling with the overall need to maintain and improve manufacturing capacity in the economy in general. During October 1982, the coordinating companies put a new proposal together, seeking much deeper cuts than they had before. They asked for a $5-wage cut, much deeper than Lloyd had expected, and said that there would be money for the unemployed and that they would offer a profit-sharing plan if the union would give up the cost-of-living allowance. Lloyd's response was that he would not give up on the COLA, but he did propose a link to profit sharing if some workable system could be developed.

In November that year, Lloyd, on behalf of the union, took the unprecedented step of offering a wage cut of $1.50 an hour, which, with compounding, saved the companies $2.25, along with some benefit cuts that in total amounted to a saving of $3.43. The proposal was rejected by the companies and it led to a serious breach between Lloyd and Ed Ayoub. Although Ed in his own studies had projected the serious circumstances facing the industry and had concluded that the companies needed some help, he believed the cut Lloyd had proposed to be excessive. His view was that some combination of a smaller cut with productivity improvements would make for a less destructive approach and would maintain union solidarity to a much greater degree.

Johnston's response was that the companies would grant profit sharing only with a $5-cut, and that they would settle for a $3-cut only if both profit sharing and COLA were dropped from the proposal. Meanwhile, Ed and Jim were working on a plan to ensure that the companies could not avoid profit sharing by inflating costs and understating profits. Lloyd had called a BSIC for 16 November. There were a number of issues involved as well as the COLA-profit-sharing proposal. The union had offered to give up two paid holidays and to reduce Sunday premium pay from time and one-half to time and one-quarter. The industry wanted more, particularly the cancellation of the extended vacation plan (EV) that provided thirteen weeks of paid vacation every five years for the top half of the seniority list in each plant. This was a wonderful but contentious benefit. The industry complained about having to defend it when asking for support from government. Some of our people criticized it as opening the door to moonlighting and other bad practices. My own private survey over the years led me to conclude that this sabbatical for workers was a special benefit, used to great advantage by most of those eligible and greatly improving their quality of life. In any case, the union offered to give up the EV if the industry would give back something of equal value. Johnston offered to give back a COLA payment of nine cents due in November that the union had agreed to defer for the EV. Lloyd said he would accept the COLA payment, plus the two holidays he had previously given up. It was settled by the union retaining COLA and one holiday and giving up the EV.

Deadline bargaining of this type is surrounded by an enormous number of details that need to be checked out, and in many cases these details require additional negotiations. So it was in this case, especially with regard to the creation of a new mixed profit-sharing and COLA arrangement. Ed Ayoub and Jim Smith began a process of checking out precisely the results of applying the new plan to the different companies and could hardly believe what they found. They discovered that, had the plan been in effect from 1978 to 1981, Armco Steel would have had to pay $9.17 per-hour profit-sharing bonuses, the other companies much less, ranging down to Bethlehem at $0.42 and U.S. Steel $0.33.

Despite this startling development, Lloyd proceeded with the BSIC meeting where the settlement was up for ratification. As it happened, Ed and Jim were still struggling to find ways to amend the new approach so it would produce a fairer result when the vote was taken. Without any examination at all of its terms, the agreement was rejected.

This outcome was the result of several factors, the most important being the issue of concessions. There was a strong dissident group in the union so opposed to the companies and the union leadership that they could not resist taking a strong, anti-concession stand. There were substantial historic reasons for taking such a stand, among them the fact that one of the most consistent characteristics of the industry was its cyclical nature. There was enormous confusion everywhere about the future of the industry. People still found it hard to accept that these massive mills were shutting down – they looked like they should be there forever. Often workers would cling to the belief that it would not happen to their plant, even as it was happening all around them. There were those who felt that government would not simply stand by and let this industry disappear.

There were also important issues related to the agreement, the most important having to do with what were called 'List 3' plants. These were plants owned by the companies but not in the basic steel industry itself. Instead, they were fabricating plants such as for structural steel operations. The union's traditional position was that they should all be under the basic steel agreement. Many of them, however, competed with smaller companies that did not have agreements that matched the wages or benefits contained in basic steel. As the union remained rigid in its stance over the years, the companies gradually but steadily closed the plants. In the 1982 negotiations, it had been agreed that these plants would be severed from the basic steel agreement so their circumstances could be addressed more specifically, thereby creating another group determined to vote down the agreement.

The proposed agreement also included an arrangement to restore some money for unemployed members by means of deductions from the employed. Not many objections to this were direct complaints about sacrificing to support those in need, but there were objections to various details of the plan, many of which were undoubtedly covers for the more selfish motives.

In my opinion, the whole process was an example of the difficulties of attempting the ratification of complex, multifaceted, and multilayered agreements in impossibly short meetings without time for details to be explained, discussed, and queried. For some years, as noted above, I had been working in the direction of more detailed, better-looking, and more clearly presented documentation of what the agreement contained, more time for consideration by the members, arrangements for questions – more meetings, hot lines, Q & A tables, and so on. But these efforts had not yet come to fruition.

The failure of this Round Two to achieve a settlement halted the effort to do anything before the normal bargaining dates. The agreement was to be renewed in 1983, with the normal bargaining schedule commencing in May. There was a good deal of speculation about what was to be done. Considerable bargaining was going on among the smaller companies. There was restlessness among members of the coordinating group, with a number of companies talking on the side with union leaders about abandoning the coordinating approach and the leadership of U.S Steel.

The union, of course, was not only involved in bargaining crises, large and small, but was also becoming more and more challenged by the general economic circumstances, in particular by the decline of manufacturing in the United States and the related decline in private-sector union membership and, therefore, in union strength in the economy and the political process. With respect to U.S. Steel in particular, fundamental strategic differences concerning the future of the steel industry were immediately evident. The company's idea was to reduce dramatically the size of the industry in the United States by shutting down plants and companies in difficulty, and selling the equipment to – and making processing arrangements with – other countries. For example, it would purchase slabs from British Steel's Ravenscraig plant in Scotland. The union's approach was to help as much as of the industry as possible to survive and provide the basis for a manufacturing base in a more rationally run U.S. economy.

During that winter, before the negotiations and their attendant excitement began again, we had one of our rare but very special family vacations, this time skiing in the mountains in Colorado with Audrey's sister and her family from Iowa. Before I left, Lloyd took me aside one day to tell me that he intended to retire early and would be recommending me as his successor. The implication and context of the conversation were that he wanted to finish up the bargaining and have that out of the way for me. I cannot say that I was totally surprised, but neither was I of the view that he would, in any circumstance, retiring early or not, necessarily recommend me. We had never discussed, through all the politics of putting the McBride team together, what might or would or could happen next. Naturally, I thanked him for the confidence he was showing in me for a position of such responsibility and importance. I assured him that, if he changed his mind, I would quite understand. I raised the Canadian question with him but, as in all things, he had a very straightforward view. He teased Canadians about our quickness in being on our feet to talk at conferences and meetings, but admired the union work we did, felt that our union was stronger for being in the two countries, and had no qualms about there being differences from time to time in view of national considerations. He felt we should always try to have a united position but not to the extent that we failed to represent the needs and views of our members in each country – even if they might be, from time to time, on different sides of an issue.

Of course, this was all cast in a framework of total confidentiality, not to be shared with anyone until the time came. I told my wife about it on a chair lift when skiing, a fairly confidential location, and as far as I know Lloyd did not tell anyone except possibly his wife, Dolores. In any case, during subsequent political events, after Lloyd had passed away, no one came forward and said that he had so advised them.

Meanwhile, the mood of our members had changed considerably as the industrial devastation continued. There were many sober reflections following the rejection in Round 2. As Lloyd heard from more and more local union leaders, he became anxious to begin Round 3. It is difficult to exaggerate the depth and impact of the crisis in steel and of the general crisis in manufacturing, although many secondary industries appeared to be enjoying more normal circumstances. Steel was bearing the brunt of the impact. These giant plants, with their massive machinery and their long history of leadership in the economy, were threatened with becoming rusting hulks. Thousands of families whose lives appeared secure, who planned confidently for their children's future, were thrown onto the industrial scrapheap. It was a heartbreaking circumstance, compounded by the emergence of the term 'rust belt' to denote the industrial heartland – with its implications of uselessness, of being yesterday's story, and of being the problem, not the solution. All of this was dramatically and depressingly reinforced when skilled steelworkers found themselves in a labour market in which their skills had no value.

We took one approach that was quite different from anything tried earlier. In most turndowns over the years, in lesser versions of these same circumstances, it was common for unemployed groups to attempt to represent the needs of those affected. Normally, a somewhat hostile relationship would develop between such groups, who often had in their leadership persons of radical persuasion, and the union, which insisted that representing these members was its responsibility. We decided to set all that aside, to develop a working relationship with these groups, to help fund them and support them. Two fine groups emerged in the Pittsburgh area, the Mon Valley Unemployed Committee, led by Barney Oursler and Paul Lodico, and the Steel Valley Authority, led by Tom Croft and Bishop Malone.

One area of activity in which the unemployed group and the union worked well together was in the challenging field of retraining. In terms of retraining needs, and considering how many economists and employment specialists insist that this represents the way to cope with change, the American response has been the least adequate among advanced countries. We did have one brighter light than the rest and this was the Trade Adjustment Assistance Act, ensuring that people were aware of their rights and received their appropriate benefits. In protecting this program from its opponents, the Mon Valley Unemployed Committee and the union did especially good work together.

The union's own staff was also directly affected by the difficulties of the times. The months of shutdown and layoffs obviously had a devastating impact on everybody and everything, including the union's income. Frank McKee, in his capacity as treasurer, concluded that there was no way to avoid laying off staff, something that had never happened in the history of the union. He recommended it to Lloyd, who called an officers' meeting at which he recommended laying off 200 people.

Fortunately, our members had the benefit of a pension window in 1983. A total of 162 employees retired under this 1983 window, which provided a mutual-consent pension supplement. This was a monthly amount added to the regular pension of the participant and was payable until the participant became entitled to regular, unreduced Social Security, Canada Pension Plan, or Quebec Pension Plan benefits. Those deciding to retire under the 1983 pension window enabled us to reduce the number of layoffs from the original number of 200 to fewer than 100. (A second window, in 1987, would be offered at the end of 1986 to employees who had thirty years of service regardless of their age, or those with at least twenty years of service and whose years of service and age totalled at least seventy-five. There were 291 employees who retired under this window.)

As secretary, I decided that the best contribution my office could make to the procedure was to ensure that it was carried out in a scrupulously fair and defensible way, consistent with the collective agreements under which the staff worked. This we did, and it was well that we did, because the reaction to the layoff, which we knew would be serious, was much more virulent in a number of quarters than we had anticipated. I am pleased that we decided to administer the procedure to ensure that it was done fairly and efficiently, but the decision had the unintended consequence of improperly identifying us, the secretary's office, as somehow the source of this action. This, in turn, had the ironic result that a number of those who were most upset and critical, and supported Frank in the subsequent political contest between the two of us, didn't realize that he was the one who proposed the layoff. I don't wish to make anything of this, other than to point to it as one of those strange twists that can happen.

The extreme resentment of some of those affected was difficult to understand. There were a few who made it almost a personal vendetta against George and me. I never found, at least to my satisfaction, one overwhelming reason that outstripped all others. Of course, one important reason was the expectation that this 'would never happen' in the union. It was an enormous shock when it did, and even the more moderate view that it would never happen quickly became it 'should never happen.' The notion that we should have found some more ingenious solution was prevalent, as was the sentiment that we should not stoop to the level of the companies but rather use our own situation to demonstrate a better way. Of course, there were some allegations that George and I were doing this to further our own political ambitions, which was certainly not the case. At any rate, we set out to find as many stopgap jobs for the laid-off people as we could. There was, of course, great variance in what different people would do. I remember Gerry Fernandez willingly taking on a position with the AFL-CIO in Latin America. Gerry plunged right in, took his family with him, and turned it all into an adventure and an experience that has served him well in the years since. We found a number of inspector jobs in Ohio. I remember that one person took a job as a liquor store manager. All in all, I felt we were able to develop a helpful substitute employment program.

When preparations began for Round 3 of bargaining, the political atmosphere was as discouraging as the economic one. The administration of Ronald Reagan, facing re-election in 1984, was constantly preaching that the information, hi-tech highway was the route on which to proceed and demonstrated little concern about the 'rust belt.' The difficulty in directing the political leadership's attention, indeed anyone's attention, to the decline of the manufacturing sector came as something of a shock to me. In Canada, as in all steel-producing countries in the world other than the United States, the threat of closing a steel mill was a national crisis. By the early 1980s, the Sydney Steel mill on Cape Breton Island in Nova Scotia had been saved many times by financial input of one kind or another and ultimately by government ownership. It was simply considered a disaster anywhere in the country for a steel mill to be lost.

Before the negotiations began and the preliminary BSIC convened at the beginning of February 1983, Lloyd suffered a spell of heart trouble and after a couple of days at home was sent to the hospital for an extended time. When the conference convened, Odorcich was in the chair. This had been the result of a somewhat sensitive exercise of political problem solving, although in fact the path forward was clear and obvious. Odorcich had filled in before and had been sitting in with Lloyd at the top table, just in case there was such an emergency. Underneath this, however, there were competing ideas about the constitutional pecking order of the officers.

Odorcich's view was that the order should be the same as that specified in the constitution for local unions – namely, president, vice-president, and so on. In fact, the provision in that case fills vacancies in the office of president by the automatic progression of the vice-president. The other and only way the constitution has been interpreted and practised over the years was to apply the order in which the officers are listed in the constitution, specifically, president, secretary, treasurer, vice-president (administration), and vice-president (human affairs). There is no doubt that Frank or I would have been delighted to take over the bargaining, or, for that matter, that Leon Lynch would have been as well. He had served as an officer significantly longer than any of us, but we all knew, whatever our ambitions, that had any of us made an issue of this it would have been enormously divisive in a situation that cried out for unity. We agreed in quick time that Odorcich should handle it, and that we would all help in whatever ways we could.

Things moved along much better in this bargaining. Although the record shows Rounds 1 and 2 as failures, I think that, given the complexities, they might more realistically be viewed as scouting missions – in the sense of digging behind the superficial in order to learn the principal issues on both sides to see if an agreement can be fashioned. The union had done some work on questionnaires. Jim Brown, president of Local 1064, a major basic local, had done likewise within his local union and then brought the results in for our negotiators to study. This activity resulted in more and better preparation. Research revealed that the items of greatest concern were contracting out, early retirement incentives, investment of savings from concessions in steel plant modernization, protection of pensions, and medical and hospital benefits. COLA was the key issue. There is no doubt that the company negotiators wanted to be rid of or at least emasculate the COLA. In this regard, they kept working at the COLA-profit-sharing mix that Lloyd had earlier proposed; however, the entire union team, including Lloyd, had now decided against the blended plan. In the end, flexibility was attained by establishing streams for COLA in the early years of the new agreement and then bringing the full COLA principle back into play by the end of the agreement.

A settlement was reached the night before the 1 March deadline. Of course, it contained many items beyond the COLA; probably the most popular items were a retirement-incentive plan and the restoring of finances for the SUB. The BSIC met for part of one evening, used the rest of the evening to discuss the proposal with their local leaders back home, met for a couple of more hours the next morning, and then voted 169 to 63 in favour of the settlement.

In retrospect, although there were three distinct rounds of bargaining, they really all merged into one exercise as the industry and the union struggled to come to grips with the new realities we were facing and trying desperately to understand. It was for me, in terms of what we were to face in the years ahead, a great advantage. It enabled me to be an observer through this process, but also to be in touch with it almost where I chose, to come to know many of the local union movers and shakers by watching them and through the many conversation opportunities that a complex bargaining procedure provides. Our headless officer group worked quite well as Odorcich led the bargaining and pushed a little into some other affairs of the union, testing the presidential waters, one might say. Nobody forced the issue from either direction. Although Lloyd was not present in person, his influence was very much in evidence, because everyone knew what his reaction would be if we ended up making a political mess of things during his absence. His willingness to head right into difficult situations had been just as evident internally as externally. We knew he expected the same from us.

Lloyd returned to work in the spring of 1983, after a heart operation following his February illness. He worked very hard that summer but by late September returned to hospital for tests and in October had multiple bypass surgery. He was recovering well as the fall moved along. Audrey and I visited him one evening in November. He was in great spirits, talked about the walking exercises he was doing around the apartment, teased us in his usual way, and gave Audrey a great bear hug when we left. In the morning we received a phone call that he had died during the night, on 6 November.

I was haunted for a long time by the memory of Lloyd's early responses to those of us who were encouraging him to run for the presidency. He often said that we were taking away his retirement and it would seem that we did. I take comfort from the fact that we cannot be absolutely certain of that, or whether his heart might have given up the same way during retirement. I also take comfort from my belief that he came to enjoy the presidency of the union much more than he had expected, not the steel crisis at the end, but during the initial years of his presidency. He found his feet quickly and felt comfortable in the leadership roles in which he was involved, including in our union, the AFL-CIO, in dealing with the White House when Jimmy Carter was president, and as a leading figure in labour's relations with the Democratic Party.

While I had worked conscientiously to be a responsible and useful officer, it was not an arrangement that necessarily meant agreement in all cases. Lloyd and I certainly shared a commitment to decent, democratic trade unionism and progressive politics, but within that broad framework our different life experiences certainly meant that there were differences about various programs, approaches, priorities, strategies, and matters of that sort. Yet there was a great deal of agreement as well, increasingly so as we worked together, came to know each other better, and shared the same challenges. Sometimes we were in agreement, sometimes we were not, but he was the president.

Lloyd liked written proposals. From the international secretary's office, George and I provided him with a fairly constant stream about items large and small, within the framework of the departments for which we were responsible and beyond. He was a quick and sharp study. It became a challenge for us to see if we could submit a proposal with which he didn't find something wrong or questionable, or less comprehensive or accurate than it should have been. I don't recall that we ever succeeded. He was an intelligent man, courageous, straightforward, and honest, some would say almost to a fault.

But the McBride era was now over. His death brought about the most intense personal political exercise in which I have ever been involved.

10

ASSUMING THE PRESIDENCY

One could feel the politics in the air. The administrative structure Lloyd had established, with each officer being responsible for certain functions and departments, reinforced by three of us – Joe Odorcich, Frank McKee, and I – being active in the pursuit of the presidency, provided both a base of support and a great deal of space for politics. It meant that there was immediately an embryonic campaign organization in place.

An officers' meeting made some immediate decisions. The constitution was clear. Lloyd had died a short time before the vacancy of an unexpired term could be filled by board appointment, so there would have to be a vote by the board members. It was agreed that a board meeting for that purpose would be held on 17 November 1983 and that out of respect for Lloyd there would be no campaigning until the funeral was over. But on the 17th we would vote. On the advice of our legal department, the position would be known as temporary acting president and the board member elected would not have to resign his regular position. A referendum of the full membership would be held in March of the following year to complete the one year then still remaining in Lloyd's term.

McKee lined up quickly with Odorcich for this vote and I think they believed they had it wrapped up. Odorcich seemed to feel a certain entitlement because he was older, had been on the board longer, and had looked after recent bargaining, besides holding all the other assumptions I have mentioned in terms of his view of the vice-presidency. I certainly considered him one of the better members of the board from the time he took over District 15; he had brought more unity and effectiveness into the district than it had known for years. I knew McKee longer and better, and we had always been friends, active in the Non-ferrous Conference where, during President Abel's last term and in the midst of our struggles with Mine Mill and the subsequent merger with them, he had been the vice-chairman to John E. Johns and I had been the secretary. We were also the two board members most active in support of César Chávez and the Farmworkers' grape boycott, and knew each other through that connection.

What was different were the new and challenging circumstances we were facing. These included the dramatic decline of the industry, the emerging challenge of globalization combined with the corporate agenda of international business, and the intensity of the additional pressures on and challenges to the American labour movement that resulted. In this context, I believed that Odorcich and McKee, though decent, loyal, and committed trade unionists, were not nearly sensitive enough to the new realities. Nor were they involved in particularly deep analysis about what the union's role, strategies, and programs should be in order to represent its members in the changing economic environment.

McKee was simply in denial. First of all, on the concessions question, he simply said no. I also discovered later that, in terms of strategic analysis, he examined the alternative of a corporate-campaign approach to the struggle against Phelps Dodge, an Arizona-based copper mining company that waged a union-busting campaign during a bitter 1983–6 miners' strike, and rejected it, resulting in a terrible defeat for the union. I and others increasingly favoured the corporate-campaign model, which targeted the financial interests that owned a given company and invested in it. But McKee would have none of it. His thinking, it seemed to me, was stuck in the past, though he had been an excellent leader under earlier circumstances. He had not become fully conversant with or thought his way through the intense, non-traditional efforts and innovations that the challenges of the time required. To meet the new and threatening circumstances, we needed a more effective political voice and would have to nurture a membership that understood its role in the continuing development of our union and our labour movement.

Everyone accused everyone else of breaking the no-politics understanding during the funeral. Personally, I think that everyone behaved well. It was impossible for there to be no discussions in such a dramatic situation and any words, however innocuous, when overheard by the other side, were reported as political. Odorcich and McKee thought that, with their combination, they were well in the lead, and they probably were a little. They were much more part of the 'old boy' network in the union than I, and both had wide experience in the United States, where the bulk of the votes were for a long time. But what was not on their radar was the impact of the new circumstances on members of the board and their increasing concern about what the future might hold. Lloyd had appointed me chairman of a committee on the future direction of the union, which was a committee of the whole board, open to any who wished to attend. In addition, I was involved in meetings held by AFL-CIO Secretary-Treasurer Tom Donahue. For the most part, these sessions focused on the future and were supplementary to the work of the evolution of work committee, which Donahue also chaired. This was the mechanism for change in the federation. I was much involved and interested in all the ideas that were floating around and members of the board knew it.

Fortunately, too, from my point of view, Odorcich and McKee's overconfidence meant that they did not count carefully enough until the night before the board was to vote and only then did they realize that, while their number of votes was close to what was required to win, they remained a bit short. There were three directors whom they quite correctly viewed as critical and with whom they discovered they were in difficulty the day before the meeting. The first was Paul Rusen, the director in West Virginia, who in fact had told them at the beginning that he was in their camp. However, Rusen also appreciated, as much or more than anyone else on the board, the need for new ideas. As already recounted, he and Jim Smith had done some interesting bargaining at Wheeling-Pittsburgh in terms of worker participation and investment bargaining, and he became persuaded that if there was to be change it would come through my presidency much more than through that of Odorcich. He advised Odorcich and McKee of his change of mind on 16 November.

The others Odorcich and McKee focused on were Thermon Phillips from Alabama and Harry Lester from Michigan. But it was to no avail. Harry was solidly in my camp. Whenever someone raised the nationality issue with him, he told them: 'You're not voting for a flag. These Canadian Steelworkers are just as good Steelworkers as Americans. We're supposed to build harmony [within the union], not tear it down.' A McKee supporter within the union in Michigan went to all the meetings in the district and Harry was there to refute what he said and get my message across. It came to a head at a meeting in Bay City, when a bodyguard for the other side told Harry he wasn't welcome at an impromptu press conference that had been called. When Harry responded that he had rented the hall and had every right to be there, the bodyguard told him he had a black belt in karate. Harry replied that he did too. The bodyguard backed off and that was the end of the confrontation.

What they did not know about Harry was that he and I had bonded long before, when I was director of District 6 and he was the assistant to Chuck Younglove, the director of District 26. Harry looked after their golf tournament every year, which raised money for the Kidney Foundation. One year they held it in Windsor and were having difficulty arranging for beverages, and I helped them out. More to the point, Harry would find me working in the office in the evening and answering the phones and we discovered we shared much in our feelings about the union and its members and the privilege it was to be involved. When Odorcich and McKee began bugging him on the phone the night before the vote, he took it off the hook, rolled over, and went to sleep. Ultimately, in the referendum that followed the board vote, he would deliver his district to me by a large majority.

Phillips was a different case. Most of his friends and colleagues wanted to support Odorcich. But Phillips was also concerned about the future. He did not disagree with his friends easily, but he wouldn't back away from doing so if he thought it necessary. In short, he was courageous. This was a man whose children attended integrated public schools throughout the civil rights crisis in the South. On the night before the vote, he, too, received incessant phone calls from Odorcich and McKee. At five the next morning, we all went to breakfast so that Phillips would not have to struggle with Odorcich and McKee on the phone any longer.

The executive board meeting unfolded that morning as was expected. I won by four votes. Odorcich was bitterly disappointed and felt that the board had once more let him down. For my part, I was elated and sobered at the same time – the opportunity to lead this great union was overwhelming in every way. To be able to function as the head of one of the most effective progressive organizations on the continent delivered a level of excitement I had never experienced before, but, likewise, a level of responsibility that I never felt before either. To sit in the chair where only four other people had sat before me, under all of whom I had served and each of whom I considered giants in their time, was unbelievable. To be the first leader from Canada to do so highlighted the contrasting emotions I felt: exhilaration at the prospect of leading this great union and apprehension concerning all that was entailed.

Yet there was not much time for celebration and, in any case, what we had won was a leg up towards achieving incumbency in the referendum election that the board had decided would be held on 29 March 1984. My first concern was the fact that the union had in many ways, as a result of Lloyd's illness, been leaderless and left to its own devices for some weeks. Fortunately, ours is an extremely decentralized organization, a characteristic that stood it in good stead. At the same time, I felt that the exceedingly difficult circumstances we faced cried out for a strong hand and a strong voice.

A board meeting was scheduled in Washington in December. This provided an opportunity for a hold-the-line policy statement, stating as firmly as possible that there would be no concessions beyond those in the 1983 agreement. The resolution read in part: 'If our union were to permit local level wage or benefit concessions, our wage and benefit programs would almost immediately become a shambles. Local after local would be whipsawed by threats of plant closing, diversion of orders from one plant to another, false promises and many other pressure tactics.' It was at this meeting, too, that I first began talking about the strategic opportunities and challenges that we and the companies faced. Our policy position was as follows: it was the union's preference to work constructively in collective bargaining and in all the places where our needs and policies intersected with those of the company in the best interests of the company's success. One of my favourite collective-bargaining observations for years had been that, far from being hostile to the company's interest, what almost every employee wanted most was to work for a successful company. And what almost all employees resented most was being treated like ciphers, with no recognition of their importance to the success of the enterprise beyond their job description.

Our statement, however, also made it clear that, if an employer rejected the idea of creative, problem-solving, participatory collective relations, and chose to use the difficult economic circumstances of the day as a reason for running over us, trampling and destroying labour rights whenever they could, they were in for the battle of their lives. We assured them that not only did we remember all the lessons learned from traditional, adversarial collective bargaining, but we would seek out as many sources of bargaining leverage as we could imagine.

There was, naturally, a great deal to do: the crisis in steel and the manufacturing industry didn't stop because we were changing leaders. As I've said, I am personally an enthusiastic supporter of the referendum system, but it does crowd in on one when, at the same time, you must deal with all of the administrative and leadership issues that are urgent matters in any administration, but particularly in a new one. One of the immediate and compelling issues to be dealt with was a new agreement that director Thermon Phillips had reached with U.S. Steel. If approved by the executive board, this agreement would reopen the mill in Birmingham, Alabama, that had been closed for a couple of years. The question was whether the agreement met the guidelines. We concluded that it did.

Another matter was that, although elected president, I remained international secretary as well. I wanted Ed Ball, our director in Texas, to run as a member of our ticket. The issue was whether to bring him up to Pittsburgh immediately on some kind of temporary assignment. We decided that it was best that he stay in his district throughout the election and through to the end of McKee's term as treasurer, and that we make no attempt to have McKee and Odorich resign before the completion of their terms.

As a result of my new position, I now had the executive assistant to the president, Harry Guenther, working with me. Guenther was one of the longest-serving persons in headquarters, if not the longest. He had done many jobs over the years, knew everybody, and was enormously helpful. Meanwhile, George Becker, who had been my assistant, was thoroughly qualified to carry on the work of the secretary's office, which he did with the occasional consultation with me.

The referendum election was an immediate preoccupation. It came up quickly, eight weeks after the beginning of the year, and it was an enormous task. It wasn't that every local of the 7,000-plus units spread across Canada and the United States expected a visit, but in such a contest you were expected to do a good job of campaigning, of making yourself and your opinions known. Fundamentally, this is what I find so appealing about the referendum system. When there is enough concern among the members that two or more individuals are nominated for one of these leadership positions, this system requires that the candidates move around among the membership to become acquainted and that they present themselves, outlining their experience, their ideas, and their vision for the future. They have to foster as broad and well-informed discussions about these issues as they can. I welcomed the opportunity enthusiastically, enjoyed it immensely, and found it endlessly interesting, challenging, and inspiring. Once again I was impressed with the quality of our union and the breadth of our Steelworker 'culture.' In almost every corner of two vast countries, despite the variety of languages, and the different ways of speaking the same languages in many cases, it was everywhere evident that our members shared a powerful common commitment to the values of democratic trade unionism as represented by the Steelworkers.

Much of the campaign effort had to fit in around the work of the union. I did take some vacation time and some straight leave time for full-time campaigning, there being no other way to cover the territory and the needs of the situation. The other side switched candidates, with McKee replacing Odorcich. The latter could not run under the existing provisions of the constitution because he was too old. It was the interim position he wanted and he viewed his failure as a slap in the face from the board. He was very bitter about this and, most unfortunately and in my view quite inappropriately, remained so for the rest of his days. Odorcich had had a distinguished career; he had every reason to be enormously proud of his accomplishments and he could have enjoyed a wonderful retirement, welcomed and honoured among our membership everywhere. It was unrealistic for him to think that I would sit still and let him have the base provided by the temporary presidency to work against my election, and there is not the slightest doubt that this was what he would have done.

Despite the bitterness, for some time after the election and after Odorcich had finished his term and retired, I continued to invite him to functions, more than prepared to recognize him and his contributions. He never came and, ultimately, in his anger and frustration, acted in a way that to me was simply unpardonable. In a court proceeding, Odorcich testified against two of his colleagues, one of whom was Thermon Phillips, who had supported me in the election. The testimony contributed to Phillips, in a disgraceful miscarriage of justice, being incarcerated.[1] I never invited Odorcich to a Steelworker function again.

My opponent in the referendum campaign, McKee, had acquired his leadership credentials as the director of the former District 38, representing California, a position he had won in a multi-candidate election with four or five people running. He was perceived to be a good director, particularly when compared with some of his predecessors. He was a man of considerable charm who spoke as a traditional union

---

1 See my sketch of Thermon Phillips in Appendix 1 for the details of this case.

'stalwart,' a descriptive word he often used with regard to others. In the McBride election, McKee saw an opportunity for advancement, and he took it. Not only was Abel retiring that year, but Secretary-Treasurer Walter Burke was as well. Very early, McKee was letting people know that he was interested in filling the vacancy thus created and, in this, he had Burke's support. After Lloyd and I had agreed to run, we really never considered anyone else for that position on the ticket and but quickly invited McKee to join with us, which he did without hesitation.

Until Lloyd's illness began to create a more political atmosphere, and particularly at the beginning of his term, the new officers worked together well. As the new officers' group proceeded to meet and work at direction and policy, there were differences of one degree or another on various matters, but on an entirely issue-by-issue basis and in most cases it was more a matter of emphasis. However, in the area where McKee and I were required to work closest, Linden Hall, we had some annoying differences. As treasurer, property was one of his major responsibilities, but the educational aspects were one of the major areas of responsibility for the secretary's office. When an issue or concern arose, McKee had a way of acting unilaterally without working through the issues. For example, in what was clearly the treasurer's area but where feedback from members would have been useful, all the sand traps were removed from the golf course – until howls of protest led to their being restored. But the most aggravating issue concerned the focus of the facility. We had determined to make Linden Hall available first for programs developed by the international, second for programs developed by the districts, then for those of local unions. It would then be available for other Steelworker activities, such as bargaining, other labour groups, and then, if time was available, as a conference centre for whoever might be interested. We had numerous discussions about this. McKee and his subordinates saw renting the facilities to outside groups as offering a financial benefit. We had no differences regarding Steelworkers educational programs having priority, but in the interests of other activities McKee and his subordinates were reluctant to present it as clearly a Steelworker facility. Most of the rest of us considered that approach to be counterproductive, that it defeated the feelings of pride and confidence that our own place, identified as ours, could engender. The arguments dragged on for some time, producing not a little bad feeling in the process.

These differences between McKee and me were a portent of others that would emerge during the 1983 board election and the referendum campaign that followed. The procedure in the referendum required each of us running for the office of president to receive five local union nominations, plus one for every 10,000 members. According to the record, there were 1,056,741 members as of July 1983, which meant that another 106 nominations – in addition to the five – were required; therefore, a total of 111 nominations was necessary in this election. There were three of us seeking nominations: McKee, Ron Wiesen, president of Local 1397 at the Homestead Works of U.S. Steel, and me. (Wiesen filed a challenge, which was unsuccessful, on the number of members used to calculate the number of nominations required.) Obviously, if one were a serious candidate, it was critical to receive enough nominations. The political game was not simply to receive enough, but to receive the highest possible total, to swamp your opponents if possible, certainly to establish clear front-runner status. It was a great mechanism for establishing a political organization in each local around the task of persuading members to support your candidate and to attend the meeting at which the local union nomination decision was made by a vote of the members present. From the candidates' perspective, it provided an opportunity to attend meetings of some select local unions to bring their presence to bear on the decision-making process.

The meeting procedures provided for nominating speeches on behalf of candidates. The extent to which there was much activity of that kind depended on the size of the local and the heat of the campaign in the location. For the most part, the leadership of the union divided as one might have expected. With one notable exception, the directors worked in their districts for the candidate whom they had supported in the election for the temporary appointment. That is, those who voted for me worked for me, and those who voted for Odorcich worked for McKee, to whom the group had shifted their support.

Andrew 'Lefty' Palm was the director of District 15, which included Pittsburgh and the big plants in the Mon valley. He had succeeded Odorcich and his sister had been Odorcich's secretary and a great political helper as well. She had died tragically from an aneurysm a few years after she had moved with Odorcich to the headquarters. For all these reasons, Lefty had been a loyal supporter of Odorcich's, but he did not agree with the shift to McKee. George and I had worked well with Lefty and his district. There is inevitably a much more day-to-day connection with districts that are neighbours of headquarters than with those that are far away. As well, Odorcich had been telling Lefty for years, while promoting his own hopes to become president, that McKee was not by any means a good or adequate person for the position. Odorcich was furious when Lefty advised him he would be supporting me. He cut off all contact and remained estranged from him for the rest of his days.

The department heads and the departments that had reported to McKee and Odorcich generally supported them and those that had reported to Leon Lynch or me supported me. The strangest twist was that a small group of staff, who had been especially aggrieved and angry over the layoffs at headquarters, supported McKee, who had been the officer who instigated the layoffs and the most determined to pursue it. Evidently, once a candidate, he had sent word that, if elected, he would immediately put them back to work. This little group remained among McKee's best campaigners.

The auditors, all of whom worked under the supervision of the treasurer's office, for the most part supported McKee. They represented something of a field staff on his behalf in that their work took them all around the union, with a great deal of opportunity to talk to people, particularly to local union financial officers. Retired president Abel supported me and, most helpfully, made some campaign speeches on my behalf. Retired Secretary-Treasurer Burke maintained a friendly neutral face that probably tilted a bit in McKee's direction. They had been close and, as mentioned, Burke had been a principal sponsor for McKee becoming treasurer. Larry Spitz, the third member of the leadership trio that had retired to Sun City, Arizona, had been an assistant to Abel and had always been one of my supporters.[2]

In my campaign, I presented a program of progressive action, with an emphasis on the need to bargain with strength and imagination. My supporters urged vigorous political activity in support of maintaining a manufacturing base in our countries, while also emphasizing the need to organize and build our union and our movement and to reach

---

2 Sun City is quite a story in itself. The new residents were concerned to discover when they all moved there after their retirements in 1977 that, although a great many retired trade unionists lived in Sun City, there was no connection for any of them to the labour movement. Organizers by instinct and with a lifetime of practice, they organized what they called the Union Club. In short order they had monthly winter meetings of 1,000 people and a host of activities. The Union Club, of which Larry Spitz was a principal inspiration and motivator right up to his passing, now has satellite organizations all over the state.

out internationally as we faced the challenges represented by multinational corporations and the Reagan agenda. As the campaign became more active, we began to hear reports about McKee's campaign. He was putting forward a very strong line of argument against electing a Canadian. An early piece of McKee literature, a letter written to District 23, which covered West Virginia and part of Ohio along the Ohio River, whose director, Paul Rusen, was supporting me, read in part as follows:

> Your director has committed your support to Williams, who is a Canadian citizen and retains permanent Canadian residency. If successful, Rusen's choice for president will travel throughout America, instructing Americans how best to resolve their domestic, economic, and political problems! Before Congressional Committees on Unemployment, Imports, Taxation, Labor Law Reforms, etc. He will be our union's chief spokesman during our 1984 Congressional and Presidential Elections! Because of his lack of citizenship Williams will be unable to vote in the American Elections! How credible will his voice and leadership be in our domestic affairs?

I was surprised at this and furious. It seemed to me to be entirely the opposite of the one-union philosophy of our organization, suggesting instead a second-class kind of citizenship for Canadian Steelworkers. I imagined and expected that the discussion would be about qualifications and programs and ideas, not about what part of the continent we came from.

It turned out that McKee did me, and the union, a favour. Since he made the issue so central, indeed his was almost a one-issue campaign, the fact that I was a Canadian became well known and, in the end, was discounted as immaterial, at least for most of our membership. Absent such a focus the issue would not have received nearly as much attention. As it was, once I won the election, it ceased to be an issue of any kind. One of the main effects it had on me was that, after many meetings, somebody would come up to me, tell me about the great fishing they enjoyed in Canada and hoped I might know their favourite lake. I rarely, if ever, did.

In relation to nationality, I always expected when testifying before a committee in Washington, or discussing a contentious issue on TV, or in some similar situation, that someone might question the propriety of me speaking. I was always prepared to say that I was the spokesperson of our membership and, in that capacity, was authorized to speak on their behalf on issues, concerns, and circumstances in a wide variety of places and institutions. I never needed to make the case; no one ever challenged my right to speak on behalf of our members. In the 1984 campaign, it was a bit different. There are really two electorates in a union referendum. The first is composed of the activists. These are the people who know what is happening, have been at least thinking about it for some time, and are often actively involved as well. I had good support among the activists. They are people who had seen McKee and me at work and had opinions about us both. The second group was made up of those who came into the process at the end, suddenly realizing that there was a vote to be cast. They were a larger number of people than the activists, by and large less well informed about union matters but interested nonetheless. They were, generally speaking, more susceptible to the quick line, 'You wouldn't want to vote for a foreigner, would you?' Our campaigners could address the matter with most people in ten minutes or so, but during a campaign there are only so many ten-minute time spots.

My memories of the campaign are nearly all positive: meeting many members, being well received, eating a lot of hamburgers and hot dogs, having many bacon-and-egg breakfasts, and seeing North America. I spent election day visiting the polling booths in the Pittsburgh area, for the most part talking with voters after they had cast their ballots. I remember in particular speaking to one woman, an officeworker, towards the end of the day. When I introduced myself, she smiled and said, 'I am sorry, but I didn't vote for you.' I asked, 'Because I am a Canadian?' She said that was the reason. I asked if she knew that Canadians were members of the Steelworkers, just like Americans, with organized locals, bargained contracts, and paid dues. She said she really wasn't familiar with that. So I asked, with a smile, 'Did you think I was some unemployed Canadian who saw an opportunity for a good job here in Pittsburgh?' At this she laughed and said, 'Well, something like that.'

As a result of instances such as this, on election day, McKee gained some votes but I was still able to claim a nice, clear majority. I had won overwhelmingly in Canada and, while I fell a bit short in the United States, it was still close. In the end I had more than enough votes. I polled 192,767 votes to 136,264 for McKee, a comfortable margin of 56,503. The oath of office was administered by former president Abel on 7 June in Washington, D.C.

An analysis of the U.S. vote, which I firmly believe to be correct, is that I received more nominations in the United States than McKee because of the activists, and we did not have time to reach enough of the second group of voters to make them as well informed as the activists. All things considered, though, I was very pleased with the results. The Canadian issue was not nearly as damaging as McKee and his colleagues had expected.

The union came together quickly after the election, I think for a number of reasons but essentially because the desire for unity is basic to the union's culture. In addition, we had kept the personal frictions and criticisms to a minimum. For example, divided as the headquarters building was, everyone knew that in a few weeks it would all be over and we would all be working together, so people were careful not to break bonds of friendship that had lasted much longer in many cases than the length of time they had known Williams or McKee. And so in March 1984, unbelievably, I truly was president and not temporarily acting as such, sitting in the chair where Phillip Murray, David J. McDonald, I.W. Abel, and Lloyd McBride had sat before me. How this had happened to a preacher's son from Sarnia and Hamilton, Ontario, was a question that wandered through my mind in reflective moments. It was a question to which I had no obvious answer. In fact, I would have been even more astonished if I had known then what the future held: I would hold the post of president for ten years, from 1984 to 1994, being elected for two full terms in my own right, first in November 1985 and then in November 1989. Each time I would be unopposed.

Not that there were moments when I had the luxury of quiet reflection on how far I had come. Starting in 1984, I found myself immediately immersed in a heavy agenda that never slowed, so much so that in the years to come that I often introduced McKee to conventions or other gatherings as 'the winner.' One often wishes in the hubbub of life in the labour movement that issues could be dealt with sequentially, in a proper, orderly fashion, but that is rarely the case. Usually, at least a half a dozen major issues need to be addressed simultaneously, with a weedy garden of smaller ones always in need of tending as well. This was certainly the case with the Steelworkers during the period of my presidency.

As we approached our various challenges, problems, and tasks in my early days as president, I was thankful over and over again for the quality of the senior colleagues who were available to me. First there were my colleague officers: Jim McGeehan, secretary-treasurer; Ed Ball, secretary; and George Becker, now vice-president. The first two I had in effect picked and the third had been a solid supporter from the beginning. Jim had been the director of the district in eastern Pennsylvania; Ed had been director of a district that included Texas, Oklahoma, and Arkansas; and George, as I've related, was my assistant when I became international secretary. George was a man of overflowing, instinctive talent whom I had by lucky chance picked from the union crowd almost at the beginning of my service as an officer. We had by now done many things together: worked at the mailing system, reworked or restructured the public-relations function, been the developers and managers of a number of international conventions, and led the international efforts and commitments of the union.

I also had available an excellent team of elected directors from the various districts, with significant membership in basic steel, and an outstanding group of senior headquarters staff of rich talent and amazing ability. Many of these people in both categories had years of experience. The key directors at the beginning of my term in office were the following: Len Stevens, responsible for western Canada and the territories as director of District 3, out of Vancouver; Mike Mazuca, finishing up many years of service out of Buffalo in District 4; Clément Godbout, director of District 5, encompassing Quebec and Atlantic Canada, out of Montreal; Stu Cooke, responsible for Ontario as director of District 6, out of Toronto;[3] Dave Wilson, long-time activist serving his first term as director of District 8, headquartered in Baltimore; Paul McHale, director of District 9, out of Bethlehem, Pennsylvania; Andrew 'Lefty' Palm,

---

3 Two of Stu's associates deserve mention here. Bob Mackenzie had helped Stu and the union leadership and staff in Hamilton build the Steelworkers and the labour movement into a force that quietly supported, and was closely integrated with, the NDP. Bob became a member of the Ontario legislature and, as minister of labour in the NDP government elected in 1990, introduced the first anti-scab legislation in the province. During the two years that this legislation was in effect, the Steelworkers organized more workers than ever before in the history of Ontario. It was a notable legacy, and one that Bob's son David has helped to carry on. Under Stu's leadership in District 6, David began a distinguished career that would see him hold a number of important posts in the union, including assistant to Leo Gerard, during Leo's service as national director, and head of the Humanity Fund which had been created by Gérard Docquier as a means of making our involvement in workers' struggles around the world more meaningful and effective. David has become a wise leader, committed to both the labour movement and the NDP.

director of District 15 in southwestern Pennsylvania; Walter Bachowski, director of District 20 in northwestern Pennsylvania; Paul Rusen, director of District 23 in West Virginia; Harry Mayfield, director of District 27 in Ohio, out of Canton; Frank Valenta, director of District 28 in Ohio, out of Cleveland; Harry Lester, director of District 29 in Michigan, out of Detroit; Jack Parton, director of District 31, encompassing Indiana and northern Illinois, out of Gary; Joel Vattendahl, director of District 32 in Wisconsin, out of Milwaukee; Eldon Kirsch, director of District 33 in Minnesota; Buddy Davis, director of District 34, out of St Louis; Bruce Thrasher, director of District 35, out of Atlanta; Thermon Phillips, director of District 36, out of Birmingham; Jack Golden, director of District 37, out of Houston; and Bob Petris, director of District 38, out of Los Angeles.[4] All of these directors looked after some steel bargaining, most with a number of companies, a few focused on one or another of the major companies as chairman, vice-chairman, or secretaries of the committees where they worked in leading the bargaining at the top table. A number chaired the bargaining committees with the major companies that had been part of the coordinated bargaining procedures – Jack Parton for Inland, Buddy Davis for National, and first Frank Valenta in 1983 and then Tony Rainaldi in 1986 for LTV, while Paul McHale led Bethlehem in 1983 and 1986.

Shortly after I took office, there were a number of changes in the above list; Tony Rainaldi replaced Walter Bachowski and Joe Coyle replaced Harry Mayfield. In 1986 there were more retirements and replacements, when Lou Thomas replaced Mike Mazuca, Jim Bowen replaced Paul Rusen, and Joe Kiker replaced Bruce Thrasher. Upon Jim McGeehan becoming secretary-treasurer, John Reck replaced him as the director of District 7 out of Philadelphia.

---

4 After my term, the district structure was changed significantly and the number of districts reduced from twenty-six to thirteen. Subsequently, one was added so that there are now fourteen.

   Although the common language of the union is to refer to the number of the district, denoting the geographical area for which a director is elected and the area within which the general programs of the union such as political action and organizing are conducted, I have attempted to use the numbers very infrequently because there has been so much change in them as a result of restructuring. During the period about which I am writing, we were gradually reducing the number of districts, as opportunities for mergers presented themselves. We were basically committed, however, to the idea that districts should be the instruments for organizing and growth. The number of board members remained essentially unchanged as new board members representing merged groups, such as the Upholstery Workers, were added.

A strong headquarters group had been a characteristic of the union from the founding days of Murray's presidency. Historic greats such as Arthur Goldberg, Clinton Golden, Joseph Scanlon, and Marvin Miller were included in their number, but the group in place when I became president did not need to hide in their shadow. Five deserve special mention, being extraordinarily gifted in their own right. To single them out, of course, is to omit the names of others who also made great contributions. But these five, in the major bargaining situations, along with the other officers and the directors, were the ones with whom I was principally engaged.

Senior among them was Bernie Kleiman, who came to the union from Chicago as general counsel in 1965 when Abel was elected president. Bernie held that position until 2004. He then continued to serve as a special assistant to the president until 2006 and, in effect, carried out the same responsibilities in retirement until his sudden death in 2007. It is impossible to describe the importance of his contribution in terms of his strength, his understanding, his wisdom, and his persistence. He was both a graduate engineer and a lawyer, but the depth of his human understanding went far beyond any formal learning.

Two of my assistants came with widely different backgrounds but brought great talents to the bargaining table. Sam Camens had been the president of a basic steel local in Youngstown and, although he became a top negotiator and travelled the country, in another way he never left home. He lived in Youngstown and on every Saturday evening he could, he played cards with the old gang from the plant; he certainly never forgot where he came from. Jim Smith after college became a war plant local union president when he couldn't pass a medical to enlist. Jim went on staff of the union for a time but left to pursue a PhD in economics. After accomplishing that goal, he came back to the headquarters staff in Pittsburgh, instead of returning to his home district staff in Texas. Then there was Carl Frankel, one of Kleiman's associate general counsels, the son of Russian immigrants, a graduate of the University of Chicago, and a brilliant lawyer, writer, and draughtsman, a detail person of enormous patience.

The fifth person I include in this group was Jack Sheehan, who was the head of our Legislative Department in Washington throughout my presidency and carried a tremendous load of responsibility during this critical period in the life of our union. Most of the formal testimony I gave to congressional committees and other government bodies in Washington was a joint product of Jack and me, and Jack also played a key role in my dealings with the president and various administration officials.[5] A former Steelworkers auditor, he had worked for some years in Quebec, where he had learned to speak French and had acquired an informed understanding of Canada's social and political circumstances, particularly in relation to the United States, that was often helpful in cross-border discussions. He had also played a very constructive role in legislative battles in earlier administrations over the Employment Retirement Income Security Act (ERISA), national health care, occupational health and safety, Social Security, and Clean Air initiatives, among many other issues. I cannot say enough about the importance and the quality of Jack's work. He was criticized in some circles as a 'free trader.' This was quite unfair. In all the work we did together, I never knew him to support anything but our position. Thanks in large part to his efforts, administration officials and members of Congress never failed to know where the Steelworkers stood on the various issues before them.

Such was the team I was fortunate to have around me when I began my first presidential term in 1984. It was a good thing that they were such an able group, because the waters ahead would be treacherous indeed.

---

5   See Appendix 2.

11

TRYING TIMES

During the early years of my presidency, and continuing right through to the end, I assigned the negotiations with our staff unions to myself. My theory was that there were many difficult messages to be delivered and difficult facts to be assessed and, remembering how our members felt about messengers, that these would be better coming from me directly rather than from someone to whom I had assigned the task. I was always pleased with this decision. In fact, I cannot imagine any way of dealing with these issues nearly as satisfactorily in a non-union setting. The union provides excellent communication, a way to gauge feelings and motivation, and a way to search out better solutions. In this regard, Bill Elliott, one of our staff representatives from District 6, came to Pittsburgh and was very helpful in the thankless task of being a personnel manager in the middle of a depression.

Not everything went so smoothly. My arrival in the presidency coincided with the beginning of a discussion about whether the industry should pursue a '201 Petition' before the U.S. International Trade Commission. The purpose would be to seek protection for the steel industry on the grounds that imported steel was inflicting enormous damage on domestic producers. At one point we put together a road show to attempt to stir up greater public concern about the loss of industrial jobs. We called it 'Saving American Industry and Jobs.' It had limited success. We did not have the resources to crack the American public consciousness adequately at that point. Too few thought what was happening in steel would happen to them, and too much of the American political and economic elite was branding the steel crisis as the fault of the industry and the union, while preaching the false theology of free trade as the solution.

The industry was divided over whether to proceed with a 201 Petition. Bethlehem was in favour; U.S. Steel was opposed, preferring the approach of pursuing individual cases in relation to the most seriously affected product lines. The CEO of Bethlehem, Donald Trautlein, was very much supportive of the petition approach, but he was reluctant to proceed in the face of U.S. Steel's opposition. I came quickly to the view that the petition would be an effective way to raise public consciousness and I advised Bethlehem that we would be pleased to join it in pursuing the cause. Trautlein agonized over the decision for some time but finally agreed to proceed.

I wanted to exempt Canada but was advised that this would not be a practical stance. The best strategy was deemed to be to raise the issue of Canada once we had won the petition and were dealing with the White House in terms of what action was to be taken. We could then request an exemption for Canada on the grounds of the close trading relationship – amounting to a single market – between the two countries. Indeed, that was what happened in the end. In fact, there have been five periods of some kind of protection of steel in the United States by quotas or other devices, such as Jimmy Carter's trigger prices, and in each case our union has been able to exempt Canada, an enormous advantage that speaks directly to our being an international union, respected and strong in each country.

The filing of the petition set in motion a series of events. It began, of course, with the preparation of substantial briefs and documentation setting out how devastating the crisis had been and continued to be. One of the mechanisms in Washington that assists in efforts of this kind is a congressional caucus, in our case the Congressional Steel Caucus, a bipartisan group from districts in which there are steel facilities. They have done great work in supporting the needs of the industry and the workers, although not always successfully. They do not represent a majority of the House or the Senate but have often pushed hard across party lines, and often effectively. Legislators such as former Minority Leader Dick Gephardt, congressmen John Murtha, Pete Viclosky, and Ralph Regula, and senators such as Jay Rockefeller and Paul Simon come quickly to mind as very helpful, among many others. I shall always remember, too, the assistance of someone who wasn't from a steel district, House Speaker Tip O'Neill.

In the midst of this effort, the Steelworkers held their regular convention. A biannual event, this was the first of five conventions that would be held during my time as president. For many years, there were only

tricts than the few who had adequate convention facilities. Cleveland was a perfect spot for this because it could be done right on the lake. District 36 from Alabama agreed to look after it. They were experts in jambalaya and towed their equipment all the way up from Alabama. A good time was had by all.

A major event at the convention was a visit from Walter Mondale, the former vice-president and the current Democratic Party candidate for the presidency. His campaign staffers were eager and bright but very young and inexperienced. My senior convention aides were forced to spend inordinate amounts of time working out security and other arrangements with them. On other fronts, the convention had its amusing moments. Some of the better-known dissidents were present. One of them, Mike Bonn, decided to position himself at the front floor mike, directly in front of the podium, and directly in my sight line, standing with a pious demeanour, holding a Bible. He made no gestures indicating a desire to speak, but just stood there. I concluded that his purpose was to engage me in complaining or harassing or setting up something contentious. I decided to let him stand. He lasted all the first day. On the second, Mondale was coming and his security people swept Bonn away from his prime position. I think Bonn was profoundly relieved – at least there were no complaints and he behaved the rest of the week as a normal delegate.

The convention coincided with President Reagan's decision about what to do with our 201 Petition, which had received the sanction of the International Trade Commission. The end of the 201 process is entirely in the hands of the president. Winning the arguments, as we essentially had, simply sets up the opportunity for vigorous action to be taken – it does not require that anything be done. But the timing was in our favour. With the election looming in November, Reagan obviously did not wish to have the union and the industry furious. This reaction could come about either by a failure on his part to deal in any effective way with the steel industry's trade issues, or, in a worst-case scenario for him, by a decision that was seen as likely to make the situation even worse. In the end, he issued a policy statement that endorsed the administration's belief in the principles of free trade and then announced a system of voluntary quotas, along with the countries and the products to which they were expected to apply. Trade negotiators were sent out to work out agreements with the various countries. Canada was first mentioned as included, but during the negotiating period our idea of a North American market prevailed and Canada was exempted – just as it has been in all subsequent trade-control programs.

In the midst of all this manoeuvring over the 201 Petition, there were also steel negotiations to attend to. As I've already indicated, steel negotiations had been very much the president's responsibility in the union, with the other officers in supportive roles but without anything like the same measure of responsibility. This had pluses and minuses, the latter being that those in a supporting role did not feel as useful as they wished to be, but it had provided the significant advantage in my former role as secretary of giving me the time to learn, to come to know the players, the issues, and the dynamics of the relationships. As a result, on becoming president, I was not without considerable under-standing and a number of ideas.

As president, I brought three ideas in particular to the negotiating process: first, the notion of quid pro quos, meaning that if we were indeed in a situation in which some kind of concession had to be made, there should be gains in some other direction in view of the sacrifices our people would be making in such a circumstance; second, in the area of information and knowledge, we should know everything there is to know about the industry and the companies; and third, that at the end of the day the workers should have a significant voice in what policies were to be pursued in their industry.

This last idea I discussed earlier in relation to my experience in the Niagara area in District 6. In fact, it goes back to the very beginning of the union and Murray's ideas of industrial democracy. One of the first books I read about the labour movement was *The Dynamics of Industrial Democracy* by Clinton S. Golden, the first vice-president of the union, and Harold J. Ruttenberg, the first research director.[2] It set out the principles and proposed methods for workers having a real voice in their industry and made a great impression on me. My sense as I began my presidency was that, if ever there was a time to pursue these ideas, it was now. Murray's early attempts had been rebuffed by the industry. Various other attempts over the years had been short-lived, but never before had there been a crisis of the dimensions we were now facing.

This mix of propositions, facts, experience, and concerns led us in a variety of directions. Given the break in the tradition of coordinat-ed bargaining, I let it be known that, contrary to past practice, I did

2 New York: Harper and Brothers 1942.

not intend to immerse myself totally in the bargaining procedure with steel, and particularly not in any one company's negotiations. The tradition had been that the president of the union did simply that, which in practical terms meant a preoccupation with the top table and with the spokesperson for the group, who traditionally was the U.S. Steel person, in this case Bruce Johnston. My view was that my role should be much more like that of a CEO, meeting with our people, strategizing, interjecting myself occasionally when particular circumstances or a particular issue warranted it. It was a message that I wanted not only the steel companies but also the heads of other companies and the rest of our membership to hear. Our union was now so much more diverse, encompassing a wide variety of industries and occupations, and it did not seem to me that the union would be well served by a president who virtually disappeared into one set of negotiations for weeks at a time. Another element in my thinking was that we had a whole structure of negotiating committees chaired by district directors or, in some instances, senior staff people. I believed that the union and its members would be best served by putting this structure to work.

I do not recall receiving any direct protests from the other side of the table, but word reached me that Bruce Johnston was quite upset at my decision and grumbled to others that it was a snub to the steel industry. I think, however, that before the first round was over it was clear that a different approach or style did not mean any neglect of the concerns we wished to resolve and the objectives we wished to achieve.

Around the time of the 1986 negotiations, we determined that it would be worthwhile to commission an independent study of the industry, in this case by Locker Associates Inc., a small independent economic consulting firm from New York, known to be of progressive persuasion. We asked the firm, headed by Michael Locker, to do an entirely objective study of the steel industry and present it to our entire Basic Steel Industry Conference. Our purpose was to achieve a broadly shared understanding among our activists and within our membership of the kind of circumstances we were facing so that as we developed and pursued our objectives there would be no second-guessing. Locker and his group did excellent work, and when we had them report to the Basic Steel group at a special conference in Chicago, the effort was positively received.

It was at this time, too, that Sam Camens became our in-house enthusiast, expert, and missionary for worker participation. He embraced the entire concept as if this was the moment he was waiting for in his trade-union career. He was greatly influenced or reinforced in this by a number of advocates and consultants with whom we became involved through our efforts with the Labor Management Participation Team programs. We also came to know others in the labour movement who were pursuing similar ideas: Irving Bluestone and Don Ephlin of the Auto Workers, Morty Bahr of the Communication Workers, and Murray Finlay and then Jack Sheinkman of the Amalgamated Clothing Workers. One of the consultants whose ideas Sam and I were attracted to was, interestingly enough, the consultant hired by U.S. Steel to work with it in the LMPT process, Sid Rubenstein. The particular insight he brought was that it was not realistic to expect workers to contribute their most productive ideas to improving the company's circumstances if the result was that they put themselves out of a job. He added that the Japanese, with their culture of lifetime employment, had taken a much more productive approach and that we needed to find a way to include employment security in our programs.

Another important player in the developing scene was Stan Ellsperman, who had come from the paper industry to be the industrial relations vice-president with National Steel, whose chief executive took a more progressive view than most about the role of the employees. Ellsperman was ready to lead the way in worker-participation provisions in a collective agreement, including employment security. Also interested in pursuing participative approaches was LTV, with David Hoag as CEO and Cole Tremain as the industrial relations vice-president.

One of the crucial changes as we approached our first round of bargaining in steel was the industries' abandonment of coordinated bargaining, an approach that had prevailed for many years and that involved one table led by U.S. Steel. The companies hailed this as representing a new realism in bargaining which would enable them to pursue agreements more related to the circumstances of each company than the old coordinated approach had permitted. They sold this idea without difficulty to financial and media analysts, who paid little heed to our constant explanation that, whatever the procedure followed, we were going to coordinate the bargaining regardless.

The reality was that we were faced with substantially different situations in each of the companies, depending on how they had reacted to the crisis in steel, what the state of their plants was, how their blend of products fitted the market, and other issues of this nature. How, then, to establish a pattern that was fair to all parties and provided as equal an opportunity as possible for all to move forward? We had always known that the impact of traditional settlements based on coordinated bargaining was different for each company. The same settlement was significantly more costly for some because their employment costs were often significantly different. We had never known what the employment costs really were, but now, with new access to information, we did. It was apparent that a pattern of matching employment costs would establish a common cost basis from which each company had its own opportunity to move forward.

While the 1986 round of negotiations was the first round subsequent to the ending of the coordinating-companies model, it was also one in which the union coordinated a pattern-setting approach. Negotiations that year started with LTV, the weakest company. The settlement with LTV was typical of the pattern that had been worked out with each of the major companies before negotiations with U.S. Steel moved towards a conclusion. It was representative of our approach that concessions should be recognized as investments, and that there should be a major focus on improvements in the non-monetary and union-rights issues during this period when the union's bargaining leverage was significant but the possibility of important economic gains severely constrained.

Contracting out was another major focus of the LTV agreement. In the general milieu of the crisis in steel, the employment of hundreds of outside contractors as our members faced the destruction of their jobs was an enormous issue across the industry. This was specifically confirmed by our pre-bargaining surveys and meetings, and was underlined by Sam Camens, who, in many ways, was a one-person public-opinion pollster among our membership. The way I often put the issue was that we were working to save what we could of the industry not for contractors but for our members, for their communities, and for their sons and daughters. One day, Bernie Kleiman and Carl Frankel came to me and said that the traditional way of improving contract language, by pursuing modifications to the existing language, was simply not working in these negotiations, given the inadequacies of the old language and the complexities involved in attempting to improve it. Therefore, they recommended that they should go and hide for a few days and draw up new language. I urged them to proceed immediately. It became the basis for the best contracting-out language in any agreements in industrial America.

On presenting the proposed agreement with LTV to the members, the bargaining committee wrote the following:

LTV is in trouble. The Union's own independent examination of LTV's books by our expert financial consultants proved that.

The Company lost $227,000,000 in 1985.

It will lose as much, or more, in 1986. It can't survive these losses for long – unless it gets help from us.

The Union agreed to cooperate and negotiate to help the company survive – but only for a very steep price.

The Union demanded that all sacrifices required from you will be recognized as an investment. You will get a return on your sacrifice, or investment. You will get at least your sacrifice back, dollar for dollar (and possibly more). So long as the company returns to profitability. And you can have a voice in the affairs of LTV as a shareholder in its parent company (the LTV Corporation).

Further, the Union demanded other concessions from the company.

The company had to recognize, and act on, your problems.

Contracting out had to be brought under control. Problems of excessive overtime had to be dealt with. A serious commitment to fight foreign steel had to be made, and the company had to make a binding commitment of equal sacrifice for its managers, supervisors, and non-union employees for the term of the agreement.

The above quotation is the introduction to a thirty-nine-page magazine-style booklet describing all of the details of the proposed settlement. The mechanism for managing concessions as investments was a Profit-Sharing and Stock Ownership Plan. If the company made sufficient profits, the concessions were to be returned as cash, dollar for dollar. If the company made insufficient or no profit, and could not pay dollar for dollar in cash, the difference would be paid in preferred stock. This LTV Exchangeable Preferred Stock could be exchanged for common stock in LTV's parent company at the employee's discretion. The agreement also included a successor clause that provided that the company could not sell or transfer a plant covered by this agreement without the proposed buyer recognizing the union and completing an agreement satisfactory to the union. This provision provided the union unprecedented rights in such events. Another provision guaranteed equality of sacrifice on the part of executives, managers, and all other non-represented employees. The union was guaranteed access to the relevant company books so that it could monitor the application of this agreement. There was agreement as well on the need for joint activity in the battle against imports and many, many other matters, such as improving the availability of transfers to other locations in the event of plant shutdowns and improving efficiency in the administration of the grievance procedure.

Carl Frankel recalls that 'as pressures from imports rose, the companies looked for ways to reduce costs and they thought contracting out was a way to accomplish that. It's debatable whether it was or wasn't. In some instances it clearly was. But in others, it was a case of the maintenance manager having a brother or friend or family member who had a business on the side. There is no way of measuring [it] ... but our people firmly believed they were being screwed. There's a lot of evidence indicating that they were ... It was an issue and it's still an issue.' Carl adds that, while there were pluses and minuses in separate negotiations with individual companies, in terms of addressing the contracting-out issue the procedure was an advantage for the union. 'LTV had the least contracting out problems on the surface. They had more underneath, but our members weren't screaming as much at LTV as they were at other companies, particularly U.S. Steel,' Carl says. 'LTV took much of the revolutionary program we designed ... Now, once we got it at LTV, we also got it at Bethlehem [and] I think Wheeling Pittsburgh Steel.'

Carl wrote an extensive paper on our contracting-out proposal for the National Academy of Arbitrators. In it, he said that the proposal has been described as revolutionary, because it imposes perhaps the toughest restrictions on contracting out found anywhere in the manufacturing sector, it provides a genuine opportunity for the unit to recapture work that has been historically contracted out, and it fashions a special expedited procedure by which, in many cases, the parties may obtain an arbitrator's award even before the company makes a final decision to contract out the work. The system is based on the principle that 'work capable of being performed by bargaining unit employees shall be performed' by them. 'The employer is barred from contracting out any work, whether performed on or off the plant site, unless it proves that the work in question falls within one of the delineated exceptions to the general principle.' In the plant, contracting out of production, service, maintenance or repair work, non-major new construction, installation, and replacement and reconstruction of equipment and production facilities is forbidden unless it meets two conditions: the employer must prove that there was a consistent practice of contracting out such work, and it must also show that it is 'more reasonable' to contract out than to use bargaining-unit employees. In terms of work outside the plant, the employer again must prove that it is more reasonable to contract out than to perform this in-house.

One must understand that all this was under way in an atmosphere full of new crises day by day, as well as assorted other developments, all of which in turn had an impact on each other. One of the issues that arose in concession bargaining was what would happen if the crisis suddenly ended and the companies unexpectedly started doing well, a far from unheard of experience in a cyclical industry such as steel. One approach that occurred to us was stock ownership as a way of providing a payoff should circumstances change, in that improvement would be reflected in the value of the stock. All of these matters tied in to what Jim Smith and his shop called investment bargaining, based on the idea that concessions should be thought of as investments, as indeed they were, and not inconsiderable ones. A number of results flow from investment, such as access to information and ability to have a voice and influence policy, indeed to be on the board, and the expectation of reward when and if circumstances turn around.

By and large, our activists and members backed all these ideas and initiatives. In particular, attempts to become involved in what had been exclusively management's turf, based on the idea, as I often expressed it, that 'management was too important to leave to the managers,' were enthusiastically supported. Far from being thought about as jumping in bed with the company, they came more and more to be seen as a right for workers in the industrial sector facing critical challenges.

The 1986 round of negotiations, starting with LTV and then proceeding to the other companies, went well until we faced U.S. Steel. That company was driven by the desire to reap a deeper concession than Bethlehem and to reject the new tough contracting-out language to which all the other companies had agreed. We obviously could not accept such terms. If we did, the entire house would have collapsed. Despite their rejection of coordinated bargaining and their media spin about their interest in their own unique agreements, the companies had a constant eye on each other and came screaming to us at the slightest hint that one of the others had achieved some kind of advantage in their negotiations. In a situation of constant bargaining, so much change was under way that issues would arise almost daily that required a new kind of contractual arrangement. If the rumour ever drifted out, as it in fact constantly did, that someone had been granted some advantage, all the other companies would be calling me immediately to complain and seek equal treatment. It was in this context, too, that each company would push for a level playing field when it felt its interest was threatened.

In the case of U.S. Steel, being unwilling to accept the terms we had reached with the other companies, it resorted to a lockout which lasted for six months in 1986–7. The bargaining during that time, although fundamentally about two issues, depth of concessions and contracting out, reached out into many other elements. I think that the company miscalculated the strength and determination of our members, feeling that they would not persist in the face of all the difficulties in the industry. I began more and more to feel that what the dispute needed most was a skilled third party, a mediator who would be respected by both sides and in whose judgment both would be confident. There was a remarkable man, willing and able, who more than met these qualifications. His name was Sylvester Garrett. He was a prestigious labour arbitrator who had settled a great many complex disputes in the steel industry. He was held in great respect by both sides, but it required some convincing within our group and with the company to accept the idea of mediation. There was considerable feeling that the parties could and should resolve matters directly between themselves; both sides were accustomed to pressure from outside to resolve disputes, but not to having outsiders as part of the process itself. However, the idea was accepted. Garrett conducted matters more like an arbitration than the mediation I had visualized, but he knew his parties well. His recommendations became the basis of the settlement, the key elements of which were concessions that matched those that had been agreed to with Bethlehem in 1983 and 1986 and the contracting-out provision that we had negotiated across the industry, with one minor exception in the language.

Interestingly, almost uniquely in my experience, the head of U.S. Steel, David Roderick, made public speech after public speech declaring that the company had 'won' the dispute. The more common experience is that both sides say they want to put the dispute behind them and move forward. In this instance, Roderick continued to argue, until the day of his retirement, that the truth was other than it was.

I cannot say enough about the solidarity of our membership at U.S. Steel through the lockout. Our local union officers and activists were superb. The top leadership responsibilities were shared. Jim McGeehan, who became the treasurer in my first full term, was the chairman of the U.S. Steel negotiations for our side and did yeoman work in pressing our case. This was in the midst of the biggest crisis the industry had ever faced. Our members in basic steel had not established picket lines since 1959, twenty-seven years earlier. We took the position that, because we were involved in a lockout, unemployment compensation should be available to the workers. Under Kleiman's leadership, our legal department handled this in public hearings in every state that was affected, and won in every state but one.[3] We asked Vice-President George Becker to set up a picket-line organization that would maintain solidarity and communication across the various situations, which he did with his customary focus and efficiency. Other than an altercation over a train in Lorain, Ohio, our lines were not threatened and nowhere were they broken.

We also conducted an information campaign among Marathon Oil customers across the country, making the point that in purchasing oil and gasoline from this U.S. Steel subsidiary they were in fact supporting the company against the workers. U.S. Steel never acknowledged that it was even aware of this effort, but we heard from many franchise holders who complained that they should not be expected to suffer because of what U.S. Steel was doing. We replied that their best avenue was to advise U.S. Steel it would be wise to change its stance in the bargaining.

Another spinoff of the lockout was what became the strategic approaches committee of the AFL-CIO. Early in the lockout, Lane Kirkland, president of the AFL-CIO from 1979 to 1995, had asked me to report to the Executive Council on what was taking place. I did, and as a routine motion in our support was about to be passed, Murray Finlay, president of the Amalgamated Clothing and Textile Workers Union, intervened to say that this was one of the most important struggles the labour movement had faced in the current circumstances. He proposed that a special committee be established to coordinate support for the Steelworker members who were locked out. This was immediately done, Murray was appointed chairman, and the committee raised considerable money and coordinated considerable activity in the Marathon initiative. After the lockout ended, the special committee was transformed into the strategic approaches committee. Murray was its chairman until he retired in 1987, after which I was privileged to take his place.

---

3 These cases were most often tried in public hearings, which became a rare opportunity for members to watch their union in action battling the company from the witness chair as well as the counsel's table. In Gary, Indiana, thousands packed a huge arena where the atmosphere resembled that of a hotly contested athletic event.

After the successful conclusion of the U.S. Steel lockout, we invited Murray to speak to our 1988 convention in Las Vegas. Our principal reason in doing so was to thank him for the support he had given and had generated from the AFL-CIO and the affiliates. Murray was stunned at the enthusiasm and fighting spirit on display at our convention. He told me that he had expected to see a gathering that was much more intimidated by all the troubles with which we were struggling, not one that had such a high level of militancy along with a very great deal of spirit and enthusiasm.

The lockout was no sooner over than we found ourselves faced with another crisis: the campaign for 'free trade' by much of the economic and political leadership in the United States and Canada, a cause that was closely tied to the continuing and increasing pressure for concessions, largely driven by what became known as 'the race to the bottom.' Two forces in opposition to these pressures were at work in the heart and soul of the labour movement. One was our pride in having built the standard of living of the industrial democracies to an unprecedented level with middle-income standards for working people, coupled with our determination to continue along this progressive path. The other was our desire to address the wretched poverty of the Third World by enabling such countries to progress economically, an issue of constant international discussion since the end of the Second World War but a distressing failure most of the time.

For those of us in the labour movement, we believed that trade had to be managed in such a way that met the needs both of workers in the industrial West and of the Third World poor. Such ideas were anathema to many university economists, who were true believers in free trade. Whenever we talked about managing trade, we were condemned as protectionists. Great things were predicted first for the Canada-United States Free Trade Agreement (FTA), which came into effect in October 1988, and then for North American Free Trade Agreement (NAFTA), which, enlarging the FTA to include Mexico, followed in January 1994. When it became clear that there had been more loss than gain for thousands of workers in all three countries – Canada, Mexico, and the United States – the only confessions I remember from the enthusiastic economists were rather quiet and weak observations that maybe they had gone overboard. They certainly had.

The Steelworkers joined the rest of the labour movement in both the United States and Canada in fighting both the FTA and NAFTA, and, while our efforts ultimately failed, we did put forward ideas that, in my opinion, have stood the test of time. The example I often give is the trade in Portuguese wine for English wool, a trade that recognized the relatively superior advantage each country had in its product. Such trade seemed to have done a great deal for the English, but very little for the Portuguese! In a broader context, Carl Frankel observes that unmanaged free trade on a global scale inevitably must be 'a race to the bottom.' 'Unless you put in trade agreements provisions that say you've got to come up to certain levels and you've got to be environmentally responsible ... business being as mobile as it is, is going to go where the surrounding elements are cheaper. Why would they not do that? Mexico is now learning that all the industries they took from us are going elsewhere because somebody else is cheaper. It's not amazing if you think about it. You don't push people out the door, which is what we're doing and the Canadians are doing. And NAFTA is a perfect example. NAFTA is a disaster.'

Similarly, Tom Donahue, former secretary-treasurer and later president of the AFL-CIO, is not an advocate of unmanaged free trade. 'As long as you have the concept of a nation-state, that nation-state should manage industry with an eye to advantage of the people it represents. To be an advocate of total free trade is just silly,' he says. Donahue doesn't think the United States has been hurt by trading with Canada under NAFTA, but Mexico is another story. 'When you don't have equality in earning power between nations, it's impossible to have fair competition.' Donahue argues that, while exporting heavy equipment to Mexico helped the U.S. trade balance with its southern neighbour, the benefit was short-lived because that same equipment was used to make products that competed with U.S-manufactured goods and thereby cost jobs on the home front. Though NAFTA has become a catch-all acronym for free trade in general, the real threat to jobs in Canada and the United States is not from each other but from offshore competitors, Donahue explains, adding that it's unfair to blame China. Instead, the finger should be pointed directly at Canadian and American corporations that locate there to take advantage of cheap labour. 'I don't think NAFTA is the principal problem. The principal problem in trade is the World Trade Organization and its lack of concern for safety and environmental issues.'

Even some of those in Congress who voted for NAFTA did so with reservations. One of them was Iowa Senator Tom Harkin, who said in addressing NAFTA on the Senate floor: 'The case is not overwhelming on either side of the issue. Iowans seem to agree, according to a recent poll, which showed them evenly divided on the issue: 36 per cent in favour, 36 per cent opposed and 28 per cent undecided.' Harkin, a friend whom our union has supported, acknowledged that NAFTA 'involved a bit of a gamble.' What tipped the balance for Harkin was his view that, from Iowa's perspective, NAFTA would mean reduced tariffs on the state's exports and, by promoting economic growth in Mexico, would make Mexico 'a better customer for our products.' After dropping out of the 1992 race for the Democratic presidential nomination, Harkin was approached by Bill Clinton's people to endorse their candidate. In return, he wanted Clinton to renegotiate NAFTA and include provisions protecting labour and the environment. Clinton said he couldn't renegotiate the treaty but promised to address those issues as side agreements. Harkin restated his position on the Senate floor: 'I wish that the labour and environmental provisions were in the basic text of the agreement. That is where they belong.' Harkin went on to tell Congress: 'As long as we are talking about change, Mr. President, it is time to change this outdated view that somehow, in our negotiated agreements with other countries dealing with trade, we can protect everything that deals with capital and property but we cannot deal with protecting basic human rights.'

In the same vein, former congressman Jim Oberstar, a Minnesota Democrat, has said that 'we're losing jobs overseas wherever the basis of competition is wage rates. Where the basis is skills, performance and quality of workmanship, we keep those jobs.' He believes that industry needs to invest in job training and replacement of older, less cost-efficient equipment, while at the same time competing in skills training. 'I think industry has been way too concerned with the bottom line and stock market returns for investors and needs longer-term investments.' Oberstar remembers a vice-president of Bethlehem Steel saying in the mid-1980s that, while the North American industry invented the new technology, the Japanese, Germans, and Koreans studied our technology to death and invested in it and we didn't. 'That was compelling,' Oberstar states. 'You don't see Microsoft concentrating only on return to the shareholder; 3M requires 25 per cent of all sales to come from products developed in the last four years. They place a premium on research, development, testing and engineering. They are successful in competing, even against subsidized products.'

Such views have become common in Canada too. Jack Layton, leader of Canada's federal NDP and a supporter of 'sustainable and fair trade,' notes: 'NAFTA needs another look. In addition to the structure of NAFTA, it has become a model for global trade rules that are leaving a lot of people behind.' He adds: 'First of all, there's the labour standards that are not being given the important place that is required. Secondly, corporations are the titans of the trade deals. They are at the top of the food chain, higher than governments. You would hope that they [trade deals] would address the public will and that private persons would be elevated to have far more status than they do now. Lastly there are environmental issues that need to be considered.'

Of course, a world without trade is inconceivable. It is the terms of trade that matter. My favourite example of managed trade is the Auto Pact between Canada and the United States, which lasted from 1965 to 2001. The goal was to enable the Big Three automakers of the day to ship new cars back and forth across the border without tariffs and thus allow them to include the Canadian plants in the overall specialization of production, which in turn would make them that much more efficient. This would end the practice of Canadian plants, behind tariff walls, producing a wide variety of models in a single plant, which resulted in short, inefficient runs. The Canadian concern was that the simple abolition of tariff walls could result in the companies producing all their products in the larger U.S. plants, shipping the cars duty-free across the border, and eliminating production in Canada. Under the Auto Pact, the companies, in return for shipping without tariffs, undertook to maintain production levels in Canada at least commensurate with the consumer base in Canada. The pact was a great success, hailed as a triumph of free trade, but it was not free trade at all, it was managed trade, trade with strings that provided consumers with cars without duty attached and did no harm to the workers' wages and living standards in either country. To me, this is managed trade at its best, an imaginative arrangement worked out to meet the needs of both trading partners.

Today the economic miracle in the world of development is China. This is no free-trade model. China is a member of the World Trade Organization (WTO) and enjoys the benefits of market access to the developed countries that the WHO provides. But China is exempted from key WHO free-trade provisions and, in fact, controls its development with an iron hand, building vast trade surpluses and suppressing imports as it sees fit. It is essentially providing export platforms for foreign companies which enable them to exploit the cheap, controlled labour that China offers. This is managed trade with a vengeance.

Current Steelworkers Vice-President Tom Conway says that competition on the home front from Asian imports has currently eased because China and India are now consuming a lot of steel. Similarly, the lower U.S. dollar has also helped. With the United States using 130 million tons of steel a year and the domestic industry producing just 90 to 100 million tons, Conway notes that some imports are necessary. The key is maintaining a proper ratio. But finding that balance has often been problematic. 'By the mid- to late 1960s, imports had grown to 20–25 per cent of the U.S. market, but by the height of the steel crisis of the '80s, it was substantially higher. Japan, Korea, and Brazil were dumping a lot of steel. With the collapse of the Asian economy and the Russian ruble, these economies quit using steel but no one quit making it. They would dump it below cost.' Imports now serve 26 to 27 per cent of the U.S. market, a percentage that Conway calls 'manageable.' But he cautions that there is concern that it could increase if the China/India bubble bursts. China, in particular, would pose a serious problem because its production of steel has increased from 150 million tons five years ago to 600 million tons today. 'Now they're pretty dirty tons. There's not a lot of environmental controls and labour protection,' Conway adds.

Steelworkers President Leo Gerard also has serious concerns about the threat that untrammeled free trade poses to his members' job security.

I think in my case at this point in time it is the negative effects of a global economic system that's been designed to reward financial interests and … to reward Wall Street and Bay Street rather than Main Street. The reality is that nowhere on Earth, except it appears the United States and Canada, are countries willing to give away their jobs. In America, it's a disaster. Someone has to explain to me how having an $800-billion trade deficit is good for the economy. If it's so good, why doesn't anyone else want it? The effect of that kind of exploitive globalization is a huge crisis for not only the union but for our two countries. And in reality, we're going to reap the hurricane of the last thirty years of deregulating the capitalist system.

Or, in the case of so-called trade agreements, regulating it in the interest of the rich and powerful. That's a huge challenge at the collective-bargaining table, at the economic-policy table and at the political table. Those are huge challenges and if we don't succeed, our generation will be the first generation in the United States and Canada to pass on less opportunity to our kids and grandkids than we inherited. That's never happened in the history of our two countries. To me, that's the fight. You marry that with the empowerment that's been given to the corporate elite, to systematically attack the labour movement and to loot the corporate treasuries. You'd almost think that you're hallucinating when you hear the money grabs that CEOs are making.

Leo's observation of generation-to-generation decline is frightening, yet I think that if we turned loose our best brains on the task of devising more imaginative policies we could respond effectively. Our free traders seem to have no trouble creating agreements that protect intellectual property rights or interfere with the national rights of countries by requiring open access to multinational corporations regardless of national considerations, but they have great difficulty requiring protection of human and labour rights such as freedom of association and access to collective bargaining, or protecting and improving the environmental practices in the involved countries.

I really do believe that trade has a vital role to play in building a better world. But its aim should be to improve living conditions in those countries desperately in need while maintaining a high quality of life in those countries where it has been achieved. This is where managing trade enters the picture, the model being, as I have explained, the Auto Pact. One of the difficulties, from labour's point of view, is that by and large those who make and administer the laws, teach economics, or belong to the 'chattering classes' are not themselves subjected to the same internationally competitive circumstances as workers are. Lawyers are protected not only by national regulations but by state and provincial ones. There is no international competitive market for civil servants or teachers.

And so the most bullish proponents of free trade are those who are not affected by it, for instance, many university economics professors. I was invited on a couple of occasions to visit the Harvard Business School to talk about the union's position with regard to trade. One of my favourite ways of attempting to make my point was to say that I often wished the Japanese would come to town, build a first-class university halfway between Harvard and MIT, charge half the tuition, and pay the professors half the salaries. Then the professors might understand in more personal terms what the manufacturing workers in both Canada and the United States have been facing for years.

Trade was an issue all the time, from my first day in office until my last. I was never not dealing with it. It was true that our activity peaked at certain times, but through it all there were issues of interpretation and application crying out for attention, along with private initiatives, mergers, 'outsourcing' of plants overseas, and other such matters that quickly became embroiled in the same international concerns. Other people in the union – the Legislative Department in Washington, lawyers, research people, and public-relations personnel – were principally responsible for the details of the various issues. I was mostly concerned with presentations, interviews, and debates about the principles at stake: Were we protectionists or free traders? Of course, my point always was that we were neither. We had a great many rallies along the way. I did a couple of *Larry King Live* appearances, and two or three Sunday talk shows. In many ways it was very much like the days of debating national versus international unionism in Canada, except that the trade debate lasted much longer and was much more intense. Trade was also a much discussed issue in the international labour movement. We were active in these circles everywhere, and had particularly good relations with, for example, the metalworkers in Japan. We had an annual meeting with them, and other sessions on call, to discuss international issues – one of which was always trade.

The Steelworkers, the labour movement as a whole, and other progressive organizations in both Canada and the United States put up a spirited fight against the FTA and NAFTA. In the opening chapter of this story, the Steelworkers' national director, Gérard Docquier, in his role as a member of the Royal Commission on the Economic Union and Development Prospects for Canada from 1982 to 1985, wrote a strong dissenting report when the commission declared its support for North American free trade. Subsequently, in 1987–8, we in the Steelworkers did our best to derail the free-trade agenda, lobbying Congress and Parliament, mobilizing our membership in the anti-free trade cause, and joining our efforts to those of others in the labour movement and beyond. We lost, it is true, but the fight goes on – as it must. In recent years, corporations, in their overwhelming desire to access the cheap labour available in China, have seized WTO opportunities without meeting WTO obligations. In this case, an international trade agreement has been used to achieve the destruction of North America's manufacturing base. It is a trend that must be reversed.

12

UNION WORK AND POLITICS

In my second full term as president, running from 1989 to 1994, I faced some new challenges and some old ones, not least of which was the continuing crisis in the steel industry. I also carried on with a variety of initiatives that dated to my first term and that, indeed, had been special preoccupations of mine throughout my career in the labour movement. Of these, none was more important than organizing.

In many ways, organizing the unorganized is the principal mission and challenge of the labour movement. Certainly, it was my first love and the activity where the greatest challenges lay, internally in terms of structure, activity, ability, and commitment, and externally in terms of the forces arrayed against us and the uneven tilt of the law, particularly in the United States. Organizing had come with such a rush in the days of the Steel Workers Organizing Committee (SWOC), in the beginning of our union, that the original challenge was more with building the institutional structure and working with and looking after this almost immediately large membership than with organizing. For example, Bert McNamara, long-time union leader and director of the Wisconsin district, was one of the first people hired by SWOC. I asked Bert on one occasion what his duties were and he replied he was in charge of Indiana. I asked, 'What did you do?' He said that he picked up cards that workers had signed or delivered cards that workers requested so that they could be signed. So, I asked, 'How many cards did you pick up?' His reply was it was a poor week if he didn't pick up at least 1,000. Bert, in fact, was one of the most persuasive with regard to me running for international office, assuring me that I would get good support in the United States.

Not that everyone was organized so easily in those early days, but there were vast numbers in the unorganized major steel facilities and no lack of workers eager to persist with organizing efforts until they succeeded. Company attempts to resist were crude and obvious, not sophisticated propaganda but intimidating campaigns. There were shocking confrontations, such as the Memorial Day Massacre in 1937 at the Republic Steel South Chicago plant in which ten picketers were killed while trying to escape the attack of the police. The principal tasks were to make something of this membership, establishing local bodies and regional groupings and structuring it all so as to be democratic and effective. There were contracts to be negotiated and grievances to be pursued – all the items we call servicing became priorities. Organizing just kept happening without requiring the special efforts, talents, and skills it does today.

The Steelworker organizing routine was very basic: finding enough interested people to form an inside committee, turning them loose with applications for membership and authorization of collective-bargaining cards, and working with them in distributing leaflets and holding meetings. Generally, this approach would succeed. House calls were not part of the routine, yet it was difficult for me to envisage a campaign without house calls. This rather simple issue was the first of many to be faced internally in the years to come. It was not so much that the original committee approach could not, from time to time, produce results. It was that, in the U.S. context, there would be a vote and far too frequently, under the relentless propaganda pressure of the employer, often combined with the discharge of some activists and the threat to continue to operate with scabs, the vote would see a significant swing against the union.

After moving to Pittsburgh, I quickly came to the conclusion that organizing should receive greater attention. While serving as the union's international secretary, I became active in Tom Donahue's secretary-treasurers' organization, which Tom, as secretary-treasurer of the AFL-CIO, used for a variety of purposes, such as sharing experiences and expanding communication between unions; developing a mechanism of some substance that could be used to advise affiliates of changes in requirements and procedures; conducting educational presentations, discussions, and forums concerning the needs and future of the labour movement, both in terms of financial officers' direct responsibilities and in terms of the broadest possible view of the movement's objectives; and examining the areas of greatest need, such as organizing. I became an admirer and firm supporter of Tom and his efforts. He demonstrated great interest and concern about the difficult circumstances we were facing, openness to ideas from a broad array of sources, and determination to find approaches to our challenges that could succeed.

Once I became president, I continued to emphasize the importance of organizing to the future of our union and the labour movement as a whole. In the audiences at local union meetings and other gatherings where we talked union, there were always some who had a deep interest in organizing. We tried to touch their interest and guide them into such activity. We worked to recognize the organizers, to emphasize the critical nature of their contribution. We conducted training conferences to help them hone their skills. We were working hard to be sure that those active in organizing were known and recognized.

Another cultural change we attempted in the Steelworkers was the concept that organizing is everybody's challenge and business. The traditional structure of our union provided a local union charter for each workplace, sometimes in the larger mills for large sections of the facility. In my view, this encouraged a certain inward-looking, parochial focus on the local's own needs, while leaving the broader questions, such as organizing, to the international. In the early days, that was a viable approach, but no longer. We now needed an organizing model of trade unionism in which organizing was not only everybody's' concern but also a concern of the highest order.

There was, of course, no way we could turn our union totally over to organizing, not while enduring the biggest, longest, most destructive downturn in steel industry history, with mills closing everywhere, enormous restructuring, thousands of jobs lost, and communities devastated. Nevertheless, we had to do what we could and we did. We began by working out a ratio of staff to membership for servicing purposes by making this as tight as possible and dividing the staff that thereby became available equally among the districts as full-time organizers. This was not meant to free the servicing staff from organizing responsibilities, but to recognize that campaigns of consequence require full-time attention. Servicing staff were expected to contribute by digging up leads, handling smaller campaigns, and helping with house calls, meetings, and leaflet distributions in the larger efforts as they had time. We also continued with central organizing staff in Pittsburgh and Toronto. Our intention was that the central staff should be available to work on major campaigns and also be involved in creative and strategic thinking and planning, as well as research and training. All of this improved the pace of organizing to some degree. The most interesting and obvious result was that, given the same relative resources in each district, a much better result was achieved in each of the three districts in Canada than anywhere else.

It did not require much examination to determine the reason. If one looked at campaigns of the same size in the two countries, it was immediately apparent that those in the United States were much longer, both before any procedures began before a board and, even more dramatically, after they had. Why was this? It was because the law in the United States allowed employers to use tactics of coercion and propaganda far beyond anything provincial law or the federal law permitted in Canada. And the anti-union consultants frequently led their clients past what the law permitted, presumably because, even when and if they were found guilty, the penalties were slight. These activities cost time and caused frustration, largely as a result of the knowledge American workers had of how badly employers can behave in the American setting. In no other country in the advanced world are workers required to face such vicious attacks simply for exercising their right to organize.

During the rest of my time as president, we attempted various approaches to organizing and went round and round on a number of basic issues, searching for an approach with which everyone could be comfortable, committed, and enthusiastic. One of these issues was the different roles of organizers at the centre and in the regions. My view is that the most effective organizing requires skilled and committed people at both levels. An organizing campaign succeeds best if the workers involved feel it to be their campaign, if it is linked to their conception of building their union successfully and bringing justice to their workplace. The central group has a key role to play as well, thinking about and working on such considerations as broader strategic approaches, researching the main issues, and bringing fresh insights and new ideas into the program.

My conclusions about organizing are that two elements are critical. The first is the law, particularly as it deals with employer interference in what should be the clear right of the workers, and second is the quality of the organizing approach. By the latter I mean both the posture of the entire union – the organizing model as it has been talked about – and the abilities of the front-line, full-time organizers. There is a role for every activist in organizing; everybody from members to local union officers to servicing staff can talk to people, find leads, knock on doors, ensure that the union's voice is heard, or hand out leaflets. There can be no union without an ongoing building effort. As for the full-time organizers, there are many myths that particular people need to talk with particular workers, usually with reference to their own kind. There is truth in this where different languages are involved, and sometimes with certain cultures as well. But, generally speaking, what is required is a good organizer who knows how to approach people, to listen and learn, and to present the union ideals effectively. In campaigns involving large numbers of workers, lead organizers are required who have a broad range of creative talents as strategists, communicators, and leaders, along with great energy and a high level of commitment. I had a policy at one stage where I would not put anyone into any staff position without them having organizing experience. In this vein, the Organizing Institute that a few unions created within the AFL-CIO to recruit and train organizers was an important development. The labour movement needs both a mass effort regarding organizing and a continuing commitment to seeking out and training the best organizers it can find, wherever it can find them.

Every poll shows that there are millions of workers in the United States and a great many in Canada as well who would like to have unions if they had the opportunity. The most important obligation of the labour movement is to meet that need, to overcome the hurdles that our opponents put in the way. If we do so, everything is possible for us; if we fail, our future will continue to be one of crisis and challenge. For the Steelworkers in particular, the challenge remains to have the organizing culture achieve the same importance in the life of the union as do the cultures of bargaining or representation.

The historic fact that, in the early years, the AFL model of bargaining won out in terms of staying power over the more dramatic, more movement-oriented models of the Knights of Labor and the Industrial Workers of the World ('Wobblies') had a profound impact on everything that followed. The model developed in the 1930s emphasized local unions whose purpose was to look after their members, a responsibility we carry out in a detailed way not matched or followed by labour movements in the rest of the world. Yet, alongside bargaining and servicing members' needs, organizing remains key. We can wait for the frustration of people to move the pendulum again, as it did in the late 1800s and in the 1930s, but we may wait ourselves out of existence. We need to find a way to build our movement, given the present circumstances. Success in that endeavour will support success in the other areas; even marginal movement will enable marginal improvement. I see much more success coming from pushing the pendulum than in waiting for injustice and frustration to move it. It seems to me that the particular element organizing requires today is an intensity of effort involving the application of all the elements of strategic campaigns, including community support, support from political and religious leaders, support from other locals and other unions, demonstrations, leverage, campaign activities – and all of it sustained through board procedures or, outside board procedures, through the negotiation of the first agreements. In this regard, the importance of organizing in the service and information sectors of the economy cannot be over-emphasized. I believe that in some of these situations the labour movement should consider pooling resources to focus the necessary talent and resources on breakthrough organizing efforts.

Industrial action can be likened to a three-legged stool. One of those legs is bargaining and servicing; another is organizing. The third leg is political action. In the U.S. context, we must continue to recognize that political action, electing representatives to Washington who understand and support the needs of the labour movement, is essential. It is key to the Steelworkers, and, I believe, to the bulk of the labour movement in the United States. Deep in everyone's memory is the reality that the movement was built on laws enacted in Washington, that for years steel agreements were settled when everyone was summoned to the White House, that legislative and political action both gives and takes away. Labour ignores politics as its peril.

In Canada, we read and hear and see so much of American politics that I think most Canadians consider themselves to be experts, at least in comparison to what most Americans understand about politics in Canada. In my own case, I quickly discovered that I was both correct in my views and yet also wildly off the mark. I was correct about the basics, how the system worked, the names of offices and other places, but there were also matters of local detail, subtleties of language and appearance that one could not learn in absentia but only by being there.

There are a host of similarities between the American and Canadian political systems; there are in both countries, after all, elections with candidates and campaigns and events and door knocking and phone banking and such activities. But when it comes to process, structure, and social backdrops and systems, there are vast differences. In sweeping structural terms, the principal difference is that the system in the United States is much more fundamentally a two-party system, whereas Canada has evolved from a two-party to a multi-party system. In Canada, labour and the democratic left have their own party, while the

Parti Québécois, the Quebec provincial party supporting the separa-tion of Quebec, has an extension in a federal party, the Bloc Québécois. Today, there is also the Green Party, although it is not a party of the left as in Europe but rather one focused on environmental issues and, on other matters, aligned on the right within the general policies and tradi-tions of the Liberals and Conservatives.

In procedural terms, the United States has regular election dates on which voting for various offices is held on the same day, includ-ing the direct election of the president, with every citizen entitled to vote; candidates are chosen through primaries. In Canada, candidates are chosen at meetings of the members of the party in a given district, called a riding. It is a system of one election at a time; federal elections have their own dates, provincial their own, and municipal their own, so that party organizations are arranged separately for each election or, in essence, transferred easily from one to another.

The prime minister in Canada is not elected directly by the people but is the leader of the party that wins the most seats. In the election itself, he or she is simply one of the candidates in one of the ridings, and when elected he/she is not the head of state, as is the president in the United States. The formality of that function falls to the governor general, the representative of the British queen in Canada, so there are no cries in Canada in times of crisis that we must support the prime minister – one can be a loyal supporter of the country and feel no pangs about being critical of the prime minister.

My involvement in U.S. politics began with the election in 1980, Jim-my Carter's attempt to win a second term. I was very much on the fringe but did attend the Democratic Party convention. I helped out in our operation where I could but mostly focused on how we con-ducted ourselves politically as compared to our approach in Canada. However, it was in the campaign for Democratic presidential nominee Walter 'Fritz' Mondale in 1984, shortly after I had taken up the post of union president, that I really became immersed in the American politi-cal scene, encouraging our organization and members to do all they could to defeat Ronald Reagan. Reagan's destruction of the Profession-al Air Traffic Controllers Organization (PATCO) was an unforgivable act, taken against a union that had endorsed him and whose problems he had promised to address. If every corporation in America that was accused of breaking the law, indeed if every corporation in America that was found guilty of breaking the law, were destroyed by the presi-dent as Reagan destroyed PATCO, the economic landscape of America would be unrecognizable. I was determined that we do everything possible to defeat him.

It was in this connection that I came to understand the full reality of how unhooked a Democratic presidential campaign is from whatever else the party is doing. Mondale was in charge of his own campaign. Although I do not know for certain, I can't imagine that the idea of affirming that he would raise taxes was subjected to any expert analysis or tested on some focus groups or anything of that kind before it was announced. The affirmation so shocked the Reagan campaign team that they were a little confused about their response for a day or two until they realized that all they had to do was say that they would not raise taxes. The episode was symptomatic, I think, of the problems besetting the Mondale campaign. As I discovered at our Cleveland convention, the Mondale campaign organization, as we came to know it, was essentially a group of college students, wonderful, committed, and idealistic but without much political experience. Mondale was a man we wanted very much to elect, and I am confident that he would have been a great president. It was not to be.

The next opportunity for political involvement came in 1988 with the nomination of Michael Dukakis as the Democratic Party's presidential candidate. Dukakis was again an outstanding candidate who would have been a fine president but once more the Democratic cause was burdened by a weak organization that was shaken up a number of times during the campaign. Our principal difficulty, beyond the instability in the campaign organization, was the candidate's reluctance to adopt as firm an attitude about trade and its consequences as we would have wished. Towards the end of the campaign, the Auto Workers, the Machinists, and our union jointly commissioned a public-opinion poll to demonstrate to Dukakis what a powerful message a tougher line on trade would be. Although he did amend his stump speech a little, and his numbers picked up towards the end of the campaign, I felt that what we were asking he could not imagine supporting, living as he did in the midst of the free-trade academic temples of Boston and Cambridge. We lost again.

By now, it had become apparent that the process of reinventing a campaign not only for each new cycle but also within each campaign's duration was a poor match for the Republicans' disciplined, well-financed, and well-prepared campaigns of that era. A number of us on the Executive Council of the AFL-CIO began discussing the need for reform in this regard. We supported Ron Brown in his effort to become chairman of the Democratic National Committee (DNC), and once he landed the job in February 1989, we raised with him the need for some planning and preparation for presidential campaigns. He shared the same view but needed funds. It was agreed that I would promote a major contribution from the Steelworkers for this purpose and thus provide an example that could be used to encourage others. I did, and the contribution was made, leading to themes, polls, and focus groups. Then, in the early 1990s, Bill Clinton came along, maybe the greatest campaigner ever, with an all-pro team, and we were on our way. In truth, I do not know the extent to which there was a tie between what Ron Brown had prepared and what the Clinton team did – I like to think there was. Tragically, Ron, as secretary of commerce in the first Clinton administration, was to die in a plane crash in 1996.

The Clinton campaign of 1992 – the excitement of its success, the euphoric expectations it aroused – was among the high points of my political experience. Clinton enjoyed the process of campaigning like few people I have ever seen. We held a rally during the campaign in the parkette beside our headquarters building in Pittsburgh. There must have been nearly a thousand people there. He was late arriving, but I think that before he left he had shaken hands with everybody at least twice. And then, on his way out, he noticed people standing along the far side of the Boulevard of the Allies, the street in front of our building, and dashed through the traffic and shook hands with all of them.

A think-tank conference – one of many of Clinton's ideas – was held between Election Day and the inauguration. It was an inspiration-filled event of new ideas, new initiatives, new hopes, and new dreams. It had a level of excitement, an air of promise and intensity I have rarely experienced. I enjoyed the privilege of serving on a panel chaired by Al Gore about the environment. My presentation concerned using the need for improving the environment as the basis for economic development with new products and new technologies, rather than considering the environment a hindrance. I submitted a report on the conference from which I would like to quote because it expresses well the great hopes we had at the time.

The most impressive aspect of the conference was undoubtedly the dramatically effective manner in which President-elect Clinton conducted its proceedings. He was leader, manager, facilitator, resource person, and consensus builder, all the while displaying both the depth of his concern and the breadth of his knowledge with regard to the wide range of problems, issues and possibilities about which America must act. It is impossible to think of any other political leader who would attempt such a challenging and, in many ways, risky task, much less accomplish it with such sparkling success.

I was most impressed not only with the President-elect's commitment to the need for a new approach to health care in general, but particularly with his understanding of the vital importance of this issue in relation to the enormous burden of "historical costs" in health care that are being borne by our traditional industries, such as steel and auto. His comment to the conference that this requires some "semi social insurance" approach, as I recall his words, was most perceptive.

The unconscionable failure of the present system to provide coverage for all Americans, the need to establish a level health-care playing field with our principal trading partners and, therefore, to deal with both the competitive needs of our private sector as well as meaningful cost containment, the fundamental obligation to minister to the health needs of today's and tomorrow's generations, are all issues that cry out for effective solution.

In this regard, five of the largest integrated steel producers and the union presented our joint proposals to the transition group for health care.

In the events surrounding the inauguration, the president's superb understanding of policy issues was on display in every conversation, while his wife, Hillary, the soon-to-be first lady, showed a grasp of the issues of the day that was more restrained but still very apparent to anyone who listened and understood. Clinton himself could 'do a room' better than anyone I had ever met. When he spoke with you, he looked at you so intently, and listened so carefully, that the noise and the crowd disappeared. At one cocktail party, surrounded constantly by an enthusiastic crowd, he stopped with me long enough on his way to the platform to remark that a person I had been talking to was one of the most brilliant economists in the world on the subject of using the peace dividend for conversion to less military and more civilian production. This has to mean that, even as he was deeply engaged in his one-on-one conversations, he was somehow keeping a close eye on the rest of the room.

At one of the major inauguration events, because of the significant contribution of the Steelworkers to the campaign, Audrey and I were given seats on the high platform right in the middle of the USAir Arena, very close to the performers and with a marvellous view out across the assembled multitude. On the great day itself, 21 January 1993, we enjoyed the advantage of representing a union that encompassed two countries. We watched the ceremony and listened to the address from seats on the lawn directly in front of the podium; later, we watched the parade from the roof of the Canadian Embassy, the best vantage spot in Washington.

And what of the Clinton presidency? Was it all we hoped it to be? Certainly not, but probably no presidency could have been. Was it all it might have been? I don't think so, undercut as it was not only by some terrible errors of judgment on Clinton's part but also by his desire to be liked, an important quality in any politician but almost overwhelming in Clinton's case. Was he better than what went before? Dramatically so, in myriad ways that most citizens would be unaware of – such as the appointments he made to thousands of jobs throughout the government apparatus that were so much better than before, and so important. He was enormously popular and could have been elected in a walk to a third term, had the constitution permitted it. He was one of the most intelligent persons I have ever been privileged to know.

I did have policy differences with Clinton, and one of them was particularly important – free trade. Clinton was and is a true believer in free trade and, like true believers anywhere, unshakable in his faith. For this reason, we did not initially support him in the primaries but instead backed Tom Harkin, whose views on trade were similar to ours. But Harkin's campaigning skills, while impressive, were no match for Clinton's, nor were those of any of the other aspirants. I had known about the firmness, indeed fervour, of Clinton's convictions on free trade for some time. We had both attended a conference in Europe before he emerged as a candidate. It was mixed conference involving business, political, and trade-union leaders from Europe and North America. One night, those of us of social-democratic persuasion gathered for a little socializing and discussion and, as the evening progressed, the subject of trade inevitably came up. Ultimately, there were only the two of us left, me and Clinton, neither of us budging an inch in a discussion that went on so late that, the next morning, we were unable to rouse ourselves from bed for our regular run. Our differences on the subject of free trade were destined to become even sharper in the years ahead, as first the FTA and then NAFTA took effect.

Free trade was closely linked to another issue on which Clinton and I disagreed: competiveness and skills training. In the era of trade liberalization, our overriding concern about maintaining a manufacturing base in the United States had involved us in numerous activities, many of them related to or centred on the challenge of competitiveness. At one point during the administration of President George H.W. Bush, there were a few councils on competitiveness. A couple of them were the result of private initiatives; the others were public, one under the direction of Vice-President Dan Quayle at the president's instruction and another established by Congress, with the representatives on it chosen by various congressional bodies. I served on this council by appointment of the Democrats in the House of Representatives. Its Congress-appointed president was Dr Fred Bergsten, the founding president of the Institute for International Economics. Bergsten had worked on trade in the Carter administration and established his institute after President Carter's defeat. He was yet another example of a progressive person, who, for all his commitment to the goal of a decent, prosperous, democratic society, with a strong labour movement at its centre, was blinded by his uncritical embrace of free trade. In fairness, given the intellectual and political atmosphere of those years, it is impossible to imagine successful mainstream institutions devoted to international economics pursuing any other approach.

When pushed to respond to the loss of jobs as employers shifted production and supply offshore, the answer inevitably was enhanced competiveness through training and retraining. And it was on this subject that Clinton and I were again poles apart, not because his administration didn't believe in retraining and I did, but because he paid only lip service to the cause while I saw it as critical. There was and is absolutely no evidence that any U.S. administration or employers' organization throughout this entire period was willing to create or support anything involving training on a scale remotely adequate to meet the need. This is not to say that good things were not done. These efforts received the support of people such as Bergsten, but they were simply not of the magnitude required. For example, Clinton campaigned vigorously in 1992 for an ambitious skills-training program. Every company was to have a program at a cost of at least 1.5 per cent of payroll, or they could pay that percentage of payroll into a government program. After Clinton won the election, the employer pressure against this idea was so intense that it was the first item in his program to be dropped. If memory serves me well, it happened even before the inauguration. I was bitterly disappointed.

On another issue, health-care reform, Clinton and I saw eye to eye, but the results were hardly what either of us hoped for. At the time of our discussion in Europe on free trade, Clinton was governor of Arkansas. But that evening, clearly, he was reaching out to broader fields and more difficult national issues. This was certainly true about health care, a subject that gained prominence during his campaign for the presidency. We were suddenly facing a window of opportunity; health care was an issue whose time had come and it had been pushed along by the election of our candidate, Harris Wofford, in November 1991 to fill the Senate position left vacant by the death in a helicopter crash of Pennsylvania Senator John Heinz. Harris was unknown to me until he was appointed secretary of labor in the cabinet of Pennsylvania Governor Bob Casey, Sr. We had been vigorous supporters of Casey and were urging that one of our own, Frank Mont, receive the secretary's position. Frank did become the head of training outreach in the Casey administration, but the governor insisted that Harris would be an outstanding secretary of labor. I was very interested in meeting him.

The opportunity came at a winter meeting in Florida. Lane Kirkland of the AFL-CIO had invited Harris to spend a few days there so he and the leadership of the labour movement, particularly in Pennsylvania, could get to know each other. I invited Harris and his wife to have dinner with Audrey and me, the other officers who were present, and Bernie Kleiman. Harris and I hit it off immediately, although our backgrounds were quite different. A distinguished lawyer and academic, he had served as the president of Bryn Mawr College, worked with John F. Kennedy to establish the Peace Corps, and written a book about the Kennedys. In terms of our basic philosophy about social responsibility, the labour movement, and labour-management relationships, we were very much on the same page.

When a Senate vacancy occurs during an administration's term of office, the governor of the state that has lost a senator makes an interim appointment. Immediately after Heinz's death, we began pressing Governor Casey regarding a Wofford appointment. The governor was not unsympathetic to this, but he had a very different idea he wished to try first, specifically, offering the job to Chrysler executive Lee Iacocca. It was not as off-the-wall an idea as it sounded in the beginning. The great challenge then, as it has remained, was to maintain and rebuild industry in North America. Iacocca was the living example of a CEO who had turned around, with considerable government help, a dying company. It would have been quite a public-relations coup had Casey succeeded, but Iacocca declined the offer. Fortunately for Harris and those of us supporting him, it turned out well. Harris received the appointment.

Steelworkers, Mineworkers, and most unionists put their hearts and strength into the campaign that followed the interim appointment. Harris enlisted the support of Paul Begala and James Carville, and, most important, he made health care the centrepiece of his campaign. He really touched a nerve in doing so, making it a national issue for the first time in decades. His timing was superb. Americans were concerned about health care in a way they had not been for a long time. Pressure from employers to cut back or eliminate health insurance was on the increase. Health Management Organizations (HMOs), which in the beginning had been viewed positively, often turned out to be money-grubbing profit-seekers rather than professional caregivers. The number of people without health insurance seemed on a permanent escalator, as each year millions more lost coverage.

Harris handily won the election to fill the vacancy, but in November 1994 he had to face re-election at the time of the regular election cycle. By then I had retired, but I was still a close observer of American politics. The Steelworkers were feeling reasonably good about the political landscape. We had a brilliant young Democrat as president and a number of Democratic governors in place, including in Pennsylvania. We had a majority of Democrats in the House of Representatives, Harris Wofford was in office, and in 1992 we had had come within one percentage point of defeating the other senator from Pennsylvania, the Republican Arlen Specter. We felt, or at least I felt, that there were more gains awaiting us. The road ahead turned out to be rougher than we had imagined, beginning with Harris Wofford himself.

When I learned that Rick Santorum was the opposition candidate in the re-election campaign, I urged Harris not to underrate Santorum as a campaigner. Santorum knew how to whine and pout, how to be nasty, and how to work hard at campaigning. He first was elected to the House of Representatives in a campaign based on the accusation that his opponent, the fine young Congressman Doug Walgren, was neglecting the needs of the people by moving to Washington. The truth was that nearly all members of Congress with children in school had moved to the D.C. area so they could be at least somewhat helpful to the other parent. Congress in Washington is not like state legislatures that meet a few weeks a year; Congress meets most of the time. Doug was the congressman in the district where I lived and I know he was totally committed to carrying out his local responsibilities.

Harris's campaign was in the hands once again of James Carville, truly a political genius in terms of the use of TV and the general orien-

two places that could accommodate 5,000 delegates accustomed to sitting at tables. These were Atlantic City and Las Vegas. The union was long hesitant about going to Las Vegas because the image did not seem appropriate; on the other hand, many of our delegates viewed attending the convention as somewhat in the nature of a reward and, from that perspective, what could be better than Vegas? During President Abel's time in office, Las Vegas was selected as the site best suited for our conventions, and from that point on the location was no longer an issue. However, in the context of the early 1980s, I raised a concern. It seemed to me that, with the devastation suffered in so many steel and metal manufacturing communities, it would be a good idea to take our convention to one of those places. Our convention was no longer as large as it once was – as a result of job losses – and many cities had built convention facilities as part of a development plan. We could deliver messages of support through the convention to places where thousands of our members lived. My argument prevailed. The first convention over which I presided was held in September 1984 in Cleveland, where the founding constitutional convention of the union had been held in 1942.[1]

It turned out to be a most successful event. While the special election between Frank McKee and me was over, he and Joe Odorcich were both completing their old terms. Frank was gracious, but Odorcich was very bitter about the election. He attempted to cause some difficulty at the convention by claiming he was being ignored by me and not being asked to do anything. I responded by acknowledging that there was not much I felt confident about entrusting to him, but that, given the circumstances faced by the labour movement, it was inconceivable that a vice-president could not find something useful to do. Apart from that issue, we began what became a new tradition at Cleveland. I knew that, while many of our delegates agreed with the idea of showing the union's flag in one of our distressed areas, there was also considerable disappointment about not going to Vegas, or even Atlantic City. I felt that, to alleviate this disappointment, we had to make a special effort to make the convention not only productive but also enjoyable. At union conventions, people love to meet old friends. So we started the practice of holding a big outdoor picnic/party, the food provided by a district – not necessarily the host district because there were many more dis-

---

1 The convention would return to Las Vegas in 1986 and 1988; Toronto hosted the 1990 event and Pittsburgh was the host in 1992.

tation of a campaign but no expert about grass-roots activity and not really appreciative of its importance. For whatever reason, Harris, who had taken to life in the Senate as his natural habitat, lost the election. He went on to do great work for AmeriCorps. It's the shame that Carville's belief in putting so much attention on television during the campaign without sufficient campaign workers on the ground, combined with our failure to support Harris with the enthusiasm that was appropriate, likely cost him the election. If he had won, I am persuaded that he could have remained a senator for as long as he chose, and, more important, the Clinton administration's plan for health-care reform – which its opponents dubbed 'Hillary Care,' after its chief architect, Hillary Clinton – might have garnered more support in Congress than it did. During the years he served, it was a delight to have such a member in the Senate – totally reliable in working for his constituents, and on our side in all the battles regarding not just health care but social security and the rest.

Wofford was not the only Democrat defeated that year, of course, as the Republicans, under the banner of the 'Contract with America,' regained control of Congress. Thereafter, the story is well known: Clinton's re-election in 1996 followed by the election of George W. Bush in 2000 and Bush's re-election in 2004. I was long gone from the American political scene by then, but, although I acknowledge not having the same proximity to either the Al Gore campaign in 2000 or the John Kerry campaign in 2004, it seems clear to me that in both those contests the Democrats fell back into the same old bad habits that had cost them victory in the 1980s: ineffective organization, constantly changing strategies, and politically timid leadership. For me, the tragedy is that both Gore and Kerry would have been fine presidents, in my opinion significantly better than the alternative who defeated them, as history demonstrated. The lesson is that campaigns do matter.

Through all these political goings on, there was still a union to run – a task that continued to be difficult because of the challenging economic circumstances of the times. Gradually, we came to the conclusion that meeting the needs of our members in an era of manufacturing decline, free trade, and globalization required fresh thinking and new approaches. Over the course of my second presidential term, we acted on this belief in a variety of ways, and while not all our efforts came to fruition, we did make significant strides. That story is next.

13

NEW DIRECTIONS

In the first year of my second term, 1989, we were faced with an unusual circumstance: for the first time in a long time, the steel industry made some money. In truth, I believe that this was somewhat aided and abetted, if not created, by our work stoppage at U.S. Steel in 1986–7. Having the major player out of the market for six months certainly did not harm the market prospects of the other players and everyone was enjoying some profit making, though, as it turned out, the good times were short-lived. During this volatile period, two principal priorities emerged from the Basic Steel Industry Conference, after which the company conferences met and discussed our situation. The first aim, obviously, was to gain back to the maximum degree possible the ground that had been given up in concessions, though in some cases the technological world had changed to such an extent that there was no ground to regain. The second, and most important, task was to deal with the future and it was in that regard that we launched one of the most significant new programs that had been created for some time.

During our preparation for bargaining in 1989, Bernie and I, as had become our custom, travelled the field, meeting with the union negotiating committees at the major locations. The purpose of these field trips was to discuss bargaining proposals and take an informal measure of where our committees stood, what subjects were on their minds, and which of their ideas had the potential to give rise to useful and creative proposals. The principal subjects that resulted from this exercise came from both ends, as it were: from the committees on the one hand, and from us on the other.

The committees were concerned that many senior members were taking early pensions, not because they wished to but because they were intimidated by new technologies coming into the mills. Among the leadership, we were fully aware of training initiatives that had been developed in some other industries on a joint basis with unions, particularly in the auto and communication industries. One of our distinguished retirees, the late Ben Fischer, at the time a professor at Carnegie Mellon and head of the Labor Center he was creating there, was helpful in this and we organized a forum to examine in depth what was happening in these programs. As a result, we decided to propose that joint training have a prominent place among our objectives. Our purpose was to find as reasonable, and as cost-efficient, a mechanism as possible. We developed some principles, first as a part of our opening proposals but then elaborated on and added to during the bargaining process. These included: the use of existing facilities rather than the building of new ones; a limited central staff, focused on development and excellence; a decentralized effort that maximized the use of local talent; a set per-capita budget so that costs would not run out of control; a program open to all employees at each location; the effort at each location to be developed and led by a local joint committee, framed by the negotiated principles and the leadership of an executive director and a joint board of directors; and the program to be particularly related to basic skills, so employees might prepare themselves for the new skills that were required internally, and also that they might, in the event of further shakedowns in the industry, possess more marketable skills than had the thousands of workers in the earlier mass layoffs who were skilled steelworkers but lacked the skills appropriate to the labour markets in which they found themselves.

We also determined that the headquarters of the new training initiative should be in the northwest Indiana/Chicago steel complex, the principal steelmaking area in the United States, and not in Pittsburgh. We established the make-up of the governing board without difficulty, comprised of four officers of the union and four senior officials from among the companies. We had to change the name a little because it conflicted with those of other institutions, but ultimately we settled on the Institute for Career Development (ICD). However, we had a difficult time choosing an executive director who suited both sides as represented on the board. We employed a headhunter, and searched diligently among educators, but the person who came in and wowed the board was suggested by Lane Kirkland. This was Jim Murray, president of the Montana Federation of Labor, an activist in working with the government in developing training programs, and he was an instant hit with both sides of the table. Meanwhile, because we had taken so long and the heart of the program was in the local committees, a number of locations had begun the process of setting up without waiting. I remarked to Bernie at this time that we must have done something right – the program seemed to have a life of its own.

The program has had a central secretariat of eight to ten people throughout its existence. The combination of local input, ownership, and considerable control, balanced by a central group that develops ideas and sets objectives and standards, using the budgeting process as an instrument to ensure that such objectives and standards are meaningful, has been effective. From the establishment of the ICD in 1989, participation rates at some locations have been over 50 per cent of those eligible, even in periods of high overtime. The emphasis has been on teaching basic skills, but through imaginative, learning-by-doing methods. Boats have been built, books have been written, stained-glass art has been created, thousands have become skilled with computers, thousands have improved their mathematics, and thousands have learned to communicate more effectively. The program, of course, moved ahead much quicker after Jim became executive director. He guided it for its formative early years and then retired. His successor was Harmon Lisnow, now retired, under whose leadership the institute was in the forefront of joint educational efforts. The current leader is Jerry Evans. I believe it to be one of the most popular programs that we have ever undertaken. It speaks directly to the enormous interest our members have in educational opportunities and in improving their knowledge and skills.

In 1998 the ICD was selected by the National Institute for Literacy as one of the six best workforce programs nationwide. In 1999 it was recognized as one of the eighteen best adult-education programs in the United States at a special White House summit meeting called '21st Century Skills for 21st Century Jobs,' convened and conducted by Vice-President Al Gore. The ICD has worked with Indiana University Northwest in Gary, Indiana, to create Swingshift College, which offers a degree program specifically designed to meet the needs of working adults. A series of writing workshops, with poet Jimmy Santiago Baca, produced an anthology of Steelworkers writings, *The Heat: Steelworker Lives and Legends*, published in 2000. The success of *The Heat* has inspired many other writing programs and the development of a creative writing project by the Association of Joint Labor/Management Educational Programs. The Career Development Program at USW/Mittal Steel USA, at Burns Harbor, Indiana, built the Thomas M. Conway Observatory, which has become the heart of an astronomical learning facility in the northwestern part of the state. A Steelworker photo journalism exhibit, 'Faces of Steel,' toured the United States in 2002 and 2003, visiting, among a host of cities and communities large and small, New York City, St Louis, Pittsburgh, Canton, Ohio, and Gary, Indiana. In 2005 the ICD sponsored a play at the Towle Theater in Hammond, Indiana. The play, *Steel and Roses*, featured dialogues and monologues, music and comedy, and was the culmination of a project in which Steelworkers participated through acting, playwriting, and set-design classes. The production was a sell-out. Of course, there are thousands of individual accomplishments. For example, Randy Noak was trained in computers and now works in the ICD computer division. Richard Nussbaum earned a degree through ICD and the University of Massachusetts and now has his own business in computer repair. John Dietsch started as a truck driver at Sparrows Point. Through Career Development, he passed his entrance exam to the mill's new cold sheet mill, earned his General Equivalency Diploma (GED), and is pursuing an advanced degree. Ernie Barrientez earned a culinary degree through ICD and now caters USW events in northwest Indiana and instructs at Ivy Tech Community College.

Another issue we confronted during my two terms in the presidential chair was union mergers, which I believe was a matter of fundamental importance to the future of the American labour movement. There were too many unions that were too small to cope effectively in an increasingly difficult environment. While I raised the question of mergers with everyone in a general way, two were accomplished and three more I pursued vigorously and directly. The two that were accomplished really came to us; one was the Upholsterers' International Union and the other was the Canadian section of the Retail, Wholesale and Department Store Union. The first of these came about in 1985 because the president, John Serembus, had had a good experience with the Steelworkers over the years and saw his union becoming less than viable. In effect, he proposed the merger with us. One of the great pluses of this merger, although it did not seem so for some years, was a jointly managed Taft Hartley benefit plan that gave the union the voice in such matters that we had long been seeking. Our people spent some years saving the plan from collapse by making a series of innovative arrangements with Blue Cross of Pennsylvania, but ultimately we converted it into a well-managed program that the union has gradually been extending to more and more members. Accepting the RWDSU's

Canadian section some years later, in 1993, created a serious personal rift with a good friend, Lenore Miller, the president of the union. Lenore had worked out a merger with the United Food and Commercial Workers, and, not unreasonably from her point of view, expected the other affiliates not to interfere. I knew that this merger was not going to be accepted by her Canadian membership because of various difficulties over the years between the two unions. At the same time, I knew that the Canadian locals would be amenable to coming into the Steelworkers. They were and they did.

My attempts to persuade Lenore that these were the facts and that this was the best solution, that RWDSU was the first union I had worked for during the Eaton drive and that I had retained a great interest in retail organizing, fell on deaf and indeed hostile ears. Lenore brought the matter up before the Executive Council of the AFL-CIO, asking that they do something about it. Lane explained that, whatever he might think about unions merging with little regard for traditional jurisdictional lines, the federation had no authority in such matters. The most painful part of the process for me, other than the difficulty with Lenore, was listening to Ron Carey, president of the Teamsters, who were active in a host of jurisdictions, lecturing me about raiding. The merger proceeded under the guidance of Vice-President Becker and Canadian National Director Leo Gerard. It survived a few years but was always difficult, and, after a few years, most of the locals merged with the Canadian Auto Workers.

Another merger that I pursued was with the Aluminum Workers of America (AWA), headquartered in St Louis. In 1984, on almost my first day in office as president, I phoned Slim Holley, president of the AWA, to ask if I could meet with him. I told him I had a two-point agenda. The first was that we should coordinate our bargaining in the aluminum industry. It was my observation that we tended to play secretive games with each other that, in the end, were of benefit only to the companies. This meant that each of us accomplished less than we could by bargaining together. My second point was that I wanted to speak with him about a merger. I explained my position in detail. I said the two points were not connected – that we should coordinate bargaining if we never merged, but, by the same token, I would never give up on urging the merger solution because it made such eminent good sense. Slim welcomed the ideas and welcomed my proposed visit. The visit went well and we proceeded with the coordinated bargaining part of the program.

I was, I thought, making considerable progress on the merger question as we talked, but Slim was anxious to retire and did so without the issue really moving forward. I had known Slim from my Kitimat days, when he was one of the staff persons on the other side who turned up from time to time. I did not know the new president, Ernie LaBaff, but that was quickly accomplished, with Ernie being of such a friendly and extroverted nature that it was a delight to know him. Obviously, he had some ideas about his union that he wished to implement. He was also a great public speaker and used to good purpose the platforms that became available to him.

George Becker was in charge of our aluminum section and over time the discussions about a possible merger were held by him, although I was also involved occasionally. The merger did not come to pass during my years as president, but it did occur during George's time in office as my successor. When Ernie retired, the whole arrangement was accomplished positively, with good feeling and understanding between the leaders and the two unions.

Another union that I considered a good fit and an appropriate merger partner was the Oil, Chemical and Atomic Workers (OCAW). In particular, we shared with them a keen and aggressive interest in issues of health and safety, notably in the chemical industry because our merger with District 50 had brought a significant number of chemical workers into our ranks. In this connection we had frequent occasion to be involved in issues with the OCAW and with Tony Mazzochi, its leading activist in the health and safety area. Our people had many discussions with Tony on the general subject of merger.

The president of the union was Joe Misbrener, and I had numerous conversations with him that ultimately resulted in an invitation to meet with his executive board. Jim English and I met with the board in Denver and the meeting did not go well. Bob Wages, Misbrener's assistant, was vigorously opposed to the idea of merging with anyone. His mindset was that the labour movement was still in a position to bring about renewal, and, while we didn't object to this goal, we were increasingly persuaded that mergers were an essential element in being able to meet the challenges of the times. In the end, our efforts to achieve a merger failed in my years as president, though, by a circuitous route, the OCAW did join us in 2005, after first merging with the Paperworkers.

The third union to which I paid considerable attention was the Allied Industrial Workers. This was the union that resulted from the continuation of the AFL Autoworkers but was, in fact, a great collective-bargaining fit with us in that we both represented plants in many of the same companies. We also shared with their president, Dominick D'Ambrosio, a concern about the exposure of workers to dangerous substances in plants. A former research director for their union, Ray McDonald, had joined our staff. Ray, of course, had many contacts in the AIW and would have liked nothing better than to see a merger of the two unions. At D'Ambrosio's last convention, held in Pittsburgh, the subject of merger was in the air. It turned out, however, that his successor as president had close ties with the Paperworkers and shortly after the convention that merger occurred. As mentioned, the Paperworkers have since joined the Steelworkers.

Making the union movement a more cohesive, tightly knit force through mergers required me to look beyond the boundaries of my own union to the broader labour landscape. The same can be said of another of my experiences as president: membership on the Executive Council of the AFL-CIO. At first, Lane Kirkland was cautious about putting me on the council because Frank McKee had been effective at convincing the press and some others around the movement that I was not really president until the challenges to the election had been heard. There were no challenges of importance, but I didn't fuss about it, having plenty to do and the confidence that it would all work out.

This council was not unlike that of the CLC on which I had been serving, but neither was it entirely the same. The CLC had an executive committee, of which I was not a member. One arrived at a council meeting for which the agenda had not only been set but in effect prioritized and dealt with to some extent. This meant that a direction had been set on most matters of consequence and was not easily changed. In my time, the AFL-CIO had no executive committee with this kind of authority. Certainly, as officers, Lane Kirkland and Tom Donahue came with issues and recommendations, but, generally speaking, it was much more of a discussion, issue by issue, among a group of leaders, rather than a reaction to a position taken by the executive leadership.

Some people complained that the council was insensitive to what was going on around it. Nothing could have been further from the truth. John Sweeney was chairman of the organizing committee, Gerry McIntee headed the committee on political action, and I took responsibility for the committee charged with devising strategy. The discussions at every meeting, as I recall them, focused precisely on issues that related to the difficult situation of the American labour movement. The members of council described these issues, analysed them, proposed solutions, boasted about actions that had worked, and decided upon initiatives such as solidarity days. I do not recall any meetings in any organization in which I have been involved that were more open than these, nor any chairman or president more open to new proposals than Lane. There was certainly no high-handed rejection of ideas, nor any complaints from council members of any such actions by Lane or Tom or the officials within the staff of the federation.

Lane and Tom knew their way around Washington and each had a broad range of friendly acquaintances from all camps. For example, Allan Gotlieb, the Canadian ambassador, was a good friend of Lane's. After I was truly settled on the council, Gotlieb, whom I did not know, hosted a reception for me as an introduction to some of the movers and shakers. It was a useful and pleasant event that was greatly appreciated. Lane had a broad and informed view of the labour movement and its place in the world. He understood the centrality of freedom in human progress and had no time for its stifling by left or right. That is why he understood the significance of Lech Walesa's action in Poland from the beginning and led the labour movement in responding to it and supporting it, to his and the movement's everlasting credit.

One of Lane's off-the-record activities was a dinner meeting held every six months with a few of the major CEOs and a few of the presidents of major unions, co-chaired by Lane and Jack Welch of General Electric (GE). John Dunlop, from Harvard, whose purpose was to see if there could be agreement on some of the major issues facing our society, facilitated it. The expectation was that, if these major companies and the labour movement could agree on a course of action, persuading Congress would be much easier than if we were pursuing such issues with differing agendas. During my time, the issue on the table was health care. Obviously, although the need was agreed upon and the prospect of government leadership was not abhorrent, we did not succeed. Imagine how many difficulties faced by people could have been avoided had we been able to agree on an approach.

I was impressed with the general quality of the great majority of the union leaders who sat on the Executive Council during my time there. In the nature of things, our union was close to the Auto Workers and the Machinists. I sat on the council briefly with Doug Fraser and then with Owen Bieber from the UAW, and with Bill Winpisinger and then George Kourpias from the International Association of Machinists (IAM), and found them all to be talented and committed labour leaders.

Morty Bahr of the Communications Workers of America (CWA), Al Shanker of the Teachers, Jack Joyce of the Bricklayers, Murray Finlay and later Jack Sheinkman of the Amalgamated Clothing Workers, and Sol Chaikin of the International Ladies' Garment Workers' Union (ILG-WU) were all quality union leaders, as were John Sweeney of the Service Employees International Union (SEIU), Gerry McIntee of the American Federation of State, County and Municipal Employees (AFSCME), Slim Holley and Ernie LaBaff of the Aluminum Workers, Milan (Mike) Stone of the Rubberworkers, Rich Trumka of the Mineworkers, Joe Misbrener of the OCAW – really everybody.

Tom and Lane were a formidable leadership team, both men of considerable intellectual depth and accomplishment. Their only serious failure, in my judgment, was in not working out a successful transition from one to the other when the time was appropriate. This could have been done with general support across the federation. Instead, following the 1995 election that elected John Sweeney as Lane's successor, the federation fell into family bickering, with the SEIU, the Teamsters, the United Food and Commercial Workers (UFCW), the Hotel and Restaurant Employees (HERE), the Carpenters' Union, and others leaving the fold. This schism continues today, with debilitating and harmful results.

Serving on the AFL-CIO Executive Council heightened my awareness of the challenges facing the labour movement as a whole – and the necessity of responding accordingly. In this regard, one of the most important obligations I felt during my terms of office was maintaining morale. If we failed 'to keep hope alive,' as the African American civil-rights leader Jesse Jackson so often said, the difficult would become almost the impossible. It also seemed to me that the hope had to be reality-based: some drum beating or cheerleading and inspirational spirit were important, but so were some victories and accomplishments. This is where the idea of employee ownership of failing firms continued to attract attention, on both sides of the border.

Canada did not have ESOP legislation as such, but we elected our own party to government in Ontario in 1990 for the first time in our history, and our folks added a few wrinkles of their own to the employee-ownership model. Algoma Steel and Republic Engineered Steels, headquartered in Akron, Ohio, were our two largest employee-owned operations. They were, however, quite different. Algoma was a single plant, a large integrated steel mill in Sault Ste Marie, Ontario, while Republic Engineered Steels was a multi-plant operation with bases in Canton, Ohio, Lorain, Ohio, Gary, Indiana, and Hamilton, Ontario.

Dofasco owned Algoma from 1988, and in 1991, with Algoma in bankruptcy, it tabled a plan in bankruptcy court under the Companies' Creditors Arrangement Act (CCAA). The plan amounted to destroying the company. Leo Gerard, then the Canadian national director, remembers the company coming to his office with lots of demands and few, if any, promises in return. He told them, 'If that's your plan, we'll be fighting it.' He then called me and asked whether I would send Ron Bloom up to Canada to help him with Algoma. Ron, then a consultant who subsequently joined the Steelworkers staff and later still became a member of President Barack Obama's industry advisory group, remembers the Algoma saga well:

> They tabled a plan that would have essentially dismantled the company, substantially cutting back on its operations, big pay cuts for workers, elimination of pension benefits ... it was a pretty draconian thing. The plan really didn't make a lot of sense. It really didn't hang together as a business matter. And second, it imposed all the pain on the workers. But in any event, we sort of pointed out the business folly of their plan. Leo said, 'You know what, your plan is dead on arrival. We ain't doing it.' He just swept it off the table. He knew what he was doing, but now he put the monkey right onto our back.
>
> He said we're going to come up with a better plan. So we went to work and we hired our own consultants, our own industry consultants. We interviewed people, we had very fancy lawyers and I knew something about finance and numbers and banking and we actually put together our own plan. We revealed what we called the USWA plan. We published it in a nice fancy book with colour charts, just like theirs. But ours was a plan where there were sacrifices for workers, but there were sacrifices for everybody. And in it, the workers would gain ownership of the company because we said that if we're going to provide sacrifices and the company survives we should be the economic beneficiary of that. That plan, the USWA plan, with some modifications, but not a substantial rewrite, became the basis for the plan for the arrangement that eventually brought Algoma out of the CCAA.

According to Bloom, this story illustrates everything about my own approach to such situations. 'First, you get on the field. You don't let the other guy define the game. Second, when you're on the field, you play offence, you don't play defence ... Their plan in fact didn't make a lot of sense. But so what? ... we had to have an alternative. So we got into the nitty gritty of business and marketing and all that stuff and put together our own plan for Algoma. And that plan – again it was modified in bargaining – became the core of the plan that the company used to reorganize.' Bloom adds: 'What a union usually does, if a company wants 10 things, we'll stop them from doing seven of them and it will be a good day. But it will all be based off the company's plan … Leo said, "You're going to work off our paper. You're going to dance to our tune." And while we had to bargain away from our original position, we bargained from our paper.'

Algoma and Republic Engineered Steels have survived until this day, but not as employee-owned operations. Some of the other companies created as ESOP initiatives, including Republic Storage, Erie Forge, McLouth Steel (which District Director Harry Lester simply would not let die), and Republic Container, survived until recently. All of them were worthwhile in that they maintained good jobs for a time and enabled a number of senior workers to accumulate sufficient service to establish pension eligibility. Finally, it should be noted that, in most instances when the ESOPs returned to private ownership, their stock was worth something. Therefore, in addition to maintaining good jobs and good benefits, in the end many of those involved received a few thousand dollars for their stock. Had there been an industrial policy of any consequence in place, all these enterprises might have survived.

From my perspective, there were two great difficulties with employee ownership. The first was that it was more difficult in our situation than most. While our companies all survived feasibility examination, they were all in need of, or would be before long, technological improvement, and they all happened to be in an industry for which technology is very expensive. The second difficulty was finding managers who combined a good working knowledge of the business with the skills required to work with employee-owners. I used to say at the time that the thrill of being an employee-owner lasted about two weeks, before the employee began to think, 'Here I am at the same old machine, the same old job, the same old boss, in what way am I an owner?' It takes some skill to switch that reaction to the positive side of entrepreneurial success, the rewards that accompany it, the future that may be possible.

It is my impression that our members in these circumstances appreciated the opportunity to have a voice in what was going on. They voted twice on many issues, once as shareholders, the other time as union members. Jim Smith and his closest colleagues, along with the legal department, did an enormous amount of work in these situations. Documents, information letters, meetings, votes, ensuring that we had a democratic model of employee ownership with board representation, votes on all major issues along with the continuation of pension benefits and not permitting the ownership of stock to be a pension substitute – all of these and similar matters were looked after with scrupulous care. I hope with all my heart that one day an opportunity for an employee-owned enterprise will emerge again and that all of this work will be of value once more.

The need for real accomplishments to keep up our members' spirits also made me determined that we were not going to suffer a Phelps-Dodge style defeat again. In particular, it explains why I was so taken with a new approach to industrial action – that of the coordinated, strategic campaign model – and why I felt it should not be confined as a specialty of a few people. Instead, it should become part of the kitbag of every negotiator and, I would add today, of every organizer. It should be a central element of what unions do, at least in as hostile an environment as the one in the United States.

I had become more and more persuaded of the efficacy, indeed the necessity, of this kind of approach beginning with César Chávez and the grape boycott. It was apparent in that struggle that the traditional methods of worker protest – holding meetings, raising legal objections, and reporting stories about the terrible things employers would do to prevent organization – were not nearly enough. We needed in these situations to be much more effectively confrontational. When I became international secretary, the boycott of the giant textile firm J.P. Stevens was under way, conducted by the Amalgamated Clothing and Textile Workers Union and supported by the labour movement. We were all pulling off tablecloths with Stevens labels in hotel conference rooms, asking for replacement tablecloths, and generally harassing hotel management and the Stevens company in every way we could. When our efforts succeeded, I became even more impressed with this approach to industrial action. Conversations with Murray Finlay, Jack Sheinkman, and Howard Samuel, who had conducted the strategic campaign to boycott the clothing company Farah, added to my interest. To me, it never seemed an entirely new idea. Many historic struggles had been conducted with an assortment of pressures having been pulled together – political, social, community – and we were simply adopting an approach that was more expansive and, we hoped and expected, even stronger and more effective than the ones we were currently using.

Then, in 1990, a further opportunity presented itself to put our principles into action. The scene was the Kaiser Ravenswood Aluminum plant in West Virginia, which had a large workforce of 1,700. As preparations for negotiations at this plant proceeded, there were some obvious issues demanding the union's attention, notably the need for a better pension plan and improved health and safety provisions. The company, however, was focused on the need to reduce costs, and one day, without warning, it locked out the workers and advertised for scabs. The union offered to continue to work under the terms of the existing agreement, but the company had no interest in such an arrangement. A few weeks into the dispute, as the company's approach became crystal clear, I told George Becker, one of whose responsibilities was aluminum bargaining, that we should go all out in responding to this event. We did, and the rest is history.

George did outstanding work, leading a dynamic and creative team, greatly aided by Director Jim Bowen, staff representative Joe Chapman, Rich Brean of the legal department, Gary Hubbard of the public-relations department, Joe Uehlein of the AFL-CIO's Industrial Union Department (IUD), and our public-relations consultants Fingerhut, Powers and Smith. The local union leadership as represented by its president, Dan Stidham, and its financial secretary, Charlie McDowell, was most effective: only 17 of the 17,000 employees crossed the picket line in a lockout that lasted twenty months. The spouses' support group, led by Marge Flanagan, also played an important role, organizing a weekly potluck supper that was attended by union representatives from across the continent.

In the beginning of the lockout, we did not know that Marc Rich was the power behind the throne. A fugitive from American justice, having been found guilty of tax evasion and making oil deals with Iran during the hostage crisis of 1979–81, Rich was living in and operating his businesses from Switzerland, which had no extradition treaty with the United States. He was one of the Steelworkers' bête noires, being responsible for assorted labour troubles around the world, and we were active in the efforts under way to have him returned to the United States. It turned out that Washington's most influential lawyer, Leonard Garment, was counsel to Rich as well as being on friendly terms with Lane Kirkland. In February 1992, with Kaiser Ravenswood starting to feel the heat, Lane told George Becker that Garment had called him requesting a meeting, to be attended by Lane and his assistant Jim Baker, George and me, Garment, and Willy Strothotte, a major player in the Rich organization. This meeting took place, and the intense discussions that followed ultimately resulted in an agreement, in late June. It was a three-year agreement, providing for wage increases of seventy-five cents per hour in the first year and twenty-five cents per hour in the second and third years; the retention of cost-of-living protection; and improvement in the pension plan. The agreement was ratified by 88 per cent of the union membership. As for Marc Rich, he received a presidential pardon in January 2001, at the end of the second Clinton administration.

The IUD had been an invaluable aid to us during the Ravenswood struggle. It was the continuation of the CIO, adjusted to encompass all of the industrial unions in the AFL-CIO, whether or not they had been in the CIO. The presidents of these unions made up the executive board of the IUD. During my time, Howard Samuel, a former under-secretary of labor and before that a vice-president of the Amalgamated Clothing Workers, was the president. His assistant at that time was Brian Turner. In my view, the IUD was a useful organization, although sometimes it proved a little upsetting to the AFL-CIO when it moved into what the senior body considered its territory. It played an important role in innovation and organizing, as well as taking on the issues of the day in a timely fashion. It had a great deal to do with keeping the corporate-campaign idea in the forefront, mostly in the beginning by supporting the boycott of J.P. Stevens and later by developing a capacity to help. It maintained a field organizing effort, not a massive one but one that persisted in seeking out decent organizing opportunities and that assisted in the running of the campaign. It was also the moving force on the union side of the Collective Bargaining Forum, a group of CEOs and union presidents, facilitated by Mac Lovell, that involved useful discussions of collective-bargaining methodologies and issued papers on the same subject.

While fighting the Ravenswood lockout and other battles, it was crucial for us to find the time to review what had been accomplished and map out strategies for the future. In my second presidential term as in my first, conventions were invaluable in this respect. In 1990 our convention was held for the first time in Toronto. And on 6 September of that year, just before we convened, the New Democratic Party won the election in Ontario, prompting the tongue-in-cheek comment that had we known holding our convention in Toronto would win an election for us, we would have met there much sooner. The convention opened on a beautiful late summer day. We held the opening social on the islands opposite the city that embrace the harbour. It was a special evening.

We built the convention around an update of the fundamental policies of the union, including our policy on the environment. The union had been deeply interested in this issue for some time, identified in those years as pollution, and had held its first conference on the subject in 1969, always resisting the notion that we could not have both clean air and jobs. In preparing for the convention, we had established some major committees according to policy area. At that point, George Becker was chair of the committee dealing with the environment. One of its background efforts was to send TV crews to a number of major steel mill and mining smelter towns across both countries and interview groups of our members, selected at random, about the environment and jobs. The overwhelming response was that people in these communities believed they could have, in fact desperately needed, both jobs and a healthy environment in which to raise their families.

Every convention has a life of its own, with issues emerging related to the circumstances the union is facing, and the one in Pittsburgh in 1992 was no different. In Pittsburgh, a critical convention topic centred on hiring outsiders as organizers. As noted earlier, a most critical element in organizing is the quality of the organizers, particularly in the United States, where private-sector employers are permitted such free-wheeling attack strategies. A successful organizer must be many things – strategist, communicator, publicist, counsellor, and public speaker. In my determination to break through in this area, I put George in charge of organizing so it would have the focus of an officer. I was an early advocate and supporter of the AFL-CIO's Organizing Institute and the work it was doing under the leadership of Richard Bensinger. I required all new staff to go through an institute program and evaluation, in the belief that every new staff member should have some organizing experience before they did anything else. The idea of the Future Directions Report, which was written by Carl Frankel, our associate general counsel, and me and presented to the 1992 convention, was that we move to an amalgamated local union structure in order that local union officers could assume more responsibility. At the same time, staff could focus on being labour leaders, including developing strategy on targets and opportunities and building volunteer organizing committees. This would free them from being handlers of routine administration tasks that local unions could well handle themselves. Part of the concept also was that the staff could inspire amalgamated locals to think of growth, and therefore organizing, as part of their mission. After all, if the labour movement is to be as effective as the times require, it must grow.

The idea of hiring outside organizers understandably disturbed some of our members, who felt that, with so many jobs being lost, union jobs should go to union members. One cannot but agree with that general sentiment, but, on the other hand, one does not apply it to the technicians and the professionals who are also essential to the union's work. Some top-flight organizers are in that same territory and, in the interests of the union's growth, should not only be considered but be sought out. This became a matter of open debate on the convention floor, and an attention-gathering debate it was. A movie running at the time, *Norma Rae*, provided a magnificent example of a skilled organizer at work – a Jewish lawyer from New York able to bring together and inspire a group of workers in a textile mill in the deep South. As that film made plain, the organizing challenge certainly involves changing the laws, but it also requires intense work and the best talent available, whether it is found inside or outside the union. In the end, the case for being open to hiring the best we could carried the day.

Following the Pittsburgh convention, we began preparation for steel bargaining in 1993, my final round as president. By then, the good news and the positive atmosphere of 1989 were long gone and things were in the dumps again. The employers were once more talking about concessions, long-term agreements, and cutbacks of one kind or another. We held a board meeting to consider the circumstances and found our people to be very much in the same pessimistic mood.

I did not attempt to push any kind of conclusion to the session that day. I couldn't find time alone in my room quickly enough. I needed time to think. The more I pondered the situation, the more I thought that we needed a way to take the initiative, to develop a quality plan that would both represent a challenge and be fresh enough that the companies would have to respond. It would have to be a plan that would raise the spirits of our people and would be worth the struggle.

Then I thought to myself, what is this all about? I answered my own question with the idea that it was about creating the kind of industry we wanted it to be. We wanted an industry that was composed of profitable, productive, successful enterprises that paid decent wages and provided good benefits. We wanted employment security for steelworkers. We did not want our people's and their communities' jobs given away to contractors. We wanted an industry in which our people had a significant voice, not simply with shop-floor improvements, although they were important, but at every level of the industry, including the boardroom. We wanted more training, particularly in the trades areas so that more of our people could aspire to be tradespersons. We wanted a more sweeping policy of joint union-industry approaches to government in pursuit of a more vigorous pro-steel-industry policy in areas of trade and other subjects in which we were in agreement.

I had become quite enthusiastic about our general approach. I liked the big picture idea. I liked the idea of bargaining about the real fundamentals of the industry rather than grinding away at trying to prevent concessions or whatever other disaster some company might have in mind. I wanted us to be on top of the situation, with some vision of where we might be able to go and how we might arrive there. I could hardly wait until the board meeting the next morning.

It took a little while, but the board, one by one, became excited about the idea. It was so much more appealing a thought to go to the Basic Steel Industry Conference with a positive program than to head in with a doleful story of difficulty and decline. We reached agreement on the approach, set people to work fleshing out the ideas, and gave it the name New Directions. I have always regretted not thinking a little longer about the name. My good friend Owen Bieber, president of the UAW, was not happy with the name because it was one used by a dissident group in his union. As it was, by the time Owen mentioned this to me, the name was too well established and was certainly serving the purpose of pulling our people together and inspiring them to think much more constructively and optimistically about this round of bargaining, indeed to think about it as an opportunity to be seized rather than as a terrible ordeal to be struggled through somehow.

Details were added over time. Employment security emerged as a foundation plank of the platform. So did the notion of having a voice across the companies at the various levels of supervision and business planning, capped off with a seat on the boards of directors. Another element of the participation model involved proposals that virtually all business information be made available to the union. As well as being specific to the New Directions set of ideas, this was part of our general view that union decision making should be based on the same facts that company decision making was based upon, so as not to be misled by incomplete or distorted information, as was so often the case in gamesmanship bargaining.

Long-term agreements would be considered so long as they included the possibility of being reopened, so as to provide opportunities for improvement in the event of unexpected upside developments. Restructuring the way work was done was another part of our plat-

form, the purpose of which was to make the workplace more participative instead of authoritarian, more productive, and safer and fairer,
using the workers' knowledge and skills to these ends. Health-care
costs were to be approached on a managed-care basis, with attention
paid to the funding of 'legacy' (retiree) costs. Successor rights were to
be strengthened along with corporate guarantees so there was no confusion regarding the entire corporate structure being behind whatever
guarantees the agreements contained. Other key elements in the program were the achievement of agreements committing the companies
to neutrality in organizing campaigns, along with recognition of the
union upon the signing of a majority on authorization cards; investment commitments by the companies; and the elimination of any of
the remaining problems in the area of contracting out. The program
also called for extending the joint public policy and legislative activity to include a wide range of issues in which the companies and the
union had a common interest, including not only trade questions but
also health care, legacy costs, and labour-law reform.

The New Directions program was positive; it provided an opportunity to put all the ideas we had been experimenting with in a context. It
recognized the challenges of the times without being disabled by them.
It built morale rather than destroying it. And it had enormous potential to begin rebuilding the corporations in a much more productive
mode. At its core were two principles. The first was that no one has a
greater stake or interest in the ongoing success of an enterprise than its
workers. The second was that the best way to accomplish that success
was to involve the workers and their union in the management and
decision-making processes, not superficially but in real and meaningful ways. These principles involved broad-ranging new proposals, the
most significant of which were employment-security guarantees and
partnership agreements, providing for union and worker involvement
at every level from the board of directors to the plant floor.

Employment security had become a critically important issue in
my thinking, largely as a result of the influence of Sid Rubenstein, the
founder of a consulting firm known as Participative Systems, based in
Princeton, New Jersey. Sid had been hired by U.S. Steel to assist in the
development of LMPTs and was truly one of the pioneers in the development of worker involvement. His thesis with regard to employment
security was simple but profound: How can workers be expected to
share all of the keys to productivity they know if the result is to find
themselves out on the street?

Much less dramatic, but very useful, was the call for the day-by-day input of the workers' point of view that is enabled by the presence of a union-nominated director. I believe that this would increase the level of understanding on both sides, an important consideration. Of course, it would also lead to unprecedented power being exercised by the Steel-workers. It has puzzled me that other unions have not, to any consider-able extent, picked up on the idea.

Our initial movement toward the needs of the companies was to indicate an interest in considering somewhat longer-than-usual agree-ments, which we knew would be of considerable assistance in prevent-ing stockpiling, so long as the agreement contained some shorter-term reopening devices to cope with unexpected changes in external con-ditions. Years before, we had negotiated an employment-security approach at National Steel with Stan Ellsperman, its progressive vice-president of industrial relations, which had worked out well for all con-cerned. There was one other general matter of absolutely fundamental importance and that was that we, and our expert advisers, were to have total access to information about the state of each of the companies. The way I liked to put it was that our side of the bargaining table should have the same information, and the same access to information, as did the other side. How else could the best, most rational judgments be made? Another facet to this was that we wanted to be able to under-stand the meaning of the companies' circumstances exactly as the com-panies did, not that we would necessarily agree or be moved to agree by such knowledge, but that we would thoroughly understand where they were coming from. It was in this area, as well, that Ron Bloom and a former business partner of his, investment banker Gene Keilin, played a most significant role as they brought business thinking with a labour conscience to our side of the table. Such an approach was unu-sual. 'The only other union I know that did it [share information] at all at that time was the airline pilots association,' Gene recalls. 'I would say that those two unions were well ahead of anyone else. It's more com-mon today but still unusual.'

When our program was fleshed out and approved by our Basic Steel Industry Conference, it contained the following items as described in a summary prepared by Carl Frankel:

- Adoption of an employment security (no layoff) program based on the National Steel model.
- Union and worker involvement at all levels from the shop floor to

the board room. At upper management levels, it includes participation in the development of the business plan as it deals with products, markets, and capital spending, and in the decisions involving technological change. Finally, it means access to all information necessary to perform the participatory roles.

- Long-term agreements considered only if they include re-openers with experimental negotiating agreement-type arbitration and other upside protection should the company prosper during the agreement.
- Restructuring the way work is done in the workplace in order to reduce costs and make the workplace less authoritarian, safer, more fair and rewarding in terms of worker skills and involvement in the solution of operating problems.
- Health-care cost reductions through managed-care alternatives. Plans on a single company or multi-company basis.
- Funding of retiree health care and other legacy costs by the company and through other means as well.
- Additional corporate and successorship guarantees to make sure the entire corporate entity and its assets stand behind benefit obligations, notwithstanding sales and corporate maneuvers.
- Revitalized apprenticeship and training programs in which the parties jointly determine manpower needs in the craft occupations and how to fill them.
- Company neutrality in organizing campaigns and recognition of the union once we achieve majority status through signed authorization cards.
- Investment commitments.
- Elimination of all significant remaining contracting-out problems.
- Development of a joint public policy and legislative agenda, including labor law reform, health care, trade, legacy costs and a steel tripartite commission.

When the program hit the streets after the conference, one of the first calls I received was from Charles Corry, the new CEO at U.S. Steel. The company had been expressing an interest in improving its labour-relations image and in that regard had voiced a desire that it be the lead company in what was now a pattern-bargaining situation, not the old one-table arrangement. The purpose of his call was to inquire if we were serious about the proposed seat on the board. I assured him that we were, to which he replied that, in that case, U.S. Steel had no desire to go first in the bargaining because this was a proposal that it would never accept. 'Never' turned out to be only until it became U.S. Steel's turn, after all the others had set and confirmed the pattern.

Virtually all of the New Directions objectives were achieved. For example, we realized our goal of employment security; there were some exemptions in the event of circumstances such as unexpected, unavoidable, or severely extended outages, but most such exceptions required mutual agreement. The union nominee on the board of directors was, with each company, the last item negotiated and, in each case, I did the negotiating. I outlined the general purpose, to complete the role of participation. I assured them we would not be nominating active union leaders so that there would be no conflict of interest owing to a negotiator being on the board. I said we would be nominating both union people and others in whom the union had confidence, but we also wished to nominate persons whom we were sure would make a positive contribution to the activities of the board. The company would have the right to reject a nominee, but the union, for its part, would have the right to arbitrate such rejection.

We won the provision with every company. The person we nominated to the U.S. Steel board was Ray Marshall, the former secretary of labor. When he reached the mandatory-retirement age, the company took the most unusual step of making an exception and asking agreement that his term be extended. Jim Bowen, the former director of our district in West Virginia and subsequently president of the West Virginia State Federation of Labor, and I served for some years as members of the board of Wheeling-Pittsburgh. In that capacity, we had the interesting adventure of stopping the intended dissolution of the company by its then owner, Ron LaBow. He had advised the board that a motion of liquidation was to be presented to the board on the next day of a two-day meeting and that we were all barred by confidentiality requirements from telling anybody. There is no doubt that, had we not been there, that is exactly what would have happened. As it was, we were able to raise enough concern and object enough that the two-day meeting became a four-day meeting. Some new arrangements were made with the union and the company survived.

The principles of the New Directions initiative have lived on. Some of the details in the participation area were put in place more thoroughly in some locations than in others, but the achievement of union-nominated directors on boards, the joint programs in public policy, the neutrality clauses, and many other provisions have had a significant impact. In the beginning, New Directions was an exciting, unprecedented attempt to move an entire industry in the direction of new, participative ideas about the organization of work and the role of the workers in it. And the attempt was made in one of the oldest, most conservative of industries at a time when it could almost be considered under siege. It was a bigger leap forward than many managers and a number of our people were comfortable with; it was their feeling that, if the old ways were working tolerably well, they should be left alone. On the other hand, when people on both sides were interested, they could accomplish great things. I learned over and over again that changing the culture of the union, or of the companies, or of both together, was no simple task.

At the same time, although it did not accomplish all I had hoped it might, New Directions forever changed the industry. Hundreds of employees had more confidence in their own abilities and understanding, less false respect for supervisors who did not deserve any, and much greater respect for those who did. The end result is that the dreams of the Steelworkers founder, Philip Murray, regarding industrial democracy are closer to realization today than they have ever been. There are people in all the shops who have a real understanding of how things work and of what an important contribution they can make. Knowledge is power, a slogan Murray would certainly have appreciated. It is in abundance these days.

New Directions is the best example from my experience of the importance of having a strategic vision of where you hope to go. The challenges are impossible if one does not have a real sense of where one is going and how one expects to arrive there. I'm encouraged that my successors at the Steelworkers head office in Pittsburgh have carried on with this type of forward thinking. To counterbalance the growing power of international corporations, our union is going global. It has an alliance with the Mexican Mining and Metal Workers Union, with the CNM/Cut (a metals and manufacturing union in Brazil), with the Australian Workers Union, with IG Metall in Germany (one of the largest metal unions in the world), and, since 2008, with the United Kingdom's two-million-member Unite (a transport, energy, and public-sector union). Workers Uniting, combining parts of the names of both the Steelworkers and Unite, is the first transatlantic global union. 'We'll be like a federation,' explains Steelworkers President Leo Gerard.

The big union will set its own policy, have its own constitution, bylaws, and its own staff. We will give in this merger lots of authority to the new organization over our international relationships, whether it's strategic campaigns, whether it's international affairs, whether it's occupational health and safety global standards. The founding unions will still be responsible for day-to-day collective bargaining, day-to-day national administration. You're not going to have somebody from Australia or Great Britain come to Washington or Ottawa, just like I won't be going to lobby the British prime minister. It's a complicated structure but it's going to send a very clear signal to the rest of the world that these two unions have a vision and we're going to chase global capital.

Without change, we do not progress: we are stuck forever in the ruts of the past. Change requires vision and courage. But the perils of resisting it and never challenging the status quo – no matter how wrongheaded some of its elements may be – are immense. My only regret about New Directions is that it came so late in my term of office. I would have liked to have some years to put its ideas into operation.

EPILOGUE

My final weeks in office were a mix of goodbye visits, clearing up problems to enable George Becker, my successor, to begin with as clean a slate as possible, and trying to disentangle files to some degree. George and his colleagues arranged a magnificent retirement dinner for Ed Ball and me. On 3 March 1994, the installation of the officers for the new term was held, and the next day, for the first time since 1947, I was not employed in the labour movement. It was a strange idea to contemplate, and stranger yet to experience.

It had been an incredible journey, filled with ever more interesting and challenging experiences, from attempting to cope with unprecedented devastation to the exultation of hard-won victories. I was fortunate to have such a stimulating and rewarding career in the labour movement, and most especially in the Steelworkers, moving on every few years in my career to broader responsibilities and concluding my service with the union as its president, a position that I never in my wildest imagination thought might one day be mine.

I began my career with the conviction, based largely upon the experience of the Great Depression, buttressed by study, activity, and observation, that workers in the structure of our society were for the most part treated very badly, faced with miserable and dangerous working conditions, receiving less than fair or secure compensation for their efforts, and lacking any significant influence upon the business decisions that determined their circumstances. It seemed to me that this reality was inconsistent with the democratic values that we proclaimed, and that we had defended in the Second World War at enormous human and material expense. On a more basic level, we taught our children at home and at school to become independent thinkers, respectful of civil and democratic rights. Then, when they graduated from these rites of initiation into our society, we sent them off to the most autocratic of workplaces, where they were expected to leave their ideas and their independence of mind at the time clock and fit into the system with machine-like acquiescence.

Early on I came to the view that the only practical way to move beyond this unfair and unproductive system to something far more consistent with our democratic values, far more respectful of human values, far more involving of our human capacities and, therefore, far more productive, was to establish and recognize free trade unions throughout our society. Nothing during my years of work in Canada and the United States, or in what I have learned from experience in other countries, has changed my mind in any way in that regard. Indeed, I hold to my view more firmly today than I ever have.

The corporate powers that have bashed away at unions so vigorously since the 1970s have done great damage, not only to the unions but to themselves and to our society. As I write these words in 2011, we see all around us the results of irresponsible and unaccountable power and its offspring, greed and corruption. I believe more than ever that nothing would bring more fundamental improvement to the mess our North American society is in – as we put ourselves in debt to the rest of the world, as we see our manufacturing prowess disappear, as we destroy the security of millions of our citizens – than to welcome and assist our unions to be re-established in their full vigour in the private sector.

My academic friends, along with various experts from many fields, have searched diligently and theorized most imaginatively in seeking explanations for the decline of union membership and of the inability of unions, particularly in the United States, to organize with old-time fervour and success. The fundamental reason could not be clearer. American labour law has been perverted into an instrument that permits and protects anti-union employers to propagandize, intimidate, and terrorize their employees, almost without limit, should they show interest in joining a union, and to postpone and delay procedures for months at a time, to the extent that they make a mockery of the right to organize into a free, democratic trade union. In Canada, the situation is much better, but far from perfect.

Until the weakness of the law can be remedied, the path of rebuilding the labour movement in the private sector will be difficult indeed, but not impossible. It is a wonder to many that the workers of today do not simply rise up as they did in the 1930s to assert their rights. The

explanation lies in the fact that, thanks in large measure to the struggles there have been since, workers today are much better off than were
their forebears in the 1930s. Workers who rose up in desperation in
that decade had little to lose and the world to gain. Today, many workers have mortgages, car payments, and tuition fees, with much at risk
should their jobs be lost. So they are much more wary.

Despite such circumstances, workers do organize. It requires
unprecedented dedication on their part and on the union's side. The
latter must focus its efforts, finding and developing the best of organizing leadership, using all the most up-to-date strategies and developing new ones to win recognition, and devising ways to integrate the
efforts of all our present activists and leaders. There is no more urgent
cry than Organize! Organize! Organize! To my way of thinking, our
very future depends upon building effective democratic societies
around the world in which workers are organized and the voice of
labour is heard. Our beautiful planet and its millions of people cannot survive the ravages of an exploitive economic system in which
there are no checks and balances, a system the fundamentals of which
are on striking display in the United States, with its raging inequality
and greed, declining living conditions for working people, and steady
deterioration in the overall quality of life.

The contrast between the United States and the European Union is
most informative. When the Euro was launched, speculation was ram-
pant as to how close it might come to the value of the American dollar.
In a matter of weeks it had far exceeded it. Europe has not given up
on manufacturing but is leading the way in the establishment of new
green industrial enterprises. Wages are in most cases significantly better than those in North America, vacations and other social benefits far
in excess. France has long had a thirty-five-hour work week. Its new
conservative government has made noises about reverting to forty
hours, but now word has been leaking out that many employers do not
wish to change, that they are achieving as much production with thirty-
five hours as they did with forty, and that they are now much better
able than they earlier were to address the needs and complications of
two working parents and their child-raising obligations, a responsibility that has been largely ignored by employers in North America.

I remain a great fan of collective bargaining. It can be the platform
and mechanism not simply for meeting needs, which it does so well,
but for creating new approaches to the host of issues and opportunities
that surround us. The many programs and initiatives that the Steel-

workers have been involved in over the years, often jointly with one or another industry, or within the labour movement, or simply on their own, have all been made possible through the resources that become available with collective bargaining. This is the characteristic of a democratic society at its best. Think of what the impact on Wall Street might have been if a real union of employees had been bargaining with giant financial institutions and playing a role in the public discourse concerning their conduct, or if the thousands of employees of Wal-Mart were being compensated in some kind of relation to the company's earnings and were an independent source of opinion and action. Based on my own experiences, I have no doubt about what the results would have been if unions had had a significant role to play in these situations. From the poverty of the Depression-era Sarnia of my childhood to the hardship I witnessed in my early union-organizing days in Toronto and the threats to workers' futures from imported steel and globalization during my presidency, I have always believed that strong but pragmatic union leadership is of critical importance to society as a whole. And that has never been more true than today.

My mind often turns to two of the most famous statements by labour leaders. The first is by Samuel Gompers, the first president of the AFL: 'What does labor want? We want more schoolhouses and less jails; more books and less arsenals; more learning and less vice; more leisure and less greed; more justice and less revenge; in fact, more of the opportunities to cultivate our better natures.' The second is from Tommy Douglas, one of the founders of the CCF and first leader of the New Democratic Party: 'Courage, my friends, 'tis not too late to build a better world.' Together, these statements sum up my own philosophy. My original attraction was to the ideas and ideals of what is commonly known around the world as social democracy, and my support for them has grown stronger as the years have gone by. In fact, in the delicate position in which the world sits today, I believe these ideas to be essential for our survival. Briefly put, they portend for me a society governed by democratic political processes and an economy that sees its role as meeting the needs of the people, providing employment opportunities and basic levels of support such as health care and educational opportunities for all. Social democracy also envisages a society that understands the unique strengths of both public and private enterprise, each operating within a framework of social responsibility and responsibility for the quality of its products or services. The world view of social democracy, finally, focuses on the pursuit of democratic social and economic development everywhere, based on fair, mutually favourable trading arrangements between nations and the promotion of peace.

One of the most destructive aspects of public life in recent decades in the United States has been the attack on government. The idea that governments can do nothing right is as ridiculous as the idea that private enterprises do everything right. Two of the best-run government enterprises in the United States are Social Security and Medicare, each of which uses a much lower percentage of premiums for administration than do private companies operating similar programs. The list of inefficient private corporations that we know about is endless, and there are many we do not know about. This points to a fundamental fact: public enterprises are much more accountable than private companies, whose inefficiencies are often passed along in their prices with little public knowledge. In this connection, I have found it interesting to note that the larger the enterprise, the more challenging is the development of an organization that welcomes the ideas and encourages the contribution of all its people. The rewards are great when it is done well, but they are not easily achieved.

Matters of health and safety have been a constant concern to me throughout my years in the union. Workers should not have to sacrifice their health, their physical well-being, or their lives in order to earn a living. Far too many do each year, some the victims of dramatic accidents, others of chemicals or other hazardous substances. Today, the struggle for safe and healthy workplaces and the struggle to save our environment are really understood to be one and the same, reflecting a commonality of concern that was recognized early by our union. We never became involved in defending polluting practices in the interest of illusory employment, but insisted that we needed and could have both good jobs and a clean environment. In any event, the argument is finished – it is now a matter of survival.

Another element of labour's agenda that is of enormous relevance is its involvement in the political issues of the times and its education and training of its membership in this regard. Just as our bargaining committees should not go to the table in any way disadvantaged in terms of information or preparation as compared with the company negotiators, similarly our members should suffer no inadequacies when they take part in the political life of our society.

I foresee a bright future for the labour movement. As challenging as organizing is at this moment, one of the most encouraging facts is that those who have a union report in very high percentages that they are satisfied with it and wish to keep it. I do not intend that we should be smug, but at the same time we should be proud that we do many things right, that having a union brings the principles of democracy and human rights into the workplace. The challenge is specific: How do we build the membership in order that workers may work towards the establishment of a positive corporate agenda built on positive principles, consistent with and supportive of democratic social and economic development at home and abroad?

Now, a decade and a half after retiring as Steelworkers president, I continue to be active in the labour movement. Indeed, retirement has given me the time to learn more about the struggles faced by all unions so that my concerns in this respect have, if anything, intensified. I have participated in events both within the labour movement and outside it. These have included 'my projects,' of which the principal one in recent years has been to serve as president of the Steelworkers Organization of Active Retirees (SOAR). SOAR was created during my presidency to provide representation for retirees and a vehicle for people who wish to maintain an active connection with the union and labour. I have also served as an arbitrator under the AFL-CIO's Article 21 procedure. This procedure provides for the possibility of one of two or more unions, seeking to organize the same group of workers, being given an exclusive opportunity to do so if it meets the relevant criteria. Also, as the result of provisions we negotiated in 1993, I serve as the union nominee on the boards of directors of Wheeling-Pittsburgh Steel Corporation and Republic Engineered Products. The appointments are made by our international president. At the time of my retirement, I was serving as president of the Industrial Relations Research Association (IRRA). I continue to be active in that organization, now known as the Labor and Employment Research Association (LERA). In Canada I have also taken on a modest role in the New Democratic Party, while maintaining connections with the union's political program in the United States. One my greatest honours was being named an officer of the Order of Canada in 2007. To me, it represented recognition of the important role played by all working people in our society.

My retirement activities have included visits to a variety of conferences and educational events, in a variety of capacities, including as a speaker, teacher, and resource person. These activities have required me to continue to be aware of the many harsh and challenging circumstances faced by the labour movement. It has also enabled me to come to know and correspond with many individuals who will make up the next generation of labour activists and leaders.

My wife, Audrey, passed away on 7 April 2000, a victim of ALS, often referred to as Lou Gehrig's disease. We had been married for nearly fifty-four years. She was a loyal friend, a devoted mother, an interesting companion, a tireless and talented helper, and a caring lover. She entered into marriage with little idea of what the life of a trade-union official would be like, but she never flinched or complained as it unfolded, with its many moves and my frequent absences, simply devoting herself to the tasks and challenges at hand. She loved to travel, particularly during the five years of healthy retirement we shared when the time constraints were not as great. Audrey shared her children's adventures and accomplishments to the full, and those of her eleven grandchildren as well. She always performed some community work wherever we lived, and she participated in the life of the labour movement when she could, particularly after the children were grown and she had the time to attend conventions and participate in other ways. She established a fine reputation around the union as a friendly, welcoming person, not one to stand on ceremony, all of which was appreciated by the people with whom we were involved.

She deserved a much more capable and helpful partner than I ever managed to be. I miss her greatly.

Fortunately, I have my four children. The philosophy of child rearing that Audrey and I shared was based on education and activity, with the idea that children should be aware of and informed about their parents' views on life but also encouraged to find the occupation and lifestyle that best express their own interests and personalities. The variety of occupations my children pursue today is, I think, testimony to this approach. Judy is a public school teacher in British Columbia. David, now retired, was an engineer who spent his entire career with Imperial Oil, mostly in Calgary, some of it in the far north. Barbara has had a career in television. After receiving a master's degree from the Newhouse School at Syracuse University, she held a succession of jobs: receptionist at a Toronto radio station, TV station librarian, associate producer and union activist, producer of national programming, station manager, and network executive. Currently, she is the executive vice-president of programming for Global TV. Brian has spent most of his adult life in Asia and Africa working for a variety of non-government organizations and government-aid programs, except for time in Canada at the Université du Québec à Montréal and a return to the

United States for a master's degree at the Wilson School at Princeton University. He currently is a senior official with the United Nations in New York.

There it is. I have written my story to the best of my ability. I am afraid that I have left out far more than I have included of events, peoples, struggles, and issues. My fundamental purpose, however, was not to touch on every detail but to be true to the purpose, spirit, and actions of a major industrial union, based in North America but functioning in the world in the second half of the twentieth century and on into the twenty-first.

I believe that to be effective and principled, to reflect democratic values in its political and economic life, a modern state or regional entity requires a free, strong, participatory labour movement. Our call for three centuries has been for social and economic justice. We are closer to achieving that than we have ever been. We must reach out, seize and nourish the opportunity, or live out our uselessness in the desert of our follies and our failures.

I do not offer these concluding reflections as points in a program or cries in a manifesto, but they are deeply felt all the same. May they inspire others to pursue and ponder their implications.

With my very best wishes for an enjoyable and instructive read, I now end this book.

In solidarity,
Lynn Williams

APPENDIX 1

GOVERNANCE AND ADMINISTRATION

I have attempted to write in this book the story of my life as a trade unionist, not a history of the United Steelworkers. There are, therefore, a number of very significant union people, who have done great work and have their own stories to tell, missing from my story simply as a result of the happenstance of who was involved with what. I cannot totally correct that deficiency without writing another book or two. In this appendix, I have attempted to correct it at least in part by describing the way Steelworkers governance and administration work and by providing sketches of many of the directors who were serving in my time and carrying major responsibilities, but whose interaction with me was essentially through board meetings and general administrative functions.

The union's top policy making body is the International Convention, which in my time met every two years but currently meets every three years. The top body between conventions is the International Executive Board, which is composed of the officers of the union, the national director for Canada (now an officer too, but such was not the case in earlier years), the district directors, and any divisional directors there may be, all elected by a referendum conducted among their constituents. The board is responsible for implementing policies determined by the convention and for developing new policies as may be needed between conventions, or for the calling of a special convention if there is a need to change a policy that is exclusively determined by the convention. The officers and the directors report to board meetings on the progress of the union in their areas of responsibility. The director positions are very important in the work of the union. Directors are in many cases the only senior official whom many local union members come to know and therefore are in a most significant way responsible for the union's reputation, both with its members and with the communities in which we are privileged to have members.

I do not believe that there is any other institution in our society that does more serious work in relation to economic and other fundamental issues, with as democratic governance procedures, than the Steelworkers. There is in the Steelworkers structure a creative tension between the centre and the field. The centre has and exercises the power of the purse, a not insignificant element. But the district directors, collectively, have the political power through their closeness to the membership to, in large measure, determine who the officers will be.

This democratic system, with its elections and its accountability, has produced a great number of effective leaders. Many have been mentioned in this wandering discourse, but many have been omitted simply because the story cannot possibly cover all who have been involved. A story of substance could be written about every district and many areas within districts, and not only about directors but about literally thousands of individual local union leaders who have been talented, dedicated officers, committee members, stewards, health and safety representatives, and so on, making an outstanding contribution to the lives of their fellow workers and their communities. I think of Buddy Davis, for example, the director of District 34, headquartered in St Louis, from which both Lloyd McBride and George Becker came. Buddy was a man with a great sense of humour, an exemplary work ethic and sense of responsibility, and deep political understanding – a labour person through and through. He was the kind of director who wanted to be sure that everything in the district was going as it should. Though he had some reservations about our approach to worker participation, when it was made policy he worked hard at achieving a successful program with Stan Ellsperman. When corporate campaigns came in, after some initial scepticism he undertook some himself, agreeing with my notion that they should not be the province only of specialists but part of every union leader's basic skills. He was a great man and the structure of our union supported him in exercising his own initiative and his own leadership.

District directors are crucially important officials in the governance of the union. They are the leaders who direct the staff in the field and in that way are most directly related to the membership in their work. It is they and their closest colleagues who have most to do with creating the personality and character of the union in their district, whether it is to be an organizing district or not, whether trade-union education will be considered important, or whether political action has a major emphasis. Of course, the officers work at leading and the convention determines what the policies will be, but, given the decentralized nature of the day-by-day functioning of the union, the districts really determine the amount of emphasis placed on various policies.

Harry Lester, for example, was director of District 29, a territory that included the enormous industrial complex of greater Detroit. When one of the two integrated steel mills in the area, McLouth Steel, was threatened with closure, Harry used the ESOP strategy to keep it alive for a number of years. In a sense, he really willed it to live. Harry was also a great believer that we should let the world know where we stood. When there was a struggle anywhere within driving distance that required an extra push and some evidence of general concern, Harry could be counted on to lead a caravan of supporters to demonstrate solidarity and determination.

Readers of this book have met a number of the directors in these pages, but there are others who have either not been mentioned or touched on only briefly. David Patterson was the director of District 6 in Canada for one term, from 1981 until 1985. He had been the president of Local 6500, the large local at Inco in Sudbury, and during the term of Stu Cooke, my successor as director, differences arose between him and Stu over the 1979 negotiations with Inco. Stu recommended a settlement, which David opposed. The membership followed David's advice and a nine-month strike followed. David then ran against Stu in the next international elections and defeated him.

David's term as director was hectic and stormy. Some of the staff went to work on his side, as it were, on the grounds that the work of the union had to continue. Others felt that he was too inexperienced and also a lax administrator. It was a situation crying out for resolution. Staff and local leadership activists organized across the district and Leo Gerard emerged as their candidate. Leo was elected in November 1985, defeating David by a vote of 26,429 to 15,726. Having won the election, Leo replaced David on the board in 1986. Earlier, in the special election between McKee and me, David had supported McKee but that effort had little impact.

None of this recounting of the political developments is meant to denigrate David. I have always regretted that we did not have an opportunity to work with him and encourage the development of his talents rather than have him seek out, or be forced by circumstances into, the rebel role. He was a man of undoubted sincerity, of considerable talent and charisma, with a fertile and imaginative mind.

There were a number of other changes in directorship at the same time. As a result, I worked only for a short time as president with those who were leaving, although we had all been on the board together, they as directors and I as secretary. This group was made up of Mike Mazuca in District 4 (New York State), Walter Bachowski in District 9 (northwestern Pennsylvania), Paul Rusen in District 23 (West Virginia), and Bruce Thrasher in District 35 (Georgia and adjacent southern states).

Mike Mazuca was a basic steelworker, elected while Buffalo was still in its prime as a basic-steel-producing city, with the vast Bethlehem works spread along the eastern end of Lake Erie. Mike knew his constituency and served it well in the days of coordinated bargaining and contract ratification by the local union presidents. He retired and was succeeded by Lou Thomas in 1986.

Walter Bachowski was another stalwart from the old school who also had helped build the union. Walter was something of an iconoclast, quick to use his position on the board for the practice of free speech and criticism when he felt it to be necessary. There is no doubt he contributed to keeping the leadership on its toes.

Paul Rusen bore a famous name in the union. His father had been an early director of District 23. Paul was a thinker, concerned about the problems facing the labour movement and very much of the view that change was essential. Not only was he open to new concepts, he was seeking them. He was interested in the future directions of the union, particularly in terms of insisting on a voice in the functioning and direction of the companies, and in that capacity he played a major role in negotiating the first participatory-style agreement at Wheeling-Pittsburgh Steel.

West Virginia and western Pennsylvania were not only close geographically, with many of the same companies having plants in both locations, but traditionally were often allied politically in the union. Thus it was that in the Executive Board struggle for who was to become temporary acting president, Paul began as an Odorich supporter. But he was at the same time a good friend of Ed Ball, our incoming secretary, and from Ed and other people he knew that there was much more interest and discussion about change in our group than in the other. He was also party to an interesting personal political arrangement. There were two leading staff representatives in the district, both thought of as potential directors, and both thought capable of defeating the other in an election, depending on the specific circumstances at the time. They had come to an understanding that one of them, Jim Bowen, would support Paul being elected for two terms, after which Paul would return the favour.

A couple of sessions were arranged for Paul and me to talk. As chairman of the Wheeling-Pittsburgh bargaining committee, and in having Jim Smith working with him, Paul was exposed to a lot of new thinking. To make a long story short, he supported me in the vote and was an important convert to our side in the political struggle that followed. He backed the new programs and after he finished his two terms took his retirement and served on a number of company boards as a labour nominee.

As the director of District 35, Bruce Thrasher was a leading member of the Executive Board. His most important contribution during the McBride years was to lead the campaign that brought the workers at Newport News shipyard into the Steelworkers. He retired in early 1986 and moved into work as a consultant and some periods of employment with other unions.

What follows are brief sketches of some of the other directors during my time with the union. I also offer a few words of appreciation for some of the support staff with whom I had the pleasure to work.

E. Gérard Docquier

Gerry was the first member of our union from Quebec to run for election as our national director in 1977. He did so at the urging of his district director, Jean Gérin-Lajoie, to whom he had served as assistant, and myself. My view was that, given the excellent record of District 5 in organizing, in education, and in building the union's influence in Quebec, it was time that we had a national director who could extend some of that influence across the country.

Gerry was constantly concerned about whether he could win. I said I was confident we would accomplish his victory in the same way the Liberal Party had won many elections in Canada – by winning overwhelmingly in Quebec and dividing up the vote in the rest of the country. He did just that.

His time in office brought many positive and progressive improvements. The Humanity Fund, the mechanism by which Canadian

Steelworkers reach out to assist with economic and trade-union development in the Third World, came into being on his watch, encouraged by his leadership and his commitment. He brought a great interest in training, which developed into the Canadian Steel and Employment Training Congress. This was a joint program with the steel companies that was authorized to use government resources as the instrument of choice in the training and job placement of laid-off steelworkers. He served on the MacDonald Commission on the Economic Union and Development Prospects for Canada in 1982–5 and in that capacity was one of the first trade-union leaders in Canada to draw attention, in his trenchant dissenting report for the commission, to the destructive power of free-trade agreements if they failed to respect trade-union rights and uphold safety, health, and environmental standards.

Also under Gerry's leadership, his assistant, Bert Munro, became the most involved and best-informed trade-union leader in the world concerning the development and implications of seabed mining. A slowdown in the world economy followed by the development of more land-based resources stopped seabed development, for the time being at least. However, should it arise again, thanks to Gerry and Bert, we stand better prepared than anyone to deal with the issues it raises.

William J. Foley

Bill Foley was one of the most colourful figures in the union, having come to the Steelworkers in the merger with District 50 (encompassing New England, with headquarters in Boston). He ran for district director at an early opportunity, turning up at the first local union nominating meeting with a brass band, an unheard of touch of showmanship in our elections. It was no contest from then on. He retained his interest in organizing from District 50 days, instigating some interesting campaigns, for instance, among the middle managers in Boston's city government and the employees of the special water research and processing facility in Boston harbour.

Bill loved a good time. He always wanted a piano at parties to lead some singing. At one of his district conferences, the delegates put together a 'general's outfit,' consisting of a Steelworker cap with gold braid and a leisure-suit jacket with gold Steelworker pins on the epaulets and Steelworker button 'medals.' He wore it with much pride. But, for all the showmanship and fun, there was no question where his heart was – it was in building the union.

Len Stevens

As a result of the variety, breadth, and intensity of his work in the union in his hometown of Winnipeg and home province of Manitoba, Len early on became known as Mr Labour in that part of the country. He was an active organizer, his home local being Local 4087 at Manitoba Bridge and Engineering Works. He served both on the Board of Education and on city council in Winnipeg. Len was the driving force in establishing the first Union Centre in Winnipeg, putting a second mortgage on his home to help at one stage when the financing became difficult. He was an active leader in the election of the Ed Schreyer NDP government and a trusted adviser throughout the premier's terms of office, from 1969 to 1977.

Len's range of responsibilities grew as the union did. He was given responsibility for the three prairie provinces by District 6 Director Larry Sefton. The subsequent winning of bargaining rights at the new Inco operation in Thompson, Manitoba, and the merger in a few years with the Mine Mill and Smelter workers greatly increased the range of the union in the north and west. When all this led to the creation of District 3 in 1976, which encompassed all of western Canada and the territories, Len became its first director.

Len served on the International Executive Board from 1976 until felled by a stroke in 1988, after the first day of a board meeting in Montreal. He never was able to speak again but persisted in carrying on, looking after his wife, Margaret, in her declining years as she struggled with Alzheimer's, and maintaining the family cottage – cabin he called it – on Lake Winnipeg.

During these years, despite his physical constraints, he attended conferences and conventions from time to time, exercised into the best shape he had enjoyed for years, and communicated essentially by taps of his cane of varying intensity. If he disagreed with you, he'd whack you in the shins.

During his years of actively leading the district, he built a foundation that has stood it in good stead. He was devoted to the principles and programs of the Steelworkers, particularly its support of the New Democratic Party in Canada and the Democratic Party in the United States. His first loves remained Winnipeg and Manitoba and, although as director he moved to Vancouver where the district headquarters was located, he returned to Winnipeg when he was no longer able to carry on as director.

He and Margaret raised a family of four and had six grandchildren. Len died in 2001 at the age of seventy-nine.

Clément Godbout

Clément was the director of District 5, encompassing Quebec and the Atlantic provinces, during most of my presidency, resigning in 1991 to become president of the Quebec Federation of Labour, the largest central labour body in Quebec.

Clément was a hard-rock miner and became an activist in the Metallos, as the Steelworkers are known in Quebec, through his local. An intelligent and articulate young man, he demonstrated great aptitude for union work. He became director of District 5 upon the retirement of Jean Gérin-Lajoie in 1981.

Clément was an active participant in the deliberations of the board, particularly in respect to the union's financial resources. When it became clear that an increase in dues income was necessary to meet the challenges of the time, he was a leader in presenting the case to the membership.

Clément is an excellent speaker. I used to tease him that he could speak in French any time to an English-speaking audience and receive a standing ovation.

John Reck

John was a big man in every way – physically, in spirit, and in dedication to the well- being of the union membership. He became director of District 7 in eastern Pennsylvania when his predecessor, Jim McGeehan, became treasurer of the international in 1985.

John was a great believer in the Steelworkers tradition as a servicing union. He went to almost any length to handle problems in a hands-on way, frequently driving whatever distances were required within or beyond the boundaries of his district to ensure that a problem was resolved, a dispute settled, or a grievance looked after.

John also believed in political action. He was a familiar figure in Democratic Party activities in Philadelphia. He could see clearly how powerful right-wing politicians could destroy the accomplishments of decades of labour struggle. On a lighter note, he was also one of the first Philadelphians to buy season tickets when the Philadelphia Flyers hockey team came to town in 1967.

David Wilson

David Wilson was the director of District 8, which during my presidency was one of the more contentious basic-steel districts, centred around the Sparrows' Point plant in Baltimore. He won election as a 'rank-and-file rebel' against a long-time staff person, Primo Padeletti, who had finished out the last year of the term of retiring director Ed Plato.

The situation was full of contradictions. It was a Bethlehem plant, so it was divided up into a number of local unions, the two major ones of which had side-by-side union halls but were frequently less than side-by-side in intra-union issues. These two large locals were much committed to political activity. They also conducted over many years one of the most effective worker-participation programs that grew out of the Labor Management Participation Team program.

David's experience as a union officer in coping with the politics of the local union stood him in good stead in the district, where he persevered in office throughout my terms and beyond. In the process he was a good and helpful supporter of all the new programs that developed over those years.

Paul McHale

Paul McHale was the director of District 9 (New York State), which became consolidated into Districts 7 and 8 after he died in office. He was one of the old guard who had opposed my presidency and went on to serve in my administration. I have no recollection of anyone running against him or of there being any sustained opposition to him or to me coming from that district. In my view, its members had been so immersed in the old culture and battles, and were so thunderstruck with the enormity of the disaster that was visited upon them with the collapse of steel, that they were quietly pleased that some ways of coping were developed and put in place.

The big Bethlehem home plant, the major lab installations, and the headquarters building now all sit as empty relics of former power and glory. It had been the plan that the old mill was to become a Smithsonian museum, but that has not come to pass. One of the most interesting and emotionally moving places to visit in the district is the plaza where the stones that make it up carry the names of former workers who made the plant the great producer that it was. Those who created the plaza took the time and trouble to group families together, so that one can see where generation after generation of steelworker families built the industry, the local union, the community, and indeed the country.

Andrew 'Lefty' Palm

Lefty became director of District 15 (stretching from the south side of Pittsburgh to the southern border of Pennsylvania) in a special election in June 1982. It was called as a result of the death of Paul Lewis, who had succeeded Joe Odorcich when Joe became vice-president. Albert Delesandro, a senior staff representative in the district, had served as temporary director during the pre-election period.

District 15 had a reputation as a base for dissidents, always ready to protest what some of its leaders viewed as the failures and worse of the union's leadership. The relationship between the district in which the headquarters of a union is located and the area director is often somewhat difficult. Joe had improved this a great deal in the case of District 15, and Lefty, who had been a close colleague and friend of Joe's, continued on the same path.

Lefty was an energetic director, with an outgoing and friendly personality. He handled issues in tough but fair ways, maintaining good communications and relationships. He supported all the programs of the union – education, political action, retirees, organizing, building amalgamated locals, and so on. We worked a lot with him from the secretary's office because he was nearby, because we were interested in helping to change the perceptions of District 15, and because we viewed him as one of the coming leaders of the union.

When Lloyd died suddenly and the board had to choose a temporary president, I approached Lefty but was not surprised when he advised me that he was committed to supporting Joe Odorcich. However, when Joe was defeated, and Joe and most of his supporters switched their support to Frank McKee as my opponent in the referendum, the question of Lefty's supporting me was very much an issue again. Lefty, despite Joe's strong objection, decided to support my campaign. Meanwhile, Lefty continued to grow with experience into one of our most effective directors.

James Coyne and Ray Reisman

Jim Coyne, an engaging Irishman and an experienced and excellent staff representative, had been elected as the new director of District 19 with the McBride team, but he died early in his second term before I became president. District 19 was one of the western Pennsylvania districts that cut into the city. In its case, it extended out to the north and east of Pittsburgh.

An interesting situation arose with regard to the election of Jim's successor. Lloyd had let it be known to the district that, if the staff could agree on one of their number receiving the appointment as interim director, he would be pleased to appoint that person. Within a week or two, he convened a staff meeting for that purpose. When Lloyd inquired of their decision, their staff spokesperson advised that they had always looked after matters by means of seniority and would like the senior staff person to receive the appointment. Lloyd asked me who the senior person was, and when I replied Marie Malagreca, a stunned silence hit the room. (In those days, we were not as sensitive to women's rights as we should have been.) Lloyd told Marie that the job was hers if she was willing to accept it. Marie, knowing that this was not the result the staff had intended, declined. Ray Reisman, next on the seniority list, was appointed temporary director. Ray retired at the end of the term and the district was merged into District 20.

Jim Bowen

Jim became director of District 23 (West Virginia and Ohio side of Ohio River) concurrent with the beginning of my first full term in 1984. He continued the new work, which had begun with Wheeling-Pittsburgh, and was also active in the political life of West Virginia. But it was the Ravenswood campaign that became the focus of his work for some time.

With his big powerful basso voice and his upbeat style of speechmaking and working with the local people, he was ideally gifted for this kind of a struggle. Much of it was based on regular weekly rallies at the union hall grounds, on visiting supporters from our union and others, on mass rallies in various places, on picketing and meeting with political leaders, and on international outreach. Jim had the energy, talent, and commitment to provide effective leadership in this contest.

Harry Mayfield

Harry was the director of District 27, based in Canton, Ohio. He was a vigorous supporter of the McBride team and of my election as president. He was a good friend of President Abel, who, along also with Vice-President John E. Johns, had come from the Canton area.

I always referred to Harry as the Happy Warrior. A number of the long-time directors did not face elections very often but once settled in would be the beneficiaries of a 'pass,' as it was called, meaning an acclamation. I do not recall this ever having been Harry's good fortune, nor do I ever recall him complaining about it. He carried on, did his job, and won every election.

Harry had a military background and brought a certain military-style discipline and order to his work. His meetings began on time, his agendas were clear and in order, and he was loyal to the people for whom he worked and the causes that he supported. After his retirement he became president of the Steelworkers Organization of Active Retirees, to which he gave energetic effective leadership for years, as long as his health permitted.

Joseph Coyle and Dan Martin

Harry Mayfield retired a few months after I won the referendum and the board appointed Joe Coyle to be director of District 27 (central Ohio). Joe was a member of our legal department who, as his career developed, did a great deal of work in District 27. He became interested in the broader aspects of service as a director, both on the political side in terms of the influence of the labour movement and in the collective-bargaining side in terms of creating agreements as opposed to interpreting them.

District 27 provided him an opportunity to pursue these broader goals. We supported him in those objectives and he was elected for a full term. However, the democratic election tradition was deeply rooted in District 27 and by the second term he was challenged by a staff representative, Dan Martin. Dan sensed some vulnerability in Joe's hold on the position, probably related to a lingering perception that Joe was an outsider. Whatever it was related to, it was there and Joe was defeated.

It is fascinating to observe the wide variety of personalities and interests that are represented in various directors. Dan, to a greater degree than any other director I knew, was very knowledgeable about the stock markets and how they might be helpful to us in terms of our judgments about what was happening in various industries. Dan also had a deep interest in organizing and in politics, and well understood the interconnections between these various activities.

Frank Valenta

Frank was the director of District 28 in Cleveland, Ohio, one of the traditional basic-steel districts. Colourful, active, aggressive, and contentious, he was one of the most active of the directors who supported Frank McKee. As a former Marine, he was drawn to the nationalist controversy surrounding my candidacy. Frank loved to argue and was good at it. A hostile meeting presented a challenge that he quite liked to face.

Once the election was settled, he and I worked out a good relationship. He played an active role in the U.S. Steel lockout and indeed was the one director who became involved in a bit of a physical confrontation. He worked with Bernie and me in the Lorain local's negotiations and did good work in building things up to a successful strike vote. He was active in Democratic Party politics and we supported him in a race for Congress. He did not win but pulled quite a respectable number of votes. Frank was a man who took a firm, clear position on issues and fought vigorously for whatever that position might be.

Obert Joel Vattendahl

Known variously as Obert or Joel, Vattendahl was a participant in one of the most civilized election procedures I have ever seen, this for directorship of District 32 (Wisconsin and part of northern Illinois). There were a number of candidates in the race, of which the two leading ones were Joel and Don Marzec. Both were excellent staff representatives with significant years of service. The district held a number of rallies to which all the candidates were invited. Joel and Don drove together to these rallies and home again as well.

Obert had a number of talents in addition to the staff representative's skills in organizing, negotiating, and grievance handling and arbitration. He had a great fund of amusing stories and a knack for picking up new ones. He also loved to sing and knew more of the words to 'Solidarity Forever' than anyone else.

One year it occurred to us that we could make special use of this talent. I had always had a special appreciation for those who stayed at the convention right to the end, thus demonstrating their conscientious sense of loyalty to and support for the democratic traditions of the labour movement, as exemplified particularly in the convention as the top governing authority of the union. So we asked all of those who had remained to the end to join hands in one giant circle and, after Joel told them a special story, to be led by him in the singing of 'Solidarity Forever.'

Ed Zeuch

Ed Zeuch was elected director of District 30 (southern Ohio, headquarters in Cincinnati) in a special election early in Lloyd's second term, upon the retirement of Harry Dougherty. Harry had been one of the stalwarts on the board, one of those who made education a priority. He was chairman of the education committee when I joined the board.

To a visitor, the district always seemed to be just the kind of well-organized group where you would expect a leader of Harry's calm and careful style to be in charge. I remember attending the district's reception at the convention prior to the McBride team's election and finding it an event with as well-dressed and stylish a crowd as any I had ever seen in a union setting.

It came as a great surprise to the union, as a result of this common view of the district, when the election for director in 1981 turned out to be one of the most intense, competitive, hard-fought campaigns the union had ever witnessed. Ed's vigorous, aggressive, somewhat scrappy style carried the day. He then served without challenge until 1989 when he was opposed by Frank Vickers. The 1989 election was one of the first in which our outside Campaign Conduct Administrative Committee was called into play to decide a complaint against Ed's conduct. It ruled in favour of Vickers. Ed protested to the board that internal matters should be decided by the union's internal people, not by outsiders. The discussion provided a great opportunity to vent all sides of the issue, but the board was almost unanimous in its support of the CCAC and that settled the issue for good.

Eldon Kirsch

Eldon was the director of District 33 in Minnesota, the district of the iron range, the home of good, tough trade unionism as demonstrated by miners wherever you find them. There is something special about miners, who stand up to life-destroying threats every day they go to work, as we are regularly reminded by horrific disasters in mines all around the world. This atmosphere surrounding miners usually results in a tough, vigorous, militant approach, in the best sense of trade-union culture. Our iron range in Minnesota was no different. The politics were hard fought. Relations with the companies were conducted as one might expect in such circumstances.

Eldon was a product of this kind of experience. Everything he had accomplished was by dedicated and courageous effort. However, when it came time for his re-election, he faced a challenge of a different kind. The district was not entirely mining country. It had a manufacturing base as well, with quite an established membership in Minneapolis-St Paul. There, the president of the major local that represented the workers in a steel mini-mill, the well-educated David Foster, decided to run against Eldon for director.

I supported Eldon, including going up to the district and doing some campaigning. It was clear that David enjoyed considerable support, not based on negative attitudes towards Eldon but in recognition of David's abilities. Eldon accepted defeat as one would expect he would and returned to his work as a staff representative. David developed into a fine director, in the process giving much support to the late Paul Wellstone in Paul's quest to become a senator. Once elected, Wellstone became one of the small but important group of progressive, labour-supporting members of the U.S. Senate.

David Foster

David shared deeply the vision of the union's role in society that was expressed in our Future Directions document. He was among the most conscientious and determined directors in pursuing all three facets of the report – serving existing members, reaching out to organize new members, and being involved in the social and political struggles of the day on behalf of all working people. He was a tough negotiator and a vigorous proponent of environmental causes.

As the iron mines closed down in the steel crisis, he fought to maintain employment the best he could, pursuing retraining opportunities wherever possible. Concurrently, he conducted organizing campaigns among the health-care workers on the range and rebuilt a significant membership in the district. After my time, when the mines revived, the district had a more representative membership than ever. He worked with the best available organizing talent there was, both from within the union and among interested students and other young people from outside who wished to help build the labour movement. He made a fine contribution as a leader of the Steelworkers.

Joe Kiker

Joe Kiker came to the Steelworkers when, as president of the Stone Workers' Union, he led them into a merger with us. He became director of District 35 when Bruce Thrasher retired.

In addition to the continuing challenges involved in organizing in the South, the most important responsibility for Joe was to lead the bargaining effort of the newly represented workers at Newport News shipyard, who had a significant need to catch up with industry standards. The equally important challenge was to work with this new Local 8888, the largest affiliate of the Virginia Federation of Labor, so that it might provide the high-quality leadership of which it was capable and be of great help to the federation.

Thermon Phillips

Thermon came on the board after Howard Strevel retired at the end of the term I was completing for Lloyd.

District 9 was headquartered in Birmingham, Alabama, where U.S. Steel's large southern integrated mill was located. Howard was an extroverted, good-humoured man who had a story for every occasion. It was a wonder to see how he could roll out a story that fit the situation perfectly, always breaking the tension and often in a humorous but thought-provoking style, pointing in the direction of a solution. But he was also hard as nails. He did not carry himself with the self-conscious air of a tough guy or anything like that, but everyone knew that he had taken a very courageous stand against school segregation, making himself available when need be to ensure that integration was implemented.

Thermon took over the district at a delicate moment. A few weeks earlier, U.S. Steel had advised that, if a satisfactory agreement could be negotiated, it would reopen the plant in Fairfield, Alabama, which had been shut down for more than a year, another victim of the steel crisis, and make some 2,000-plus jobs available. An agreement was reached. Concurrently, as temporary acting president, I had presided over a hold-the-line policy on concessions and related adjustments, to draw a line in the sand, as it were, and prevent the continual erosion of our standards. I called a board meeting to be held in Washington, D.C., at which time we could review the agreement and also hold my installation as president.

After a vigorous airing, the agreement was approved by the board as within the guidelines. The agreement was the product of dogged determination and skilled, imaginative bargaining by Phillips and the subdistrict director, E.B. Rich. But, I am sad to say, the district's reward for saving 2,000 jobs and reopening a doomed plant could not have been more cruel or unjust. It all stemmed from the extension of leaves of absence and pension time to union staff representatives.

The issue involved a long-standing difference between the arrangements many major steel companies and other important U.S. manufacturing companies made concerning pensions for persons who became employed as staff representatives in the unions that represented their employees. The practice of many was to maintain coverage in the company plan for the years the former employee worked for the Steelworkers, or other unions, thus enhancing the eventual pension income of the affected person. U.S. Steel had never agreed to that, but well after the Fairfield agreement was reached it did agree to grant that pension time to a limited number of Steelworker staff representatives.

A number of U.S. Steel employees who were union members initiated a lawsuit against the union, alleging that Phillips and Rich had traded off concessions in the agreement for this benefit for themselves. These accusations were regularly pasted on the front pages of the community newspapers. Worse yet, the U.S. attorney, under pressure from these members, or for other reasons, decided to pursue Phillips and Rich in a criminal case. Phillips was sentenced to two and a half years and Rich to three years.

The public assumption has always been that they were charged and later found guilty of the charges that received all the publicity. They were not. In fact, the government specifically withdrew the trade-off charge from the indictment even before the trial began. Instead, they were tried on a different theory. United States labour law has an inordinately tough provision that a union official must accept no gift from an employer of any kind. That is the provision under which they were found guilty, not that there had been any trade-off in any way related to the collective agreement. One of the things that makes this such a travesty is that no other union representative, before or since, has ever been prosecuted for simply receiving something of value from an employer when there was no corruption involved.

The civil case against the union was tried some time later and its outcome underscores the miscarriage. There, in order to win, the suing members had to prove that Phillips and Rich had traded concessions for their own pensions. They were unable to prove their charges because there simply was no such evidence. So a jury in the same Birmingham federal court that heard the criminal case returned a unanimous verdict in favour of the union on all thirty-six significant factual questions.

Phillips, a proud man who had served his union and its members with great ability and dedication, was virtually destroyed by the experience. His colleague, Rich, although it was terribly difficult for him and his family as well, did not seem to be as devastated. He first used his prison sentence as an opportunity for physical exercise. He then took an interest in improving the quality of life in prison, working to have some educational programs established. He also worked to improve the food, noting that the Jewish prisoners eating kosher received much better meals. When his first proposal on this subject was rebuffed, he advised the authorities that the prisoners would all convert. The problem was solved.

During the months all of this was happening, we appointed Dick Davis to be the acting director of the district. He carried out his responsibilities with his usual skill and competence.

Jack Golden

When Ed Ball became secretary, Jack Golden succeeded him as director of District 37, which included Texas, Oklahoma, and Arkansas. This followed the referendum when I finished being temporary acting president and became president.

Jack had a great interest in organizing and political action. The district had always been committed to the need for political action and participated in many tough political struggles over the years. Its members were enthusiastic supporters of Lyndon B. Johnson and counted themselves among the early discoverers of Bill Clinton. Jack kept these traditions alive. The district regularly raised more Political Action Committee money than anyone else.

Industrial development in the district depended very much on a thriving oil business. But, during Jack's terms in office, the price of oil on world markets was not sufficient to make the available resources profitable, with the result that economic development in District 37 was extraordinarily slow.

Robert Petris and Robert Guadiana

Bob Petris became director of District 38, the west coast district, when Frank McKee became treasurer of the international union. He was particularly active in copper and aluminum negotiations. He also maintained an interest in organizing, conducting several campaigns around the district.

At the beginning of my first full term as president, we divided District 38 in two, establishing its lower part as District 39 and appointing Robert Guadiana to be its director. The hope was that this would improve organizing development in both areas, partly by enabling each district to focus on a smaller territory and partly, through the appointment of an Hispanic American as director, by reaching out to the Hispanic immigrant workforce that was becoming so significant all across the country, but especially so in the southwest.

John Serembus and Ernest Shock

In October 1985 we concluded a merger with the Upholsterers' International Union, of which John Serembus was the president. We established an Upholstery division, with John as its director, and he became a member of the International Executive Board. This merger came about at John's initiative. He saw his union declining in the face of the movement of much of the industry to the south and offshore. Having had occasion to work with Elmer Chatak and finding him and the Steelworkers to be most helpful, he turned to us in his time of need.

Our hope that we could turn the division into an organizing project in the industry was hampered by the reality of its decline. What was left had been largely worked over and the workers in many cases were too concerned about the future to undertake what they perceived to be the risks of organizing. Still, we were pleased to have the merger bring us pre-Taft-Hartley jointly administered welfare and pension plans, though we quickly found ourselves in a crisis as a result of some wildly incorrect actuarial advice the welfare fund had received, providing for benefits that could not be sustained. It required some creative work by Ray McDonald, our research director at the time, and later Tom Duzak, to find ways to work through the problems and establish the programs on a sound basis.

John Serembus retired at the beginning of 1991 and Ernest Shock became head of the Upholstery Division.

Ernie came to the position with a distinguished record of leadership in the Upholsters and in the Steelworkers after the merger. In terms of the organizing challenge, he faced the same difficulties with the decline of the industry in the United States as had his predecessor but, to his credit, continued to seek opportunities wherever they might be.

Harry Hynd

Harry became director of District 6 by appointment of the board after Gerry Docquier retired and Leo filled the national director's position. Harry had emigrated from Scotland as a young man and, after a few months, found his way to Stelco. He became active in the union almost immediately, carrying on, as did so many of the immigrants who became active in Local 1005, the labour traditions of the old country. Harry's particular interest was always the grievance procedure, and for many years he was chairman of the grievance committee at the local union. Because of his talents, he was one of the staff we sent out to British Columbia during a time of difficulty there in order to help in the work of the district. He and his wife, Margaret, have both been very active in the NDP and he led the district with wisdom and energy. He retired in 2002.

Support Staff

It would have been impossible for me to accomplish as much as I did over the years without the patient, skilled, and talented assistance of a number of very accomplished secretaries and other support staff in the various offices in which I worked.

In the Niagara peninsula I worked from time to time in each of our three offices, with Thelma Tracy in St Catharines, with Ines Stocco in Port Colborne, and, for the longest period, with Connie Tirone in Welland. In the district office in Toronto, Brigitte Schneider was my secretary, and concurrently, while I was working with the organizers in Sudbury, Carmel St Amour was my secretary there. Mary Shane became my secretary when I became district director. Throughout all my years in Pittsburgh, my secretary and in reality executive assistant was Maxine Carter, in turn assisted by Linda Lambert.

I cannot speak highly enough of the talents and commitment of all of these individuals, who were dedicated to the best interests of the members of our union whom we were privileged to represent.

APPENDIX 2

TESTIFYING ON WORKERS' RIGHTS

One of the most challenging and interesting responsibilities that often came my way was to testify before one or another committee of Congress on one of the issues of the day, most frequently trade. My most frequent colleague in this work was our long-time legislative director, Jack Sheehan, a well-educated New Yorker who loved the union, began working for it as an auditor, and moved into the legislative arena as a result of his interest in and talent for the big issues.

The initiative for testifying might come from the committee involved, or from ourselves. Once an engagement was set, Jack and I would normally have a conversation along the way about the line we would take; the extent of the conversation was somewhat dependent on whether we were involved in a new subject, a circumstance we both enjoyed, or working over an old one. Jack would prepare our written submission, usually at greater length than was normally permitted, and we would edit it on the way to the hearing. Of course, the liveliest part of the hearing was the Q and A discussion that usually followed the formal presentation.

Many others from the union also testified and other individuals in addition to Jack prepared material, but in an interesting way it was really the turf of the president and Jack, since we usually had many axes to grind, such as which member of Congress we wished to persuade in which direction, or wished to persuade us, and matters of that kind. A great deal of this material is, of course, in the public domain but the union also published regular reports, edited by Jack, including much of the most important testimony.

The following is an example of testimony and a sampling of background material regarding Trade Adjustment Assistance. This presentation was made to the Senate Finance Committee in March 1987.

There are two features of the U.S. trading system and trade laws which deserve specific attention by the Congress. One is already part of trade law and should retain a permanent status. The other – so far – has not received legislative recognition in the basic trade law, although there is a statutory expression of it in the aid-related provisions of the General System of Preferences (GSP) and trade-related insurance coverage for overseas American private facilities under the Overseas Protection Insurance Corporation (OPIC). I refer to Trade Adjustment and international labor rights.

Trade Adjustment Assistance

Since 1962, trade adjustment measures have been part of U.S. trade law. Prior to that time there were no options in seeking relief from trade-related injury except through the safeguard or the escape clause provisions – the so-called Section 201 relief. However, the need to provide another alternative, especially for workers impacted by increased trade flows, was recognized as an equitable response to unemployment injury. I do not mean to imply that workers would seek the option of trade adjustment assistance (TAA) instead of the remedial measures of tariffs or quotas attainable under Section 201. Workers would rather preserve their jobs than be eased out of them. It would be unrealistic to expect otherwise. Nevertheless, the Congress decided that, since the petition for safeguard relief involved a somewhat extraordinary process and its outcome [was] uncertain, workers should receive compensation for the injury incurred. In other words, workers were injured through layoffs or job losses. While the adjustment measure had been hoped to have some political value in lessening opposition to an open trade policy, it cannot be evaluated in terms of whether it was buying off workers' resistance to trade-related job losses. Rather, since some losses were expected, it was socially equitable that workers not bear the full burden of increased trade penetration of our markets. There certainly was a quid pro quo being proposed, but not in terms of compensation for workers' acquiescence, but rather as injury compensation for accelerated trade. This tradeoff was reaffirmed in 1974 when Congress liberalized TAA by assuring income compensation from the first day of certification by the Department of Labor that a plant was being adversely impacted by trade. This assurance was provided through a compensation formula which paid benefits above the unemployment compensation levels. Although in 1981, the compensation level was reduced to the UI levels of each state, the underlying compact was maintained.

I feel it is necessary to reiterate these general assumptions of the TAA system – at least as they have been understood by the labor movement. Moreover, an assertion of the social equity of the TAA needs to be made because the bill before this committee undermines the 1962 commitment to workers in two provisions.

1) Sunset Provisions

Section 214 terminates the TAA program in 1991. Mr. Chairman, trade injury will not terminate in 1991. The global market is more a reality today than in 1962 when the TAA was first enacted. Then the focus was upon expanding trade in the various national markets. But now the domestic markets no longer define the parameters of trade. The global market is developing increasing preeminence. It would indeed be tragic to dissolve trade adjustment assistance in the face of such volatility in trade activity. As a matter of fact, I should note that the bill proposes a unique and effective way to finance adjustment assistance; namely, through an import duty. Yet the new TAA benefits recommended by the Act and the financing mechanism will, for the most part, be in effect only one year before the whole program will be terminated if Section 214 prevails.

The USWA sincerely urges that the sunset provision be deleted in recognition of the need for a continuation of TAA by a country having the largest exposure to trade impacts. Instead the TAA should be a permanent feature of our trading policy just as unemployment compensation is a permanent part of our domestic economic policy. The basic unemployment insurance program is not turned on and off with each cyclical swing so neither should trade adjustment assistance be dependent upon each swing in a legislative trade policy.

Somewhat related to this issue of sunsetting the TAA compact is the proposal by the Administration that TAA should be merged into the Dislocated Workers program under JTPA [Job Training Partnership Act]. For years we have heard the criticism that trade-impacted workers should not be treated any differently from other unemployed workers. Now a distinction is being made between cyclically laid off and structurally dislocated workers. Nevertheless, the Administration persists in its effort to dissolve the trade impacted program. However, the recent DOL [Department of Labor] Task Force on Dislocated Workers did not make that recommendation despite the fact that the Administration strongly urged its acceptance. Adverse consequences in the trade market, while they may have the same economic impact in terms of loss of wages and loss of jobs, are different in their causes than those consequences which result from the economic functioning of the marketplace. Trade policy more directly is linked to legislative and Administration decisions even to the extent that there is a conscious recognition that there will be job losses. Sheer equity requires that such decision be accompanied by a discrete program for readjustment. Furthermore, as will be indicated, TAA carries with it a unique feature; namely, extension of the UI levels of benefits and availability of income support during training. It is that distinct characteristic of this program which the Administration has rejected since it took office. It is our concern that you reject the Administration's proposal as did the Task Force ...

2) Worker Rights

On June 26, 1986, the U.S. delegation tabled a position paper before the GATT preparatory committee in Geneva requesting that the new round of trade negotiations should include a declaration: "Ministers recognize that denial of worker rights can impede attainment of objectives of the GATT and can lead to trade distortions, thereby increasing pressures for trade-restrictive measures."

The proposal grows out of the realization that there is a linkage between trade patterns and denial of internationally recognized workers' rights. A major thrust of this year's trade bill focuses upon the fact that new forms of unfair trading practices have evolved. The so-called "even playing field" has been spotted with potholes, some of which can have a very serious adverse impact on competition. Among the trade practices which put American producers at a disadvantage in their markets are those arising from foreign governmental policies or practices which promote:

- denial to workers [of] the right to organize and bargain collectively;
- permission of any form of forced or compulsory labor;
- failure to provide a minimum age for employment of children; and
- failure to provide standards for minimum wage, hours of work and occupational safety and health.

While the labor movement is understandably committed to promotion of human rights, including labor rights, as an expression of social purpose, it is necessary to assert that the linkage with the trade laws in the area of labor rights relates specifically to economic distortions and unfair trade advantages which suppression of these rights entails. The active denial or suppression of these internationally recognized rights by some of our trading partners should constitute and unfair economic advantage under Section 301 of the trade code.

It is not surprising that the proposal offered by the U.S. delegation was rejected. Economic advantage was at stake. We are disappointed that our negotiators did not insist upon the explicit inclusion of labor rights suppression in the agenda of the Uruguay Round. It is for that reason it should be included in our trade law.

Actually, Section 301 does reach for practices which are not addressed by GATT codes. In particular, denial of labor rights in the Riegle-Harkin bill (s. 498) is considered to be an unreasonable practice, i.e., "Any Act, policy, or practice which while not necessarily in violation of or inconsistent with the international legal rights of the United States is otherwise deemed to be unfair and inequitable." We need the explicit declaration that this type of unfair trade practice is amenable to a Section 301 action in order to adequately defend our workers against the growing reality that competitiveness in international trade means a decrease in our standard of living. Certainly competition does mean price competitiveness, but the basic approach of our trading system is that it must be conducted under certain rules and arrangements. Aside from the fact that denial of labor rights constitutes a violation of human and democratic principles, fundamentally in the trade field, it constitutes an unfair economic advantage. It is indeed ironic that our trading partners who oppose this provision as part of the GATT negotiations do so on very obvious economic grounds; namely, the potential elimination of a trade advantage. However, domestic opponents appear to be concerned more on ideological grounds, namely, the possible expansion of unionism and labor standards.

It is important to emphasize that the Riegle-Harkin proposals should be viewed entirely in terms of whether there is an unfair economic advantage being promoted. Furthermore, the issue is not whether unionism and labor standards are being actively promoted by our trading partners but whether, instead, there is active intervention to suppress these labor standards so as to obtain an economic advantage.

Additionally, Mr. Chairman, we stress that these rights are not to be described in terms of their American equivalency in the NLRA [National Labor Relations Act] and minimum wage laws. It has been charged that we are trying to impose our labor standards and collective bargaining rights on the rest of the world, but don't even apply them to ourselves. Actually, since this provision is directed at suppression rather than promotion, we would suggest that legislative language could make clear that the operative principle is government action to deny these rights. As a matter of fact, the Pease-Rostenkowski version clarifies that there is no intent to impose American labor standards on our trading partners. But by the same token, we should not be vulnerable to the imposition of a lower standard of living upon our economy.

The USTR [United States Trade Representative] has already been implementing the GSP equivalent of this provision. The agency was able to administer the provision in an open manner and interested parties were able to participate in the review of the worker rights practices in eleven countries. On the basis of that review, the President determined to remove the GSP status from two countries, suspend eligibility for another country and place on a continued review another country. Mr. Chairman, the provision is implementable and should be extended to cover all products subject to trade. Furthermore, I should note that the Section 301 action contemplated by the provision is discretionary, but the existence of the procedure will induce an atmosphere to remove this form of unfair trade if the penalty could be restrictive [of] access to this market.

S. 490 does establish certain overall objectives to be achieved under the Uruguay Round, among which is: "The establishment of minimum standards applicable to the workplace to provide greater international discipline over abuses of human rights of workers." This is an objective which we can applaud in that it attempts to explicitly commit the international trading system to the advancement of human rights. However, there are two observations which I would like to make to reinforce [the] USWA position that a position for decision on the GATT bargaining table should not be a substitute for inclusion in the Section 310 list of unreasonable practices.

- On September 20, 1986, at the conclusion of the opening session at Punta del Este, the Chairman, Uruguayan Foreign Minister Iglesias, stated: " ... there were certain issues raised by delegations on which consensus to negotiate could not be reached at this time. These issues included the export of hazardous substances, commodity arrangements, restrictive business practices, and workers' rights." Frankly, Mr. Chairman, we don't expect to see much progress dur-

ing the current negotiating sessions. Ambassador Yeutter in testifying before the Ways and Means Committee did indicate that the "…
Ministerial Declaration contains a provision that will enable us to
include additional subject matter in the negotiations as the Round
moves forward." Perhaps your statutory objective could assure
greater progress than has so far been achieved.

- But my main and second observation pertains to the fact that
  whether these rights are promoted through the trading system as
  part of an advancement of human rights, governmental suppression of these rights constitutes not only a social deprivation for the
  workers concerned, but an economic disadvantage for American
  workers. It is that essential point which we are reiterating as the
  justification for inclusion of the denial of labor rights in Section 301.
  Secretary Brock, at a recent Labor Sector Trade Advisory Committee, indicated that he would support a multilateral forum for
  developing these rights but would object to any mandatory lock on
  our trade negotiations. Perhaps your mandate in Section 105 will
  provide the necessary stimulus and yet allow sufficient flexibility to
  "provide greater international discipline over abuses" in this area.
  However, Mr. Chairman, our concern extends to the impact in our
  marketplace – which obviously will be greater if there is minimum
  or no international discipline. With or without the discipline, the
  economic disadvantages need to be addressed and for that reason,
  we urge that S. 490 incorporate an expansion of what constitutes an
  "unreasonable" trade practice.

In summary, we urge consideration of the proposals presented by the
Roth-Moynihan bill (S. 23) with the modifications indicated in our testimony. There is a social contract with labor which should not be aban-
doned. The suppression of labor rights by some of the governments of
our trading partners does constitute a valid cause for action not only at
the GATT negotiations, but also in Section 301. There is a suppression
of the living standards of American workers which should be arrested,
especially if the downward pressure is due to unfair trade practices.

INDEX

Abel, I.W., 204; and arbitration vs
strikes, 172; and Democratic Party,
145; and educational centre, 164;
final speech as president, 155–6;
final term as president, 144, 145;
and LW as president, 198, 200; and
LW running as vice-president, 147,
148, 149; and Mayfield, 284; and
Steelabor, 163
Aberhart, William, 8–9
Adams, Bill, 75
Adams, J.C., 45
AFL (American Federation of
Labor): CIO and, 26; and craft
unionism, 60; and local unions,
60; model of bargaining, 230; and
Simpson's, 29
AFL-CIO: Article 21, 269; George
Meany Center, 166; LW on Executive Council, 247–9; McBride and,
188; merger forming, 26, 62;
Organizing Institute, 230, 255;
strategic approaches committee,
218
Alcan (Kitimat), 54–65; certifica-
tion, 56; craft unions, 55, 60; and
immigrant workers, 58, 64–5; and

incumbency, 61–2; and languages,
58, 62; leafleting, 58; and local
unions, 60, 63; safety in, 59; votes,
64
Alcoa, 55
Algoma Steel, 57, 60, 143, 249–51
Allied Industrial Workers, 246–7
aluminum industry, 57–8; USWA
and, 55; working conditions, 107
Aluminum Workers of America
(AWA), 55, 60, 245–6
Amalgamated Clothing and Textile
Workers, 40, 218, 252
American Federation of Labor. *See*
AFL (American Federation of
Labor)
AmeriCorps, 240
anti-union/labour groups; consult-
ants, 52, 61, 229; employees, 52;
employers, 265
arbitration: defined, 50n1; Garrett
and, 217; strikes vs, 172–3
Archer, David, 85, 141
Archer, Doris, 85
area councils, 77–8, 116
Armco Steel, 180
Arnold, Ernie, 31–2, 42, 49